The Politics of Central American Integration

Latin American Studies

Social Sciences and Law

David Mares, *General Editor*

For a full list of titles in this series, please visit www.routledge.com

Land Privatization in Mexico
Urbanization, Formation of Regions, and Globalization in *Ejidos*
María Teresa Vázquez Castillo

The Politics of the Internet in Third World Development
Challenges in Contrasting Regimes with Case Studies of Costa Rica and Cuba
Bert Hoffmann

Contesting the Iron Fist
Advocacy Networks and Police Violence in Democratic Argentina and Chile
Claudio A. Fuentes

Latin America's Neo-Reformation
Religion's Influence on Contemporary Politics
Eric Patterson

Insurgency, Authoritarianism, and Drug Trafficking in Mexico's "Democratization"
José Luis Velasco

The Politics of Social Policy Change in Chile and Uruguay
Retrenchment Versus Maintenance, 1973–1998
Rossana Castiglioni

An Industrial Geography of Cocaine
Christian M. Allen

State and Business Groups in Mexico
The Role of Informal Institutions in the Process of Industrialization, 1936–1984
Arnulfo Valdivia-Machuca

Left in Transformation
Uruguayan Exiles and the Latin American Human Rights Networks, 1967–1984
Vania Markarian

International Relations in Latin America
Peace and Security in the Southern Cone
Andrea Oelsner

The Politics of Moral Sin
Abortion and Divorce in Spain, Chile and Argentina
Merike Blofield

Political Change and Environmental Policymaking in Mexico
Jordi Díez

Female Prostitution in Costa Rica
Historical Perspectives, 1880–1930
Anne Hayes

The Unfinished Transition to Democracy in Latin America
Juan Carlos Calleros

The Politics of Central American Integration
Rafael A. Sánchez Sánchez

The Politics of Central American Integration

Rafael A. Sánchez Sánchez

Routledge
Taylor & Francis Group
LONDON AND NEW YORK

First published 2009 by Routledge
2 Park Square, Milton Park, Abingdon, Oxon OX14 4RN
52 Vanderbilt Avenue, New York, NY 10017

Routledge is an imprint of the Taylor & Francis Group, an informa business

First issued in paperback 2012

Typeset in Sabon by IBT Global.

Library of Congress Cataloging in Publication Data

Sánchez Sánchez, Rafael A.
The politics of Central American integration / by Rafael A. Sánchez Sánchez.
p. cm.—(Latin American studies. Social sciences and law)
Includes bibliographical references and index.
1. Central America—Economic integration. 2. Mercado Común Centroamericano.
I. Title.
HC141.S36 2009
337.1'728—dc22
2008033302

ISBN13: 978-0-415-62159-5 (pbk)
ISBN13: 978-0-415-99615-0 (hbk)

This book is dedicated to my wife Jane
and our children Paul and Sara.

Contents

Glossary ix
Acknowledgments xiii

Introduction 1

1 Intergovernmentalism in International Theory of Integration 10

2 States' Preferences on Integration: The Cases of Costa Rica and El Salvador 31

3 The Establishing of the Central American Common Market (CACM) 51

4 Growth and Instability in the CACM 79

5 War and Disintegration in the CACM in the 1980s 102

6 Rebuilding Integration in the 1990s 127

7 Restructuring the CACM in the 1990s: The Move towards Open Regionalism 154

8 Concluding Chapter 176

Notes 191
Bibliography 203
Index 221

Glossary

ADC: Agriculture for Domestic Consumption.

ANEP: National Association of Private Businesses.

ARENA: Alianza Republicana Nacionalista.

CA-4: Trade and migratory agreement among El Salvador, Guatemala,Honduras, and Nicaragua.

CABEI: Central American Bank of Integration.

CACI: Multi-Sectoral Central American Committee.

CACIF: Co-ordinating Committee of Agricultural, Commercial, Industrial and Financial Association.

CACM: Central American Common Market.

CADEXCO: Costa Rican Exporting Chamber.

CAEC: Central American Economic Council.

CAFTA: Central American-US Free Trade Agreement.

CASEC: Central American Social and Economic Community

CBI: Caribbean Basin Initiative.

CCJ: Central American Court of Justice.

CEC: Central American Committee for Economic Co-operation.

CET: Common External Tariff.

CFM: Costa Rican Free Movement.

CIA: Central Intelligence Agency.

CINDE: Coalición Costarricense de Iniciativas para el Desarrollo.

CM: Common Market.

CMCA: Consejo Monetarion Centroamericano.

CODEHUCA: Central American Commission on Human Rights.

COMEX: Costa Rican Foreign Trade Ministry.

CONDECA: Central American Council of Defence.

CU: Customs Union.

EAI: Enterprise for the Americas Initiative.

EC: Executive Council.

ECLAC: Economic Commission for Latin America and the Caribbean.

EEC-EU: European Economic Community-European Union.

EU: Economic Union.

EXA: Export Agriculture.

FECAICA: Central American Federation of Industrialists.

FECAMCO: Central American Federation of Exporters.

FEDEPRICAP: Federation of Private Enterprise for Central America and Panama.

FDI: Foreign Direct Investment.

FMLN-FDR: Farabundo Marti Front for National Liberation-Democratic Revolutionary Front

FSLN: Sandinista Front for National Liberation.

FTA: Free Trade Area/Free Trade Agreement.

FTAA: Free Trade Area of the Americas.

FUCAI: Foundation for Central American Integration.

FUDCE: Costa Rican Foundation for the Defence of Foreign Trade.

FUSADES: Salvadorian Foundation for Social and Economic Development.

GATT: General Agreement on Trade and Tariffs.

GEI: General Treaty of Economic Integration.

GINSA: General Tyre and Incatecu, S.A.

GSP: General System of Preference.

GS-SICA: General Secretariat of SICA.

GT: Guatemalan Protocol.

IBRD: International Bank for Reconstruction and Development. Part of the World Bank Group.

ICIC: Civil Initiative for the Central American Integration.

IDB: Inter-American Development Bank.

IFI: International Financial Institutions.

IMF: International Monetary Fund.

INCAE: Central American Institute for Enterprise Administration.

INTAL: Institute of Latin American Integration.

IPE: International Political Economy.

ISI: Import Substitution Industrialisation.

LAM: Latin American Monitor.

LAR: Latin America Report.

LAWR: Latin American Weakly Report.

MNR: Movimiento Nacional Revolucionario/National Revolutionaty Movement.

NGOs: Non-Governmental Organisations

North Triangle: Trade Agreement among El Salvador, Guatemala and Honduras.

OAS: Organisation of American States.

ODECA: Organisation of Central American States.

OPEC: Organisation of Petroleum Exporting Countries.

PAECA: Especial Action Plan for Central America.

PARLACEN: Central American Parliament.

PCN: National Conciliation Party.

PDC: Christian Democratic Party.

PLN: National Liberation Party/Partido Liberación Nacional.

PUSC: Social Christian Party/Partido Unidad Social Cristiana.

RII: Regime of Integration Industries.

SAP: Structural Adjustment Programme.

SICA: Sistema de la Integración Centroamericana/System of Central American Integration.

SICA-CC: SICA's Consultative Committee.

SICA-GSI: General Secretariat of Integration

SIECA: Permanent Secretariat of the Central American Common Market.

TACA: Transportes Aereos Centroamericanos.

TP: Tegucigalpa Protocol.

US: The United States of America.

US-AID: US Agency for International Development.

WB: World Bank.

WTO: World Trade Organisation.

Acknowledgments

I would like to express my deepest appreciation and gratitude to all those who gave me support and strength without which I might not have been able to complete this book. The University of Sheffield, granted me a three year award: The International University Scholarships for Overseas Student, opened up the opportunity for me to complete the PhD which provided the basis for this book. The University also partially funded the first research visit that I made to Central America in February-April 1998, which allowed me to carry out interviews and collect substantial information about the region.

I want to thank my wife, Jane Lethem for her support over the years and for proofreading this work in its different phases from the very beginning. A great deal of my understanding of the English language has been gained in her company.

On the academic side, I am grateful to my former supervisors, Professor Jean Grugel and Professor Stephen George for their helpful suggestions and feedback. Jean Grugel showed a special interest in my topic and the co-operation of both former supervisors assisted in the successful completion of my PhD in June 2002. I want to thank as well Professor Martin Smith and Dr. Georgina Waylen for providing me with additional support during the final process of introducing minor corrections to the document.

My thanks go also to the following: Rob Collins for his help in processing my applications for funds within the University both for my trip to Central America in February 1998 and for my participation on the Conference on Comparative Regional Integration held in Denmark in May 2001; Victor Hugo Mata who provided me with accommodation in his home, use of his personal library and invaluable information about El Salvador, during the month and a half I spent in that country; Dr. Alvaro de la Ossa from the Foundation for Central American Integration for providing me with some of his own writings and materials published by the Foundation.

I want also to thank Professor Victor Bulmer-Thomas from the Institute of Latin American Studies of the University of London and Dr. José Antonio Sanahuja from the Universidad Complutense de Madrid, Spain, for providing me some of their writings and additional information on Central

American integration. I thank José Rafael Centeno from the Costa Rican Foreign Office for his help in the interviewing process in that institution. Likewise, I want to thank the Salvadorian Embassy in London for helping me contact interviewees at the Foreign Office and the Ministry of Economics in El Salvador.

I express my gratitude to the Economic Commission for Latin America and the Caribbean (ECLAC) and the Consejo Superior Universitario Centroamericano (CSUCA) for authorising the reprint in this book of the information contained in tables 4.1, 4.3, 5.1, 7.2, and 4.2, respectively.

This book would not have been possible without the co-operation of all those interviewed and I am most grateful for the interest each showed in the research and the time they committed to participating.

Introduction

This book is about Central American integration and analyses integration since its inception in the 1950s. Its main concern, however, is the process of reform via integration in the 1990s onwards. Integration is analysed from the perspective of international relations, focusing on intergovernmentalism as a theoretical framework. In other words, the focus is not customs union theory and its implication for intra-regional and international trade, which is a central concern of economic analyses of integration.

Economic theory of integration normally concentrates on the process of 'abolishing economic discrimination' between states (Balassa 1961, 1), but without due consideration to institutional and community building (Mattli 1999). Provided that this process of eliminating economic discrimination is successful, integration is thought to exist. Rather, in this book, the emphasis is placed on the political determinants of integration, focusing on states' preferences, intergovernmental bargaining and co-operation as well as on the constraints that governments face when defining regional policies.

These constraints may come from pressures generated in the domestic political economy of the states or pressures stemming from the global economy. The politics of integration, thus, frames the analysis of regional building in Central America within a context of competition and co-operation between the states. Competition, conflict and co-operation arise as a result of the states' search for leadership and welfare. The imperative of survival, in an international anarchical system which operates as a self-help system, triggers competition. Because in international politics there is no central authority empowered to provide security and justice, the states make their own provisions acting themselves as prosecutors and judges.

Regional integration reveals many of the characteristics of the international system. These include anarchy, rivalries, competition and cooperation between states. The politics of regional integration, as Nye argues (1970, 819) 'is not only the politics of co-operation but also the politics of status between states that have been traditional rivals'. The states not only worry about welfare gains but also about status and position in the international arena. Therefore, they have to bargain regularly with counterparts in order to strike a balance between their welfare, political and security interests. This reliance on bargaining marks the political nature of regional integration.

The strength of the intergovernmentalist approach to integration resides in its parsimony and heuristic power in acknowledging the limits of integration and in viewing it as a political process requiring governmental commitments and the willingness of states to co-operate. In other words, market forces alone do not explain or bring about integration. They may give rise to a process of economic regionalisation based on the rational decisions of private economic agents whose interests may overlap between different national markets. But, for regional integration to take place the central role of government and its willingness to compromise state sovereignty is crucial. As Waltz puts it (2008, 239) 'economic interests and market forces do not create blocs; governments do'. The willingness of the states to co-operate is determined by the governments' perception of the gains that they can derive from integration (Mattli 1999) and by the constraints they face as a result of pressures from the international political economy.

In the case of developing countries, as in Central America, these constraints arise mainly as a result of their situation as underdeveloped and dependent economies. The desire to lessen the impact of external barriers and to lower the effect of negative externalities, which might be generated by regional interdependence and by the strategic interactions of the states, may lead governments to co-operate and integrate their policies under some form of regional governance. Likewise, co-operation may also be encouraged by the governments' interest in producing some external impact designed to ease the process of internationalisation of the national economies or attract external resources in the way of aid, investment or even intangibles such as prestige and credibility.

In Andrew Moravcsik's version of intergovernmentalism governments face constraints stemming from the domestic political economy and the strategic environment (policy interdependence). For developing countries, however, structural constraints such as those arising from the international political economy are important and impact on the process of preference formation. This calls for some modification of the notion of the strategic environment in line with the analysis presented in the last section of chapter one. Integration, nonetheless, requires approval by the governments and the domestic coalitions supporting them. This fact highlights the political nature of the process and underlines the need for co-operation which in turn forms the basis for bringing the state into the analysis.

Grounding integration within states' preferences and concerns related to the national interests make the process dependent on intergovernmental bargaining; the larger states are assumed to be in a better position to determine the terms of integration. The outcomes of intergovernmental negotiations, however, will reflect both relative power and preference intensity (Moravcsik 1991). Preference intensity refers to the extent to which a state that has a strong preference or interest in forging integration, regardless of size and relative power, will be prepared to make concessions in order to attain that goal. Traditional analyses of integration have tended to emphasise relative power, hegemony, market and structural factors at the expense of governments' preferences and the agency of the state.

Because asymmetries are supposed to exist in the distribution of power between the states, even in developing countries such as in Central America, interstate bargaining will be asymmetrical. But because integration takes place between sovereign states invested with veto power, which are also assumed to act in a utilitarian manner, relative power alone does not determine outcomes. The capacity of every government to veto regional decisions makes preference intensity a defining feature of the interstate bargaining. Under this logic the states that have a strong interest in achieving a specific outcome would be more willing to reach a compromise whereas those who show the least interest, other things being equal, would enjoy greater bargaining power. This intergovernmental view of integration reflects the way the process of European integration has been carried out. With some adjustments such as those suggested in chapter one, this way of viewing integration can be transposed to the Central American experience and perhaps to other processes of integration in Latin America.

To assess the application and strength of intergovernmentalism in Central America, a detailed examination of the interests, preferences and strategies pursued by the states, and the constraints they face is presented throughout this book. Special attention is given to the process leading to the formation of the Central American Common Market (CACM) in the 1960s, the peace process of the 1980s, the process of reform of the CACM, the System of the Central American Integration (SICA), and the Guatemalan Protocol in the 1990s. These developments show clear interstate bargaining based on governments' preferences, asymmetric and strategic interdependence.

Interviews were carried out in the region in order to illuminate some of the intergovernmentalists' assumptions, particularly in the 1990s. Interviews and observation, of the role played by non-governmental actors and external events, were also carried out in order to determine the extent to which they impacted on the interstate bargaining process. There is evidence in the region, as it is shown throughout the book, that the interests and preferences of governments matter. Levels of policy convergence, whether political or economic convergence, are also important. When the policies pursued by the governments converge, integration tends to move forward. The converse happens when convergence decreases. This normally happens when the cost of cooperation is increased, by high politics differences between states or changes in the international political economy, heightening distributional conflicts.

Integration in Central America has, to a great extent, developed in the way predicted by intergovernmentalism. The governments have played a central role. Interstate bargaining has involved high politics manoeuvres as well as preference intensity. These include the threat of exclusion by a group of states, the use of veto, financial inducement or the equivalent to get the support of both poorer states and recalcitrant governments for integration. Integration has emerged largely as a result of the interests and strategies pursued by leading states within the region. These states, however, act under constraints. These constraints relate to underdevelopment and dependency, as well as institutional handicaps. This explains why many decisions adopted by the governments fail to be implemented.

Structural limits derived from underdevelopment and dependency underline the lack of technical and financial resources in the region as well as the central role played by external events and actors. Together with obstacles arising from the structural environment such as shifts in the global balance of power or financial crises, the externalities created by technological innovations and the foreign policy preferences of larger states, heighten distributional and high politics conflicts in the region. This has reduced the ability and willingness of the governments to co-operate under integration since the 1950s. Because of this, integration in Central America has not been far-reaching and has tended to undergo major setbacks from time to time. As a result, interstates bargaining have given rise to compromises under the lowest-common-denominator which have limited the pace and scope of integration. For some analysts this is disappointing, but it is a reality embedded in the structural and political environment in which the countries of the region interact between themselves and with the global economy.

Thus, in Central American integration, intergovernmentalism is a useful framework. Nevertheless, it is also important, as it is argued both in chapter one and in the concluding chapter, to analyse the impact of the structural environment as a significant constraint limiting the states' options. Given the situation of the Central American states as developing and dependent nations, structural pressures as well as the options of governments shape outcomes. The result is a modified version of the liberal intergovernmentalism developed by Moravcsik which well could be termed structural intergovernmentalism.

This research considers the utility of an intergovernmentalist perspective for the analysis of Central American integration, identifies the modifications necessary for intergovernmentalism to be applied to Central America, and analyses the process of reform of the CACM in the 1990s.

Intergovernmentalism has not previously been seriously applied to integration in Central America. Economic, sociological and technocratic approaches have predominated. These approaches are not normally grounded in the analysis of the role of politics and the agency of the state as determinants of governments' actions. They tended to ignore politics, governments' interests and the impact of distributional conflicts on integration. In these approaches the role of governments is seen as contingent on the capabilities of regional technocrats, hegemonic imperatives or class interests both national and global. The standard coinage for this is currently global governance, a buzzword, which like globalisation, complex interdependence and functionalism before, proclaims the diminishing role of the state and governmental actors in the organisation of the world economy and world politics (see Rosenau 1992).

When conflicts disrupt integration, some analysts see it as a consequence of institutional failure to conduct integration, class conflicts and imperialist designs rather than politics or clashes of governments preferences (see Sancho 1974; Bodenheimer 1981). There is the need to rethink integration in terms of intergovernmentalism in order to explain the slow pace of the process itself, the impact of distributive conflicts, and to make the connection with politics and with the strategic interactions of the states at both regional and global level. Intergovernmentalism argues that integration is a political project designed by self-interested governments to achieve their domestic and external goals. These goals would not be attainable without intergovernmental co-operation no matter how intensively non-state actors require them. This, as Moravcsik (1993a) argues, requires relaxing the autonomy of the states.

Integration arises primarily as a result of the convergence of preferences in the larger states of a region. To achieve integration, governments co-operate and get involved in asymmetrical bargaining where the larger states will attempt to shape outcomes in line with their preferences; this analysis focuses on the interests and preferences of the larger states in Central America: Costa Rica, Guatemala and El Salvador. Likewise, because integration is conceived of as a governmental action to pursue the national interest and the domestic and foreign policies of the state, the role played by government officials is paramount in articulating a process of regional co-operation leading towards the integration of their economies.

In Central America, external and structural factors influence policy-making, but the Central American states were strong enough by the 1990s to push integration forward. The Peace Process of the 1980s strengthened the states politically and led to the process of reforming and re-launching regionalism in the 1990s. Integrating the countries into the global economy became a central concern of all governments. This is the point where the regionalist project and globalisation meet. At this juncture, 'the interests of the state are seen to coincide and intersect with the interests of the international economy, and in which the national interests are intrinsically linked to the dynamics currently underway at the global and regional levels' (Phillips and Buxton 1999, 5). This convergence of interests between the state and global economy has meant that some governments have been willing to commit to regional integration. So, the argument of intergovernmentalism is that governments acting under constraints have been the central forces pushing and deciding the process of integration. The state, as Phillips and Buxton (1999, 4) put it, 'remains entrenched at the eye of the storm, and both the political process and the reform agenda remain dominated by the state machinery and government elites'.

The establishment of SICA and the reform of the CACM under the Guatemalan Protocol are viewed here as a result of states' preferences and of asymmetrical bargaining between governments. As Moravcsik argues (1998, 9), governments' preferences 'define not only the goals states seek but to a very substantial degree-via asymmetries in the intensity of preferences-their relative power' which leads governments to bargain and co-operate.

Three main hypotheses are examined in this book. First, the processes of reforming the CACM and the re-launch of regionalism in the 1990s were essentially the result of governments' preferences and interstate bargaining conditioned by their strategic environment and structural constraints. Through interstate bargaining the governments promoted the national interest of their states, as they saw them, and their own preferences constrained by pressures stemming from the international political economy and by their own political and institutional handicaps.

Second, even though structural constraints such as dependence, institutional handicaps, rules related to global governance, etc, impacted on the domestic and regional bargaining processes in Central America, the governments have been key in deciding and forging integration. The state remains the strategic actor in setting the agenda for integration. The strategic interdependence of the states together with policy convergence explains the re-launch of integration at the beginning of 1990. Equally, high politics and divergences in governments' preferences account for variable geometry in the process of integration since the 1990s.

Third, despite the transition of the region towards democracy in the 1990s, the influence of civil society and social forces in the process of revitalising integration has been very limited. The grounding of integration on neo-liberal principles and on governments' preferences have curtailed social participation. Integration thus remains an intergovernmental issue, strongly depending on governments' preferences and support to carry it forward, within the framework of an increasingly globalised political economy.

This book is made up of eight chapters. Chapter one reviews themes of regional integration from the perspective of International Relations. Focused on intergovernmentalism as a theoretical perspective, the central tenets and shortcomings of the main theories of integration are discussed. The aim of the chapter is to make the case for intergovernmentalism as a framework for analysing Central American integration. The argument is made that, despite the impact of structural constraints on the governments from carrying out integration, the main tenets of the intergovernmental approach are useful in explaining Central American integration. Government officials who get engaged in bargaining to achieve their national goals lead the process of agenda formation and the negotiations for regional building. This bargaining involves the tactics of power politics, by large states, such as coalitions, the threat of exclusion to recalcitrant states, and side-payments to smaller ones to attract their co-operation. However, structural constraints also shape government action. The chapter, therefore, also discusses how to factor in the consideration of structure into notions of the 'strategic environment' in which intergovernmentalism proceeds.

Chapter two presents a comparative analysis of the interests and preferences of Costa Rica and El Salvador regarding integration. Although both governments favour integration they differ in terms of the level of commitment they grant to it. El Salvador supports a full integration, while Costa Rica is unwilling to compromise sovereignty, making a limited commitment to integration. This state has favoured instead its global integration through unilateral and bilateral means of negotiation. These differences are grounded fundamentally in domestic constraints, history and patterns of dependence, especially the asymmetrical interdependence of the states within the CACM and their growing dependence on external markets. The chapter, thus, analyses some of these domestic and structural factors shaping preference formation in these states and seeks to demonstrate that more than institutional or bureaucratic leadership from the region's institutions, integration has advanced as a result of interstate bargaining between the leading states of the region. These are essentially Costa Rica, El Salvador and its regional partners within the so-called North Triangle, which includes Guatemala, Honduras and Nicaragua.

Chapter three focuses on the creation of the CACM in the 1960s. First, it reviews the theories that have traditionally explained Central American integration, particularly sociological, hegemonial and technocratic views. The intergovernmentalist analysis is then considered with the aim of explaining the patterns of co-operation and integration in the region informed by political economy. Preference formation in El Salvador is analysed in order to examine its actions to achieve integration. Although geographically handicapped by its small size, El Salvador possesses one of the largest economies and has traditionally been the most industrialised state of the region. It also possesses the strongest and most entrepreneurial minded groups in Central America. This gave it strong leverage to influence industrial and trade policies in the area. The creation of the CACM is seen as a result of intergovernmental bargaining substantially led by El Salvador.

Chapter four looks at the process of modernisation brought about by integration and examines some of the causes underlying its failure at the end of the 1960s and in the 1970s. Initially, the CACM was extraordinarily successful. It brought about industrial diversification, development in infrastructure and a considerable expansion of intra-regional trade. But distributional conflicts, external pressures and high politics differences between the member states combined to disrupt the integration process and led to its collapse. These kinds of issues, which account for integration and disintegration, have not previously been properly analysed in Central America. Economic analyses have predominated focusing on the relation of economic growth and integration and studying its consequences. The impact of political factors has been neglected on the basis of the primacy of the economic analysis as well as by the developmental character of integration in Central America, which allowed economists to be at the forefront of the process. This chapter thus tries to address some of the shortcomings in the analysis of growth and instability in the CACM by providing an intergovernmentalist explanation that takes into account politics and factors that shape the 'regional security complex'[1] and integration in Central America.

Chapter five analyses the impact of the political instability of the 1980s on integration and the regional process aimed at pacifying the region and rebuilding the CACM. The success of the peace process in ending the civil wars of the 1980s, is seen as a result of intergovernmental bargaining and asymmetric co-operation through which leading states, especially Guatemala and Costa Rica, sought to assert their interests and preferences. The chapter provides an analysis of the instability of the 1980s and looks at how the process of negotiation to find a peaceful solution to the crisis falls within an intergovernmentalist perspective. Focusing on states' power, preferences and convergent national interests provide a good understanding of the success of the peace process and its impact on regional integration. This process had lasting effects for the rebuilding of integration in the region. The contribution of the peace process to integration is viewed in terms of bringing peace and democracy to the region, rebuilding the process of policy co-ordination and reconnecting markets previously disrupted by war and ideology. In the longer run it gave rise to the relaunch of regionalism in Central American.

Chapter six focuses on the regional and external factors that explain the revival of integration in the region. New regionalism in Central America arises, first, as a result of evolution. In this respect it represents a recovery of the process brought about by changing political conditions in the region following the rise of new patterns of political and economic convergence caused by the success of the peace process. As a result, there was a renewed interest by the governments in consolidating the region as a free trade area and as a community, a desire strengthened by the success of the peace process. Secondly, it also represents the interest of the governments in using integration to tackle the economic crisis and decline of the region.

Integration would help the government build convergence policies and co-ordinate regional programmes designed to tackle the structural problems facing the economies of the region. Integration is, thus, a political response by the governments to pressures, especially the need to avoid exclusion from the world economy and to attract foreign investment from multinationals and aid from other states. Attention is paid to the issues of transforming Central American integration into a system of integration under SICA and the process of institutional reform. The chapter pinpoints some of the underlying differences between Costa Rica and the other states regarding the scope of integration.

Chapter seven concentrates on the bargaining process leading to the reform of the economic integration. This was initially undertaken under the Special Action Plan for Central America (PAECA) adopted in 1990 and the Guatemalan Protocol (GP) adopted in 1993. The latter updated the 1960 General Treaty of Economic Integration, turning the CACM into a strategy to promote the external integration of the region under the new globalising conditions. The bargaining process in the 1990s concentrated both on defining the scope of the GP and on negotiating the common external tariff. Progress has been made in terms of tariff reform and free trade was established, particularly in the transaction of industrial goods. But high politics conflicts, political preferences together with recurrent trade disputes still trouble the region and limit the prospect for the consolidation of the Central American bloc.

The final chapter addresses the main conclusions of the book and some of the implications derived from the application of intergovernmentalism to integration in Central America. It is argued that, despite the fact that the structural environment and structural factors in general constrain the options of the states in shaping integration, the governments remain key players in the region. Despite the difficulty in transporting intergovernmentalism from Europe to Central America, the theory still explains a great deal of the nature of integration in the region.

1 Intergovernmentalism in International Theory of Integration

Intergovernmentalism possesses heuristic power to explain integration in this region. This chapter first discusses intergovernmentalism as a theoretical perspective on regional integration. Second, it outlines the theoretical foundations of intergovernmentalism as applied to Europe and assesses its usefulness for explaining integration in Central America. In order to apply intergovernmentalism to Central America some modifications are made to integrate the impact of the structural environment in the integration process.

Intergovernmentalism has hardly been applied outside the European Union (EU). It is essentially a theory devised to explain the patterns of interdependence and integration in Europe. But some application of the theory has been attempted, especially in Mercosur where analysts seem to find intergovernmentalist traits explaining integration in South America (Bouzas and Soltz 2000; Phillips 2000a; Kaltenthaler and Mora 2002). In Central America some studies also make intergovernmentalist assumptions (Lizano 1976; Morales G 1994), but a comprehensive presentation of the theory and the grounding of integration on it has been lacking. Although in Central America the states are characterised by their condition of underdevelopment and dependency, intergovernmentalism offers a credible explanation of the conditions underlying integration in the region. The author therefore, sets out to underline the conditions under which intergovernmentalism applies to integration in Central America.

INTERGOVERNMENTALIST PERSPECTIVE ON REGIONAL INTEGRATION

The word perspective instead of theory has been chosen here with the aim of presenting Intergovernmentalism as a paradigmatic view for a discussion of regional integration, without the constraint and rigidity of normal science. In this attempt the author has been influenced by Gill and Law's (1989, 17) discussion of perspective and paradigm which, in their view, refer to 'the basic concepts and assumptions which underpin theoretical explanations'. The author has also been influenced by a debate between Wincott (1995) and Moravcsik (1995) regarding the former criticism of the scientific footing of intergovernmentalism. In placing intergovernmentalism within the category of 'mid-range' theory, Moravcsik, in the author's view, has ably rebutted Wincott's criticism, which relies heavily on a very formal and rigid view of scientific inquiry.

Moravcsik's (1995, 611) defensive arguments about intergovernmentalism as 'the indispensable and fundamental point of departure for any general explanation of regional integration' clearly falls within Kuhn's conception of the development of science. Kuhn (1962, 49) argues that normal science is seldom monolithic and unified and that a paradigm or perspective could exist even without yet achieving the level of scientific rigidity characteristic of normal science which is based on discoverable rules.

The reason for this, according to Kuhn 'is the severe difficulty of discovering the rules that have guided particular normal-scientific tradition' (Kuhn 1962, 46). Therefore, presenting intergovernmentalism in the way Moravcsik has done in his studies of European integration seems to be consistent with the pattern of paradigm building theorised by Kuhn. Thus, the theoretical significance of a perspective, or paradigm, cannot be disregarded just because it does not fully meet the formalities or exactness of normal science. Its validity must be judged on the basis that it makes reasonable and substantially verifiable predictions regarding the subject under investigation. As Huntington argues (1996, 37) 'a crucial test of a paradigm's validity and usefulness is the extent to which the predictions derived from it turn out to be more accurate than those from alternative paradigms'.

With the above definitions in mind, intergovernmentalism is presented as a perspective on regional integration. As such, it explains integration as the result of strategies pursued by rational governments whose loci of action are the realisation of the national interests of the states and the consolidation of political power by the ruling elite. Integration is viewed as the outcome of a process of bargaining among the political leaders of the major states in a region (Moravcsik 1991; Mattli 1999).

Intergovernmentalism has flourished since the late 1960s, as neo-functionalist explanations of integration began to fall apart. Neo-functionalism has traditionally been regarded the *Grand theory* of regional integration *par excellence*. Pressures from organised domestic and regional social and economic forces are taken as central variables for integration, leading towards the building of supranational authority (Haas and Schmitter 1964, 708; Haas 1968, xxxiv, 6; Mattli 1999, 42). In 1968 Haas defined regional integration as:

> The process whereby political actors in several distinct national settings are persuaded to shift their loyalties, expectations and political

> activities towards a new centre, whose institutions possess or demand jurisdiction over the pre-existing national states (Haas 1968, 6).

In this neo-functionalist view integration has an incrementalist logic whereby the integration of a sector of activity will create pressure for the integration of other sectors. A kind of domino effect will gradually give rise to the formation of a political union under a form of federal government. The trigger of this incrementalist logic is found in the spillover, which works as the main neo-functional independent and endogenous variable accounting for integration. One of the most celebrated definitions of the spillover defines it as:

> The process whereby members of an integration scheme attempt to resolve their dissatisfactions either by resorting to collaboration in another related sector (expanding the scope of mutual commitment) or by intensifying their commitment to the original sector *(Schmitter 1969, 162)*

Thus, in this neo-functionalist logic of integration, states cannot stop integrating different sectors of their economies under the care of professional and enlightened bureaucrats from regional institutions. To do so would hurt them all owing to the high levels of economic interdependence of the modern world. When conflict arises it is overcome by upgrading the common interest by means of negotiations (Taylor 1983, 8). This approach to integration fell into disrepute by the end of the decade of 1960 as integration in Europe stagnated and similar processes elsewhere faltered. Given the inadequacies of neo-functional explanations, intergovernmentalism is increasingly becoming an alternative framework for the analysis of integration in Europe and in other regions, particularly in Latin America.

REALIST TRAITS OF EARLY INTERGOVERNMENTALISM

The origin of intergovernmentalism as a theoretical perspective on integration can be found in the writings of Hoffmann (1966), Wallace (1972), Dahrendorf (1972), Webb (1982) and Moravcsik (1991, 1998). Previous to the decade of the 1990s intergovernmentalism tended to be grounded on realist assumptions, especially one branch of realism termed by Sartori (1990, 64) *'cognitive realism'*. This intergovernmentalist strand differs from traditional realism in that it embraces a more dynamic view of politics and considers a non-hegemonic integration based on low politics and interstate co-operation. This form of co-operation is limited to the pursuit of welfare and economic efficiency, without interfering with the security and the foreign policy interests of the states (high politics).

Regional integration was assumed to come within the realm of 'negative integration', which was limited to the elimination of obstacles to intra-regional trade. This, in essence, was a modification of traditional realism, a detachment from the power politics model developed by Morgenthau (1971; 1992), Carr (2001), and other realists which concentrated entirely on power politics, relative power or position of states. In the realist view of international politics the anarchical nature of the international system leads the states to worry about their position relative to other states and define their interests in terms of power vis-à-vis one another. Co-operation was inhibited because states would forgo absolute gains if the gains of others threaten to worsen their own relative position (Grieco 1993).

This early version of intergovernmentalism questioned functionalist claims that state power and the force of the territorial state in world politics was becoming obsolete. Hoffmann (1965; 1982), therefore, questioned the neo-functional thesis of supranational building by reasserting the centrality of high politics and the role of the state in world politics and in processes of regional integration. His analysis also detached the national interest from the structural determinant of the balance of power calculation, explicit in the realist view of world politics. Thus for Hoffmann 'states interest are constructs in which ideas, precedents and past experiences, and domestic forces and rulers all play a role' (cited in Rosamond 2000, 76).

But Hoffmann realised that while realism had failed to take process level factors into the definition of the national interest, i.e., domestic claims and social pressures, neo-functionalism had the opposite shortcoming. Neo-functionalism failed to take into account the context or the strategic environment in which the states operate, that is, their capabilities and patterns of interactions of which co-operation is one possibility. In other words, exogenous variables, of which domestic economic conflicts, governments' preferences and interstates bargaining are central ones, were disregarded in order to emphasise the importance of endogenous variables. Among these were the assumed automatic linear and incremental growth of integration, the unintended consequences, and the assumed goodness of economic planning. This ignored political economy variables. There was the notion that integration has an inner logic, which presses for the automatic spread from sector to sector in a well defined roadmap to an end-product which takes the form of a political community with a supranational governance structure.

Thus, Hoffmann (1966) criticised neofunctionalism for ignoring the logic of diversity. This diversity 'would arise out of both the natural plurality of domestic imperatives and the fact that every state's situation within the system would be unique' (Rosamond 2000, 76). This led Hoffmann to believe that the prospect for a far-reaching integration, as put forward by neo-functionalism, was indeed slim. In his view when integration touches the realm of high politics, the process could face disruptions. Therefore, he argued that the neo-functional logic of integration triggered by the spillover would be counteracted by the logic of diversity (diverse foreign and economic policy preferences of the states). In this sense, he argued, the spillover would be the victim of its own success (Hoffmann 1966).

This uncovering of the logic of diversity by Hoffmann brought about the need to complement the spillover with the principle of convergence, which has a political dimension that was overlooked by neo-functionalism. In other words, for integration to be successful, the policies favoured by states (e.g. foreign policy or macroeconomic polices) have to be convergent and achieve considerable levels of harmonisation. Raymond Aron had advanced the thesis of convergence as a central factor accounting for integration in Europe before World War I, and as a condition for further European integration. In the post-war period, he argues, 'Europe as a whole cannot carry out economic planning (to achieve convergence) as long as the various units are only partially planned and every government regards the national interest as the ultimate criterion of its action' (Aron 1954, 309).

The writings of Hoffmann and Aron on integration are examples of this kind of cognitive realism where the pursuit of variable-sum games co-operation is possible, provided it is restricted to the level of low politics or grounded in convergence. Because of this concern with high politics and convergence, other European analysts inspired by Hoffmann and Aron, began to think of integration within the confines of governments' interests and foreign policy to the detriment of institutions and neo-functionalist explanations. Dahrendorf, and Wallace where probably pioneers in this respect. Dahrendorf, for example, argued that 'the fiction of an uncontrolled European government free from national direction as well as parliamentary doubts was bearable to the member states as long as only very little was to be decided at a European level' (Dahrendorf 1972, 74).

Thus, contrary to neo-functionalism, this early version of intergovernmentalism disregarded the importance of non-governmental actors or the impact of transnational forces in the process of regional building in Europe. All that matters was the intergovernmental level of policy co-operation guided by the political interests and foreign policy objectives pursued by the governments.

MORAVCSIK'S ACCOUNT OF INTERGOVERNMENTALISM.

Andrew Moravcsik, the contemporary theoretician of intergovernmentalism, has reinvented intergovernmentalism along a more liberal line, emphasising the dependence of integration on both domestic and international political processes. Moracsik's intergovernmentalism is derived from what Keohane calls the modified structural realism, but closely connected with a liberal perception of international politics (Moravcsik 1991). In this perspective, 'all aspects of co-operation are affected by domestic considerations because co-operation is a continuation of domestic political struggles by other means' (Milner 1997, 10).

Moravcsik is, thus, heavily influenced by this liberal thinking, which includes earlier work of Keohane and Nye (1989) on complex interdependence and Keohane's (1984) theory of regime formation. The latter was itself presented as a modified structural realist explanation of regime formation and maintenance. This emphasises the centrality of the state in international politics, national interest, relative power and the role of institutions in shaping states' behaviour. Moravcsik embraces this version of realism, but he also differs substantially from it by highlighting states' preferences as the central variable in determining integration and clinging to the intergovernmentalist view of the subservient role of institutions.

Moravcsik recognises that structural factors constrain state's actions. However he does not follow neo-realist or structuralist arguments, which emphasise the overriding role of the structure and anarchy of the international political and economic system in shaping outcomes (see Gunder Frank 1969; Gilpin 1981; Waltz 1986a). Moravcsik is aware that structural factors influence the processes of regional integration, but he argues that the theory of integration has to be actor-oriented instead of deterministic. That is, 'it should highlight the purposive choices of states and social actors within constraints rather than the unintended dynamics of broader structural processes' (Moravcsik 1998, 15). Therefore, by concentrating on the purposive choices of actors and on their interactions, conditioned by the strategic environment, intergovernmentalism and structuralism are complementary. In other words, both structural pressures and the state or government work together in shaping outcomes. This is consistent with mainstream social science where 'it is now accepted that structuralism and individualism (the individual or the state) represent complementary rather than competitive approaches' (Little 1985, 76).

Thus, Moravcsik acknowledges that governments face obstacles that could be structural in nature created by the environment in which the governments operate, the so-called 'strategic environment'. One side of the strategic environment could be said to be made up of the constraints that governments encounter in their own political economy. Here, the correlation of power (the different domestic coalitions in favour and against integration) conditions governments' options and capacity to act in a coherent and rational manner. Externally, the strategic environment as such, refers to the limitations faced by governments in their strategic interaction or mutual relations which take place within a context of policy interdependence. Here governments seek to achieve their aims by means of bargaining and collaboration, adopting what Schelling calls (1960:16, 83) 'interdependent decisions'. The strategic environment, thus, involves domestic constraints in the definition of the national interest and constraints from the external environment whereby governments have to bargain in order to achieve national goals. In the external environment, 'mutual dependence is part of the logical structure of relations and this demands some kind of collaboration or mutual accommodation' (Schelling 1960, 83). In the EU this is reduced essentially to the strategic interactions and bargaining among member states, especially the largest ones which are characterised by high levels of interdependence and economic and political openness.

In this Moravcsikian proactive approach to the role of theory, where actors play a central and purposive role rather than performing deterministic commands, the structure is seen as imposing 'limits on and possibilities for state action' as argued by Ikenberry, rather than determining everything. According to Ikenberry (1991, 167) 'structure is not, strictly speaking, a source of causation'; the state's interests themselves are not determined by structure. They emerge through the interplay of a state elite that is adapting and strategizing in the context of structures.

In Moravcsik's view of the process of integration in Europe, although structural factors such as the distribution of capabilities among the states and domestic constraints are important in shaping outcomes, the decisive factor is the intensity of preferences of the governments. His intergovernmentalism differs decisively from the modified structural realism of Keohane, in that it locates the sources of regime reform not only in the changing power distribution but also in the changing interest of states' (Moravcsik 1991, 48). Because states' preferences are important for integration, changes of preferences will have an impact on the integration process and this change cannot be traced to shifts in the relative power of states (Moravcsik 1991).

Thus, in this view, integration relies fundamentally on states' preferences. This view of regional integration is influenced by the interdependent school which perceives power as control over outcome based on issue-specific bargaining, rather than power as the ability of an actor always to get others to do something they otherwise would not do (Keohane and Nye 1989). This view of power as control over outcome questions the realist view of structural power because it argues that in an interdependent world power is no longer fungible. Strong states may face difficulties in cashing in their structural power to get what they want. They may find it difficult to impose their will on issues in which they are not preponderant or are even weak.

This view of international politics, as substantially modified by complex interdependence, triggers Moravcsik's emphasis on governments' preferences and interstate bargaining as the basis for shaping outcomes in regional integration. In his own words, 'the willingness of states to expend resources or make concessions is itself primarily a function of preferences, not capabilities' (Moravcsik 1997, 523). The intensity of preferences implies that states get involved in bargaining situations, which reflect their asymmetrical power as well as their preferences. Accordingly, the party that has least to gain has the most power and the party that has the most to lose is in the weakest position and would, therefore, be more willing to compromise (Schelling, 1960; Moravcsik, 1993a; 1998, Cameron and Tomlin 2000, 28).

Moravcsik moved intergovernmentalism, from being a critique of neofunctionalism, to a theory of integration, which underlies the conditions (political and structural) under which governments may be willing to co-operate and promote integration. He concentrates on Europe. But this liberal intergovernmentalism need not be exclusively what explains the European process of integration. This is, in fact, Moravcsik's greatest achievement, in that he integrates into a coherent whole most of the assumptions of traditional intergovernmentalism. However, he places the emphasis for integration on domestic politics (the political economy) where domestic infighting, for or against integration, takes place, and on the strategic interactions that occur at the interstate level (the strategic environment). It is at this interstate level where governments negotiate their preferences and distributional conflicts through asymmetrical bargains. This bargaining, in turn, determines the level of institutional commitment to sustain their goals (Moravcsik 1998). Moravcsik is adamant about the central role of the national political economy. He argues that 'even when societal interests are transnational, the principal form of their political expression remains national' (Moravcsik 1991, 47).

Moravcsik (1991, 46) stresses 'the central importance of power and interests', but he emphasises that the latter is 'not simply dictated by position in the international system'. This is consistent with the liberal argument that domestic politics determine the foreign policy of the states. He is strongly influenced by the works of Milner (1988; 1997) on the centrality of domestic determinants of international politics, Putnam (1988) and Schelling (1960) on bargaining politics and Keohane (1984) on co-operation and regime formation and maintenance.

Contrary to the neo-functionalist view of integration which relied on some background conditions which proved difficult to find outside Europe, Moravcsik derives his intergovernmentalism from a liberal approach to political economy and international relations. This includes contemporary theories of international political economy, a liberal theory of economic interdependence, an intergovernmentalist theory of international negotiations heavily concentrated on bargaining and a view that institutions reflect governments' interests (Moravcsik, 1993a). This gives his theory a degree of generalisation, making it possible to apply, at least in theory, to processes of integration outside the European process. But in order for intergovernmentalism to be transferable to regions outside Europe, a re-thinking of the strategic environment will be needed, as will be seen below, to move the analysis beyond the interstates' strategic interactions and integrate the impact of the structural environment.

INTERGOVERNMENTALIST CONTENTIONS

The intergovernmentalist approach to integration can be reduced to the following propositions. First, governments are central actors. Intergovernmentalism's central tenet is that self-interested states or governments are the strategic actors promoting integration (Hoffmann 1966; Moravcsik 1991). In doing so governments face constraints stemming from their domestic political economy and externally from the patterns of interaction which define the strategic environment in which governments operate (Moravcsik 1993a, 474). The key variable, however, is 'the perception by governments of the issues and the assessment they make of their implications for the defence and promotion of vital interests' (Webb 1982, 305). Thus, the analysis of integration should focus on the actions and interactions of governments' representatives pursuing the realisation of domestically defined preferences and national interests.

In this view of regional integration, domestic limitations (demands or distributional conflicts) influence the process of state's preference formation in a dynamic manner (see Milner 1997, 13–14). Government recognises these demands and try to manipulate them in order to gain degrees of autonomy vis-à-vis domestic constituencies. This manipulation may take several forms. It ranges from influencing the process of approval of legislation, increasing the win-set [1] of intergovernmental agreements through concessions to predominant interest groups, and colluding with other governments in order to weaken the opposition of domestic constituencies to integration. This view of state's preferences formation challenges realists' arguments which assume that states preferences are fixed and untouched by domestic politics (see Morgenthau 1971, 79; Keohane and Nye 1989, 43).

Intergovernmentalism does not ignore the spill-over, but it asserts its political dependence. Because of this political dependence, rather than advancing in a linear and automatic manner integration proceeds *'in fits and starts'* (Moravcsik 1991, 76). Keohane and Hoffmann argue (1991, 17), that 'successful spill-over requires prior pragmatic agreement among governments, expressed in an intergovernmental bargain'. Without prior political agreement the neo-functionalist thesis of self-sustainability of the process of integration may not materialise. This clearly connects integration to the interests of governments. For integration to succeed, it has to be viewed by governments, especially in the largest states, as being in their own interest or in the interest of their states. Identifying governments' interests and policy convergence as the main variables for integration gives intergovernmentalism parsimony, which distinguishes it from other approaches. A change of governments' preferences, which could be the result of a revaluation of the political commitment to integration or a consequence of a change of government, would inevitably have an impact on integration, and this could happen, as Moravcsik argues (1991; 1997), regardless of relative power considerations.

Because power is an essential ingredient of the regional processes of co-operation, intergovernmentalism sees integration as power politics, though not in the sense of realism. It is a power politics based on asymmetrical co-operation guided by the pursuit of mutual gains. Some assumptions are shared with realism, but these are not taken dogmatically. For instance, although a realist view of the centrality of the state in world politics is assumed, the static view of politics is rejected (Hoffmann 1992).

Intergovernmentalism does not assume that governments are free from domestic constraints. The negotiation of regional arrangements which require domestic ratification will largely depend on the domestic win-set (support) of the agreements and this gives domestic constituencies and parliamentarians some kind of veto power over the governments. Moravcsik argues that constraints on national preferences reflect the costs and benefits of agreements to societal actors. Thus, the governments could enjoy a greater autonomy vis-à-vis domestic politics 'when the net expected costs of co-operation to interest groups are insignificant, ambiguous, balanced or uncertain', or when pressure groups are divided on some important issues (Moravcsik 1993a, 484). Where these are 'weak, uncertain or diffuse, governments will be able to pursue broader or more idiosyncratic goals' (Moravcsik 1993b, 494).

Intergovernmentalism, however, maintains that the main forces pushing for integration are self-interested governments pursuing their preferences and the national interests of the states (Moravcsik 1991; O'Neill 1996). Governments are taken as utilitarian decision-makers whose central concern is to consolidate their power. To the extent that integration increases their security and power domestically, allowing them to achieve goals otherwise unavailable, governments feel the need to co-operate, adjusting each other's interests and actions (Keohane 1984; Moravcsik 1993a; Mattli 1999, 13). As utilitarian actors, governments pursue co-operation in order to achieve positive gains in which all actors are winners. In this respect intergovernmentalism distances itself from power politics approaches, which assume that bandwagoning, hegemony or an outright threat of exclusion is sufficient to force reluctant states to get involved in processes of co-operation in which they could be absolute losers (Gruber, 2000).

Self-interest is, therefore, the force leading governments to co-operate on regional integration. The rationale for integration would be the realisation of economic gains, but the politics of integration also involves the pursuit of political gains in the form of regional influence and prestige. For Moravcsik (1993a, 492) integration will take the form of what he terms 'negotiated policy co-ordination', which involves a relaxation of the domestic autonomy of the states in order to attain common goals unachievable or too expensive to be attained unilaterally. The assumption is that governments would be willing to relinquish or pool sovereignty in some areas, provided that some lasting benefit can be obtained from their involvement with integration, as, for example, when collective action 'offers a greater guarantee of the state's security' (Webber 1997, 30). Thus, from the intergovernmentalist perspective integration is part of a process of interstate co-operation. The extent to which this co-operation may take the form of institutional amalgamation or supranationalism, which is what analysts normally view as integration, would largely depend on the level of credible commitment that the governments wish or are prepared to embrace.

Second proposition, integration relies on intergovernmental bargaining. Centred on the EU process, Moravcsik explains integration 'as the result of strategies pursued by rational governments acting on the basis of their preferences and power' (Moravcsik 1993a, 496). Integration reflects the domestic preferences of the states. Moravcsik argues that in Europe 'Each government views the EU through the lens of its own policy preferences and therefore, EU politics is the continuation of domestic politics by other means' (Moravcsik 1991, 47). The same statement can be extended to Central American integration. Through interstate bargains governments seek to achieve their domestic preferences. Therefore, more than other considerations, integration is the result of an asymmetrical bargaining based on the intensity of preferences backed by the threat of exclusion.

According to Moravcsik (1995, 616) it is 'insufficient intergovernmental demand for policy technologies, not insufficient supranational supply of them' which imposes a decisive constraint on co-operation. Thus, Moravcsik questions neo-functionalists who sustain the opposite view, emphasising supranational leadership, the role of institutions and businesses' demands to explain community building in the EU (Wincott 1995; George 1996a; Mattli 1999). Moravcsik argues (1998, 4) that 'the integration process did not supersede or circumvent the political will of national leaders; it reflected their will'. Here, Moravcsik, like his predecessors within the intergovernmental tradition, follows the traditional realist view of institutional building, a view, which tends to deprive regional institutions and transnational forces of any substantial role in the process of preference formation. In this area, then, liberal intergovernmentalism clashes not only with neo-functionalists but also with institutionalists, neoliberal and structuralist views of global integration. Analysts following these perspectives tend to emphasise the role of global pressures in shaping states' behaviour and the growing retreat of the state from economic management (Naisbitt 1994; Ohmae 1995; Strange 1996).

From the intergovernmentalist perspective, states' support for regional integration can be seen as a strategy for reinforcing sovereignty, which is undermined by the increasing globalisation and interdependence of the world economy. This was certainly a major reason why Mexico, for instance, embarked on an asymmetrical negotiation with the US to create NAFTA (O'Toole 2002). Integration reinforces states' sovereignty to the extent that it brings bargaining power to the governments in their dealing with foreign counterparts. Thus, governments would be able not only to counter pressures, but also to forge links with other states and regions, helping them to extract advantages from globalisation.

Intergovenmentalist bargaining differs substantially from the billiard-ball model favoured by realism, which views international bargaining 'in terms of the clash of national interests' and power politics (Webb 1982, 304).

Intergovernmentalism focuses on a two-level game, where the governments have to bargain simultaneously with their domestic constituencies and with foreign counterparts. Intergovernmentalism assumes that governments act purposively in the interstate bargaining, but on the basis of goals that are defined domestically through manipulation and negotiation with domestic forces. When they 'have sorted out contentions stemming from domestic forces', governments could, therefore be regarded as unitary actors in the external negotiations (Moravcsik 1993a, 481). However, even when the process of negotiations has passed through the sieve of domestic politics, the presumption of the state as a unitary actor in the external arena could be difficult to maintain. Domestic as well as sudden international changes could derail the assumption of the unitary state.

The interstate bargaining largely deals with the distributional conflicts or 'negative policy externalities' [2] created by regional interdependence. Governments then find it in their own interest to co-operate to overcome such externalities. This includes support for integration. This leads the states to engage in asymmetrical bargaining where the larger ones seek to influence outcomes in line with their preferences and power. The outcome of such bargaining, however, is largely determined by patterns of preference intensity rather than relative power among the states. Patterns of intensity of preferences predict that 'the more intensively a government prefers agreement, the greater its incentive to offer concessions and compromises' (Moravcsik 1998, 63). However, because of asymmetries in the power relations of the states, the governments of the larger states would take the lead and try to change the balance in their favour. Side-payments can be given to small states in order to bring their support to integration, whereas the threat of exclusion can be used against a reluctant government in order to force it to co-operate (Moravcsik 1991).

This kind of bargaining has taken place in Europe where, owing to economic interdependence, governments tend to be sensitive and in some cases vulnerable to negative policy externalities created by the unilateral or joined actions taken by leading member states. For instance, France and Germany have used the threat of exclusion to Britain in order to get its acquiescence to deepening the European integration. Equally, they have granted side-payments to poorer ones in order to get them alongside their preferred policies (Moravcsik 1991; Garrett 1992). Similar cases exist for Central America as will be seen through out this book.

It is important to differentiate this intergovernmentalist view of the threat of exclusion in pursuit of a compromise from Gruber's notion, which contends that the threat of exclusion will lead to a non-reciprocal submission by reluctant states. In other words, there will be no bargaining, no compromise, and no linkages, but outright submission or defeat (Gruber 2000). For Moravcsik, rather, the result of the threat of exclusion will be a compromise around the lowest-common denominator. He argues that only if the threat of exclusion 'undermines the substantive interest of the excluded state, the coercive threat may bring about an agreement at the level of integration above the lowest common denominator' (Moravcsik 1991, 47).

A state that is not strongly trade-dependent within a region or relies on markets outside the region would not be sensitive to its neighbours' policies of integration. Likewise, a government facing a low win-set domestically because of societal opposition to integration could use its inability 'to make concessions and to meet demands' as bargaining power in its external negotiations (Schelling 1960, 19). Because of this, the likely outcome of the negotiation would be a compromise under the lowest common denominator, where the preferences of all governments are taken into account. The fear of non-agreement, which would leave all states worse off, would press governments for a compromise from which they can derive some joint gains (Schelling 1960; Moravcsik 1993a). This compromise will take into account the interests, political and structural limitations of the least committed states, therefore, setting limits to co-operation and to the possibility of getting far-reaching agreements.

Third proposition, limits on transfer of sovereignty to institutions. Sovereignty is a major factor in the intergovernmentalist analysis of regional integration. It has remained a central feature in political theory since the birth of the sovereign state, which is traced back to the peace treaties of Westphalia in 1648. Because of the centrality of sovereignty in regional integration, intergovernmentalism tends to deprive supranational officials, business groups and regional organisations of the central role that neo-functionalists, institutionalists and even globalists ascribe to them. For intergovernmentalism, their role is contingent upon states' power and preferences. Moravcsik (1998, 21–22) argues that 'governments debate institutions only once they strike a substantive bargaining'. Governments use institutions as catalysts and conduits through which they seek to increase their influence and autonomy vis-à-vis domestic forces. Many regional agreements, not just on institutions, pursue this goal. To this extent institutions and regional bureaucrats are important in the interstate bargaining. But Moravcsik, as did most intergovernmentalist analysts, rejects the idea of governments being dependent on institutions in order to carry out the process of integration. In his view 'governments with the greatest interest in seeing an agreement or disinterested third governments act as entrepreneurs, initiating, mediating, and mobilising negotiations' (Moravcsik 1999, 273). For Moravcsik (1991, 75) 'the primary source of integration in Europe lies in the interests of the states themselves and the relative power each brings to Brussels'. This statement does not need to be limited exclusively to the European experience of integration. The role of the state is central in any process of integration be it in Europe or in Central America. As Holsti (2004, 29) points out, 'States are both institutions of the international political realms and the main though not exclusive agents that create and change the institutions in which they operate'.

With the perception that institutions are important, but not a determinant factor for integration, leading governments will not be enthusiastic about transferring sovereignty powers to supranational bodies. According to Holsti 'sovereignty is not a status or condition that fluctuates (a variable) with the rising and falling fortunes of individual leaders. It is an attribute of a continuous and distinct political community inhabiting a defined realm. It cannot wax and wane, be shared, or diluted' (Holsti 2004, 42). Therefore, governments would prefer arrangements that take sovereignty as quid pro quo for integration. Because of this concern about sovereignty, intergovernmentalism argues that the logic of integration will not be smooth and linear. As mentioned earlier, it proceeds in 'fits and starts' guided by the logic of diversity and the lowest-common-denominator (Hoffmann 1965, 1966; Moravcsik 1991).

Nonetheless, the fact that governments care about sovereignty does not necessarily mean that they would not be prepared to accept some limits to it. If the gains expected from collective action are large and there is the need to ensure compliance with regional agreements, then, governments may feel the need to compromise levels of sovereignty through a process of 'policy co-ordination' (Keohane 1984; Moravcsik 1998). But worries about losing sovereignty or flexibility in the implementation of their national and foreign policies are likely to lead them to favour a process of integration carried out through intergovernmental instruments, such as summits of heads of state, council of ministers, and other intergovernmental committees and instruments, instead of supranational authorities.

The aim of these intergovernmental instruments is to 'produce hard and prolonged bargaining among governments rather than creative interchange among regional bureaucrats, national officials and interest groups' (Webb 1982, 304). Pooling sovereignty would be preferred when the need for co-ordination thus requires it or when the governments wish to ensure compliance by their counterparts. According to Moravcsik (1998, 73) 'governments are likely to accept pooling or delegation (of decisions to institutions) as a means to assure that other governments will accept agreed legislation and enforcement, to signal their own credibility, or to lock in future decisions against domestic opposition'.

Pooling sovereignty means the adoption of decisions by qualified majority voting as opposed to unanimity which gives to the governments veto power on sensitive issues related to their national interests. Their attachment to the territorial state would force governments to resist arrangements that would compromise sovereignty when it runs against the national interest. They would, thus, make sure that regional agreements and institutions reflect their constitutional limitations and that they do not increase their vulnerability both domestically and regionally.

INTERGOVERNMENTALISM IN CENTRAL AMERICA

Criticisms have been levelled against intergovernmentalism on grounds that it is too state centric, probably exaggerating the role of governments and the state in fostering regional integration. It tends to ignore broader constellations of causation such as the role of transnational forces (O'Neill 1996, 135; George 1996a). It gives undue attention to economic interests at the expense of political ones (Foster 1998). It gives little or no attention to bureaucratic politics and it seems too rigid in claiming the self-sufficiency of the states and disregarding regional institutions and their bureaucracies (Webb 1982, 305). It may be considered unbalanced by overemphasising demand against supply conditions for integration (Mattli 1999). Finally, the political economy considerations that are so central in European integration may not be so in regions such as Central America.

So, given the shortcomings attributed to intergovernmentalism, can the application of the theory be transferred to Central American integration? Does integration in this region reveal intergovernmental features? Can theories be easily transported from one place to another? These are all relevant questions, which need some answers.

European integration is unique; geopolitical and economic factors have, in combination, been a force for integration. The EU model of integration may not be directly transferable to other regions, but it has given rise to a set of theories, which can be tested in other places. Intergovernmentalism may provide an understanding of aspects of the Central American integration process. At the same time, the Central American case can be used to test some of intergovernmentalism's core contentions. It will be argued that, with some modifications, intergovernmentalism has sufficient explanatory power to explain key aspects of the integration processes in Central America not only in the 1990s, but also since its inception in the decade of 1960,

Problems arise when viewing Central America through the lens of intergovernmentalism. One is the issue of a weak interdependence. Regional interdependence is strong in Europe because economic development and the size and openness of the economies generate pressures for co-operation and enhance the prospect for positive gains. As developed economies, a large proportion of their international trade takes place among member states. This contrasts with the peripheral status of the Central American economies, which directs its economic and trade relations outwardly toward the core states in the global economy. This explains the low level of intra-regional trade in Central America. Moreover, it also accounts for a low economic interdependence and co-operation while enhancing national and regional conflicts because the unequal trade relations leave the peripheral nations 'less cohesive-and hence less able to develop long-term strategies' (Galtung 1991, 295). Furthermore, Krasner (1991) argues that global economic openness, although it may bring economic gains for small states, also brings about risks that could undermine their political systems. Krasner also argues that the static economic benefits of openness are normally inversely related to size. Thus, small states, because they tend to have higher ratios of trade to the national product, are expected to gain more in relative welfare than large states. But the impact of openness on social stability runs in the opposite direction. In other words, greater openness means for small states greater social instability because they are structurally less able to protect themselves from the vagaries of the global economy. Thus, the fear of insecurity and political instability makes developing countries less willing to open their economies and more prone to favour protectionism which weakens interdependence and regional collaboration.

In Latin America the strong centralist tradition inherited from Spanish colonisation also hampers the possibility of far-reaching integration (Véliz 1980, 8–11), strengthening the case for national self-reliance. This in turn highlights the reliance for integration on the actions of the heads of government and their ministers of economics and foreign affairs. This impact of centralism has led analysts of South American integration to focus the analysis of integration under the heading of Presidentialism (Malamud 2001, Kaltenthaler and Mora 2002). In the author's view such a heading is misleading. The central roles played by the presidents and their ministers in South America fall neatly into the intergovernmentalist paradigm. To call it presidentialism seems to be quite inaccurate because the main bargaining takes place between ministers. The Presidents normally seal the final agreements and occasionally deal with any remaining hard issues that their ministers could not solve themselves, either because they require presidential agreement or because they constitute a watershed in terms of global diplomacy.

In the EU the willingness of larger states to take a larger share of the cost of integration allows smaller states to lower the cost in terms of social stability. This encourages small states to support and benefit from integration. Mattli argues (1999) that the existence of a regional leader willing to act as regional paymaster becomes a supply condition for successful integration. Thus, asymmetrical co-operation takes place where the larger states have the capability to persuade the smaller to co-operate, facilitating a process of integration which is in line with the preferences of the larger states.

In Central America the non-existence of a regional paymaster willing to carry the cost of integration implies that conflicts could become intractable, thereby, setting limits to co-operation and to interstate bargaining. Rather than co-operating, governments could well become averse to each other's policies. This would make policy co-ordination less enduring and conflict more salient in Central America than in the EU. Thus, underdevelopment and dependency in Central America, and presumably in Latin America as a whole, limit the effectiveness of intergovernmentalism.

Another problem has to do with the constrictive view of the strategic environment in the intergovernmentalist framework. In Europe, this is limited to the strategic interactions of the states within the region. The European states are developed economies and therefore do not face the same level of structural constraints (internal and external) as developing countries. They can isolate themselves considerably from the vagaries of the global economy, while at the same time generating externalities to other states and regions. Therefore, to provide a clearer understanding of intergovernmentalism in Central America, this concept of the strategic environment needs to be modified. A great deal of Central American integration emerges as a result of interstate bargaining which, in turn, is triggered by the interests and preferences of the political elite of the region. But this state bargaining is not limited to the interactions of the states of the region within a context of regional interdependence.

In contrast with Europe, where the economies are developed and highly interdependent, regional interdependence in Central America cannot provide a solid basis for integration because it is weak. The governments do not pursue integration because they face strong domestic economic pressures for it. They do not face strong pressures stemming from the negative externalities (costs) created as a result of policies adopted by other regional states as in the case of the European integration. In Europe, the intensity of these pressures leads the states to co-operate in order to manage their interdependence. In Central America governments co-operate mostly because integration allows them to achieve goals that they define as being in their national interests and because it also allows them to interact more purposefully with external actors (both governmental and non-governmental). Thus, more than economic interdependence, what leads the governments to support integration is strategic interdependence. Strategic interdependence refers to a situation whereby an actor cannot fulfil goals without the co-operation of others (Milner 1993).

Thus, even though economic interdependence in Central America is weak, strategic interdependence can be seen as a force pressing the governments to co-operate to achieve their national goals. But, because interdependence in the region is weak in general, which in turn implies that domestic social actors are also weak, the 'strategic environment' in Central America needs to be rethought. To solve this problem, the notion of the 'structural environment' [3] must be integrated into the analysis of the strategic interactions of the states. This would help to explain the broader set of interactions that take place within the region and the relations of the region with the global economy. The structural environment can be defined as the broader set of relationships, rules, changes and institutional constraints that impinge on the governments' actions and on the definition of national preferences. In other words, the understanding of the strategic environment in which bargaining and inter-governmental relations take place needs to take on board the structural environment in which Latin American policies exist. This especially includes structural changes in the international political economy. Studies on dependence have rightly emphasised that 'less-developed countries are tightly constrained by international forces' (Gill and Law 1988, 12). These forces, therefore, are likely to have a considerable impact on the definition of regional policies and integration.

Thus in Latin America generally, and perhaps even more so in Central America, governmental decisions and preferences are formed within an environment in which the broader contours of their political economy are determined elsewhere. That is, states make choices and governments engage in negotiations, within their regions, and beyond within the Americas and globally, within an environment shaped principally by a combination of pressures and options generated by the US and the thrust of the global political economy. Changes in the international political economy, as Stopford and Strange argue (1991, 22) 'create new sources of asymmetry in the relative importance of actors and broadens the space for negotiation in which the interests of non-governmental actors limit intergovernmental bargaining considerably.'

Because of this, Stopford and Strange maintain that a new strategic paradigm has been shaped in which the traditional state to state diplomacy is being replaced by a triangular diplomacy. According to this triangular paradigm, the strategic interactions of the states are no longer limited to themselves. 'The traditional players in the embassies and foreign ministries are still in business, but they have been joined by members of other government ministers and by executives of firms, both local and multinational' (Stopford and Strange 1991, 21). Strange (1994) argues that what triggered these new kinds of interaction was a structural change, particularly a change in the structure of production in the world economy. In other words, it is not so much a political led change, but a market led change.

This change is more palpable 'in the accelerating rate and cost of technological change, the mobility of capital and transborder communications' (Strange 1994, 103–104). As a result, both states and multinational businesses have seen their relative power modified and felt the need to engage in strategic bargaining which seems to conform with a notion of strategic interdependence, in which the actors are compelled to co-operate in order to achieve their aims. In regions such as Central America, this bargain takes place in the context of the need of governments to attract foreign investment and new technologies and accelerate the internationalisation of their economies, and the need of firms to gain access to the markets. This dependence on foreign investors and other actors constrains the capacity of governments and the way national preferences are formed. This structural change has increased competitiveness within developing economies, forcing developing states to compete intensively to improve their position in the global economy (Strange 1994). This competition is 'not just for markets and foreign exchange, but for capital, skilled labour and access to new technology' (Gill and Law 1988, 121).

Nonetheless, despite Strange's emphasis on technology and the market as the main source of change, the shift in the distribution of power following the end of the Cold War, in which the US became the only remaining superpower, cannot be ignored. The removal of economic guarantees by the US, based on loyalty in the East-West confrontation, also triggered competition between Latin American states, including Central America for market shares and international aid, in the 1990s. The US strategic interest changed from security to geo-economic priorities; its demand for transparency in the trade and economic policies of the states also became a major constraint on the ability of the governments to carry on integration based on their preferences. These US strategic changes in the region [4] imposed pressures on the other Latin American governments to accelerate their processes of integration as a way to avoid being excluded from the new international economic restructuring of which regionalism is a central feature.

To some extent, the reinvention of regionalism in Latin America, especially in Central America, is explained by the logic of regaining some of the bargaining power lost as a result of the end of the Cold War. This, among other things, highlights the defensive and reactive nature of regionalism in Latin America (Bouzas and Soltz 2000; Gruber 2000) which also may explain the resilience of conflicts which undermine the consolidation of integration. These developments in the structural environment substantially modify the intergovernmentalist's claim regarding the centrality of the state in forging integration based on political calculations, self-interest and interstate bargaining. Structural pressures stemming not only from the global economy, but also from domestic structures that governments face in terms of financial handicaps, lack of adequate social, political and physical infrastructure, limit the agency of the state in pursuing integration in the terms stated by intergovernmentalism. Therefore, intergovernmentalism is useful; but like all theoretical approaches it has limitations. As a theoretical perspective to integration it is too agency-centred and needs to take more account of structural constraints. But it is also important, at least theoretically, to see the influence of structural factors as constraints rather than determinants of the state's interests and preferences (Ikenberry 1991, 167).

CONCLUDING REMARKS

Thus, intergovernmentalism is not wholly successful in explaining the initial impulse to regionalism, but it cannot be completely disregarded either. Emphasising states' preferences and intergovernmental bargaining lend integration an organic sense within the political processes of the states. It also allows, *ceteris paribus*, the prediction of how far integration can go. One failure of neofunctionalism, and currently, of globalisation studies, is that they fail to take into account the political factor, that is, the willingness or unwillingness of governments to provide credible commitment to integration. The assumption was that spill-over alone, or global pressures, were sufficient conditions to force the governments to harmonise their economic and trade policies under some sort of regional governance regardless of their preferences. But, as many authors have suggested, regionalism is also a conscious action of the state's elite to protect themselves against the vagaries of globalisation and to reassert political control over the process of integration into the global economy (Gamble and Payne 1996; Sideri 1997). In addition, Holsti (2004, 19), based on arguments by Robert Jackson, argues that 'the foundation principles of international politics- what we terms today the Westphalia system-did not undergo transformation as a result of major changes in the social and technological environment in previous centuries'. In other words, major transformations such as current globalisation has not altered or made obsolete the institutions of the state system, e.g. territoriality, political authority based on the holding of legal coercion, sovereignty, diplomacy and the agential role of the state in world politics.

The process of peace negotiation under the Arias Peace Plan of 1987 clearly revealed an intergovernmental bargaining based on governments' perceptions of their national interests and political preferences. Through co-operation and bargaining the governments substantially transformed the strategic environment characterised by hostile and competitive relations, which in the 1980s inhibited peace and integration. Likewise, concerns about economic failures and the interest in improving the competitiveness of the economies in combination with governments' perception of a changing international political economy also triggered the interstates' bargaining under which the rebuilding of integration was based in the 1990s. While most states favoured integration, the threat of exclusion and asymmetrical bargaining characterised the relationship, especially between Costa Rica and the other states.

The basic tenets of intergovernmentalism, can, therefore, be found in the Latin American processes of integration. The central role of governments in development is institutionalised in the constitutional arrangements of the states. In Latin America the role of the state in forging integration is reinforced by the structural weakness of the market and that of most social actors, including business groups and social movements (Falleto 1989). Because of the weakness of the market and of most social actors, the interests of non-state actors like businesses groups 'are articulated in regional negotiations through the structures of the states' (Phillips 2000, 387). Atavisms from the region's political history, mainly the centralist political tradition, also account for this concentration of activities on the state. Thus, as Véliz argues (1980, 9), 'Regardless of the intentions of revolutionaries and reformers, every major reconstruction has resulted in increased central control'. This, as will be seen later, seems to portray the reform that regional integration underwent in the 1990s under SICA; despite the process of democratisation in the countries of the region, the trend of governmental control of regional institutions has not diminished.

Thus, atavisms such as underdevelopment, dependence and political history, paradoxically, reinforce the role of the states in Central American integration. This, as Falleto argues, is a paradox because it is in the logic of the world market and globalisation to weaken the nation-state when it is imposed on dependent countries. But, for Falleto, this contradiction is 'due to the fact that the state apparatus ensures the form of dependence' (Falleto 1989, 71). Thus, while in Europe according to Moravcsik (1998) the centrality of the state in the integration process is a rational choice by governments in line with defined national preferences and interests, in Central America, there seems to be many structural factors in defining such a role. Both states' preferences and structuralism seem to combine in shaping governments' choices and national interests. Regional integration, therefore, reflects a symbiotic relationship between the political definitions by governments and the demands or pressures stemming from the structural environment.

2 States' Preferences on Integration
The Cases of Costa Rica and El Salvador

Central American states have their own national interests regarding integration. For practical purposes the analysis can be reduced to looking at the interests and preferences of the main states, particularly the interests of those states which have different perspectives regarding what the future and orientation of the integration should be. Costa Rica and El Salvador can be identified as the two states which each represent a competing view regarding the mode and extent of Central American integration. Why focus on Costa Rica and El Salvador? The central reason is that these states pursue domestic as well as distinctive regional policies, which feature competitive views and paradigms for integration.

Because of their different interests and views and their attempts to lead integration in accordance with their preferences these states can be regarded as major players on the stage of integration. They also prevail in the region in terms of political and macroeconomic stability as well as external competitiveness. This chapter, therefore, seeks to identify the formation of interests and preferences in Costa Rica and El Salvador. The main forces influencing the national interest regarding integration will be highlighted along with some of the restrictions that they face in terms of their approaches to integration and how these constraints shape their preferences and actions in that process.

Two claims are advanced here. First, both Costa Rica and El Salvador favour integration but they differ about the method to achieve it and the extent to which integration should occupy a central position in the political life of the states. Second, because of differences in their political economy and external dependence, these states both face limitations. In the case of El Salvador these lead to pressure to pursue integration actively whereas in Costa Rica they result in a strong tendency for caution. Because of this, integration moves at the pace of the lowest common denominator, depending largely on the quality of bargaining between the two states and on their willingness to compromise on issues of common interest.

COMPETING PERSPECTIVES ON INTEGRATION

Despite the fact that historically there has been a sense of communality between El Salvador and Costa Rica, they differ quite remarkably in their views regarding the scope and nature of integration. Both states have supported integration since the signing of ODECA and the CACM in 1951 and 1960, respectively. However, while El Salvador has placed the emphasis on community building and the completion of the common market, Costa Rica has favoured intergovernmentalism and the building of a free trade area. Since the 1950s, El Salvador has pushed economic integration, to which Costa Rica has sought to adapt. The explanation of this contrast can be found in the differential patterns of political, social and economic development followed by the states, and in geo-economic factors. This has given rise to domestic pressures and forces that encourage integration or disintegration. But, in most cases, the differences between the states are structurally bound, which in turn conditions the preferences of the governments when approaching economic and political integration.

In El Salvador a free-market rationale has moulded the social fabric of the state and the definition of export policies. This was a result of the privatisation of common land at the end of the nineteenth century, public investment in infrastructure in the 1940s, and monetary and social conservatism traditionally favoured by the government in order to boost private businesses (Dada Hirezi 1983; Bulmer-Thomas 1987). It was also the result of having an ambitious and well diversified economic elite, which kept expanding its economic and commercial interests (Paige 1997, 19–23). This gave rise to the proliferation of small businesses in the manufacturing sector, transforming El Salvador into the most industrialised of the region in the 1960s and 1970s. Although protectionism has not been excluded in Salvadorian trade policies, the state has been traditionally conservative in supporting producers. This has given El Salvador the upper hand in promoting the opening of the markets of the region, proposing a strategy of market integration and, particularly in the 1990s, preferring institutional development within the CACM.

Costa Rica, on the other hand, is the state of the region which, since the very beginning of its republican history, has consistently promoted its integration beyond the region. 'It was the first state of the region to succeed in exploring external markets following the apogee of coffee production and the first to have a financial institution supporting coffee growers and exporters'.[1] It was also the state which relied more on protectionism and governmental support to producers. The support to industrialists was strong in the 1950s with the adoption of a highly protective import tax and the first industrial legislation (Araya Pochet 1982). The support to industrialists was further expanded in 1972 with the adoption of the export promotion law which granted lavish incentives to exporters, including tax credits and the elimination of taxes to goods imported by industries supplying third markets. As a result of this, Costa Rica has faced recurrent financial difficulties, which have undermined its bargaining position within the region and hindered the process of openness of the CACM. The San José protocol of 1968 was a clear example of this, and so is the weak commitment of Costa Rica to the Guatemalan Protocol of 1993 which reformed the economic integration in line with the prevailing interest of external openness.

Geo-economic factors also underline the difference between the two states. These have to do, for instance, with the economic and geographic location of the states. El Salvador is the only state of the region without a Caribbean coast. This, to some extent, explains why the banana enclave which concentrated on the Atlantic coast of Central America did not develop in this state. This in turn underlines the national basis of Salvadorian capitalism and the entrepreneurial leadership of its economic elite. The need to gain access to the Caribbean, but also the need to allocate its industrial surpluses in the other markets of the region may have encouraged El Salvador to consolidate its relationships and channels of communications with its immediate neighbours, Guatemala and Honduras. According to Siri (1984, 9) 'no other Latin American country is so well linked with its neighbours'. The country is located in the densely populated and highly entrepreneurial region of the north of Central America which has encouraged for the development of the entrepreneurial class, taking advantages of abundant unskilled and skilled labour and concentrated markets.

Costa Rica, on the other hand, located in the sparsely populated and narrower strip of the isthmus has tended to look inward. In colonial times Costa Rica was the poorest part of the isthmus both in economic resources and populations. However, by the turn of the nineteenth century it had gained the reputation of being 'the most highly civilised, the most politically mature and the most advanced and prosperous nation of the region' (Robinson 1977, 180). In the 1950s, these conditions, together with the fear of losing ground in the face of the competitiveness and larger markets of the other states, prevented Costa Rica from striking a compromise with the attempt at regional unity by the other states (Parker 1964, 88). The fears were expressed in the nationalist postures adopted by the Economics Minister Jorge Borbón in late 1959 and 1960. However, these fears also forced Costa Rica to co-operate with the other states, signing up to the General Treaty of Economic Integration (GEI) in 1962 and the Guatemalan Protocol in 1996.

The allegiance to the territorial state has been a strong force determining Costa Rican cautious behaviour towards integration. El Salvador has historically neutralised the Guatemalan ambition of integrating Central America under a centralised republic, thereby leading a liberal coalition seeking decentralised federalism. Because of the interest in preserving its sovereignty, Costa Rica has also opposed Guatemala's project of integration, lining up instead with El Salvador on several occasions (Valle Martínez 1999). However, Costa Rica has not been a strong supporter of the Salvadorian project of integration either. Three factors inhibit it from fully supporting integration:

1. The threat of federalism dating back to the independence of the region in 1821. Costa Rica participated and honoured its obligations

under the federal regime established after independence. However, it saw itself as a loser within the federation (Obregón Loría 1977). As a result, following the breaking down of the federal system in the 1830s, Costa Rica therefore avoided re-engaging with the region at that level of political commitment.

2. Rejection of the highly socially differentiated model of development of the other states which has been a source of recurrent domestic instability, especially in El Salvador (Dunkerley 1982). The Costa Ricans fear that this model may be transferred as the paradigm for the integration of the region. As they managed to consolidate an economic model which combines 'export-led growth with agriculture diversification' which has reinforced the democratic system and domestic stability (Bulmer-Thomas 1987, 151), they fear that the instability of the other states could spill-over into the country. Therefore, Costa Rica is cautious about integration. Rodrigo Carreras illustrates this.

   In a document Adolf Mary, Deputy Foreign Secretary during the government of Juan Rafael Mora Porras (1849–1859), sustained a very important thesis regarding Central American integration. He said that Costa Rica is a unionist country, but it does not like the permanent wars, which take place in the region between liberals and conservatives. Therefore, it prefers to stay away from these conflicts. He said that until Central America achieves the same levels of economic wealth and living standards of Costa Rica, the country prefers to remain away from the region. Unfortunately Costa Rica is still ahead of the region and this has encouraged its timidity and cautious attitude regarding the Central American affairs. This situation has not changed.[2]

This view of the region has led Costa Rica to pay lip service to integration while avoiding engaging the country in some regional arrangements, such as security and social integration, which might be required to consolidate the process of economic integration.

3. The competitiveness and entrepreneurial ethos of the Salvadorian economic groups contrasts with the weakness of those in Costa Rican and their dependence on the state for subsidies and protectionism. According to Luis Guillermo Solis, Costa Rica is not the most advanced in economic affairs because it is the most protectionist state of the region. It is a country whose social development has been funded with customs duties and taxes in general.[3]

Because of these social, economic and geopolitical differences these states tend to stress different interests and values when considering integration.

INTERESTS AND PREFERENCES OF EL SALVADOR

The interests of El Salvador regarding the CACM were neatly expressed in 1966 by the former Minister of Economics, Jorge Castellanos. According to Sol Castellanos (1972), building and consolidating the CACM is a vital foreign policy objective for El Salvador, which promotes integration not only for ideological reasons. The thrust for leading the case for integration is determined by its national interest. The pursuit of economic gain is a vital foreign policy objective of the state, which sparks off regional integration. This includes opening the markets for the allocation of Salvadorian goods, capital and labour. Thus, for El Salvador, regional integration is a matter of survival and vital space in the sense of overcoming the geographical constraints imposed by the territorial state and the size of the domestic market (Sol Castellanos 1972). As Francisco Sorto points out, 'integration is the way of resolving the space problem through the promotion of the free movement of factors in the region. It is also the way to promote the economic expansion of El Salvador in the region which is a central pursuit of its national interest'. [4]

The view of integration as 'vital' for its economic life explains the special attention that El Salvador gives to Central America both at the level of government, the general public, the education system and the media. As Dada Hirezi points out (1983, 103), despite obstacles faced by the process of integration, 'all generations of Salvadorians have been educated under the ideal of the Central American fatherland, and the leaders of the state have proclaimed themselves ready to carry it out'. Its political constitution (Articles 55, 89) commands the government to promote the integration of the region, including the creation of supranational bodies or the reestablishment of the Central American Federation. This explains the leading role that El Salvador has played since 1950s in negotiating free trade agreements with its neighbours and embracing proposals leading toward political union, such as ODECA (Ortez Colindres 1975; Dada Hirezi 1983) and the current system under SICA.

In the 1950s the government was concerned about the restrictions which high population density, the lack of natural resources and soil erosion, imposed on the conditions of life and economic activity of the state. It was believed that the country 'would have great difficulties surviving and shaping a sufficiently solid economy within the actual limitations of its own resources and markets' (Sol Castellanos 1972, 82). It was the understanding of these constraints together with the growth of a thriving entrepreneurial class and the integrationist ideology shared by the political and economic elite, which moved El Salvador to play a central role in promoting the integration of the region. The objective pursued was to overcome these limitations through the expansion of economic and trade relations with the other states. Economic integration offered the advantage that it would provide markets for the Salvadorian industrial surplus. Likewise, it would induce economic change and modernisation without challenging the status quo domestically. ECLAC (1986) terms this fashion of modernisation 'superimposed development'.

Business groups, particularly industrialists strongly supported the government's policy of integrating with the region. El Salvador does not seem to have experienced inter-elite conflict regarding the processes of economic modernisation and regional integration. Menjivar (1982) observes that contrary to what happened in other Latin American countries, conflict between the landed oligarchy and industrialists did not take place in El Salvador. Delgado Rosa (1984, 84) likewise stresses that in this country both industrialists and traders were 'thoroughly integrationists', a situation which was rare everywhere else in the region. This gave the government a strong political lever and autonomy to negotiate the integration of the region with the other states in terms according to the Salvadorian preferences. To the extent that there is a strong constitutional and inter elite backing to integration, it is possible to argue that El Salvador enjoys a large leverage in the region to pursue integration. Nowhere else in the region does a government have such a strong capacity to lead on economic and political integration.

In the 1990s El Salvador still faced some of the constraints that prevailed in the 1950s and 1960s: the small size of the domestic market, entrepreneurial pressures, high population growth, unemployment and a strong dependence on the CACM for the allocation of its industrial production. Their importance, however, have diminished not only because of the current level of integration of the country to the global economy, but also because of substantial levels of migration of Salvadorians to other Central American countries and the US. This has not only reduced domestic pressures, but has also become a profitable business as the remittances of Salvadorians living in the US accounted in 2006 for about 16 per cent of the countries GDP. In addition, as a result of the economic reforms instigated, particularly in the 1990s, to transform the economy and integrate it to the world market, the Salvadorian interests are no longer limited to the CACM.

The economic reform implemented during the 1990s brought about significant changes in the Salvadorian economy. The economy is more diversified and less dependent on agriculture both domestically and in terms of its foreign trade. In 2005, for instance, main agricultural exports, including coffee, sugar and shrimps amounted only to $233 million out of $3,387 billion exported by the state. The remainder was distributed between 'maquila' [5] and under the heading of others (BCR 1999). The agrarian conflict so acute in the 1970s and 1980s was to a large extent alleviated with the agrarian reform of the 1980s and the programme of land distribution agreed under the Peace Accords of 1992, which ended the civil war.

The Salvadorian economy has become more dependent on the secondary and tertiary sectors, particularly maquila, industrial trade, banking and remittances from Salvadorians living in the United States. The maquila industry, for instance, expanded dramatically in the 1990s. According to data from the Central Bank, in 1992, maquila exports amounted to $198 million. By 1999 the figure reached $1,333 billion, and $1,815 billion in 2005 which is about half of the country's total exports which in the latter year, as said above, amounted to $3,387 billion. Most of it goes to the USA which is the main Salvadorian market accounting for 54 per cent of its exports and 50 per cent of its imports. Economic growth has recovered from the negative trends of the 1980s. As a result, El Salvador became one of the fastest growing economies of the region during the 1990s, although the economic growth started to slow down in 1996. The size of the economy also increased during the 1990s. The GDP soared from $5, 955 billion in 1992 to nearly $20 billion in 2007, placing El Salvador as one of the largest economies of the region, behind Guatemala, and Costa Rica. The country is moving very fast to regain the position as the second largest economy of the region, a position that it lost to Costa Rica during the instability of the 1980s.[6] By 2003 it was considered to be the economy of the region with the highest potential for economic growth, a position withheld up until then by Costa Rica (Leitón 2003).

Since the 1990s, banking has become one of the most dynamic sectors of the Salvadorian economy. This has given the government the authority to pursue the financial integration of the region. The Cristiani administration (1989–1994) re-privatised all the economic sectors that were nationalised at the beginning of the 1980s, including the banking sector. The re-privatisation of the banking system placed the Salvadorian banks at the forefront in Central America, leading the region in integration of the financial market and external competitiveness. The commitments, made by the government under the policies of structural reform, to open the economy, encouraged the private sector to take risks and to establish domestic, regional and global alliances in order to acquire competitive power. Although the Salvadorian bankers may not necessarily rely on official policies to expand their activities in the region, the government has used integration to expand their activities and to encourage intergovernmental co-operation in the financial sector. The North Triangle is an example of the outcome of governments having made clear commitments to allow the free movement of capital. In this area financial integration has been established. This has unleashed strong positive reactions on the part of Salvadorian and Guatemalan bankers, who have established strategic alliances throughout the region, including in Costa Rica in spite of this country's non-membership of the North Triangle.

By year 2000 the Banco Cuscatlán, the second largest Salvadorian bank, had already set up branches in Costa Rica and pursued a very aggressive marketing campaign. The use of this financial capability had been enabled because of the close links between bankers and businesses in general and the governing party, ARENA. Thus, despite the lack of a regional instrument regulating the integration of the service sector within the CACM, El Salvador has integrated Central America in at least three sectors, namely:

banking, manufacturing trade, and air-transportation. The Salvadorian airline TACA has absorbed most of the national airlines of the other states, becoming a quasi-regional monopoly. Salvadorian traders are also the main attendants at the Costa Rican stock market, the largest in the region. This has created pressure for the integration of the stock markets of the region, a process which by 2000 was nearly reaching completion (Bravo 2000).

This activism on the part of El Salvador in Central America both at the official and private levels pursues two objectives. First, it seeks to increase the political influence of this state in the region through the consolidation of the SICA system. The second objective is to improve the competitiveness of the Salvadorian economy and to integrate it more successfully into the world economy.

Led by its trade dependence on the CACM, El Salvador fosters integration as a way of creating and managing regional interdependence. This would allow its partners in the North Triangle area to engage in a myriad of economic, trade, and social relationships with El Salvador. This in turn would not only allow El Salvador to increase its influence over the other states and to pursue its historical project of integration, but also to prevent its isolation in Central American relations. The North Triangle area, including Nicaragua, represents the core economic space of El Salvador within the CACM. About 86.3 per cent of its Central American exports went there in 2003. Export-dependence is, therefore, a major explanation of the central role played by El Salvador in consolidating the CA-4 as an area of co-operation and integration. As integrating some economic sectors with its neighbours would give rise to negative externalities it is expected that other states outside the CA-4 area would feel compelled to co-operate in order to avoid being affected or excluded from integration.

From the Salvadorian perspective, consolidating SICA is vital to ensure not only the free movement of capital, merchandise and factors throughout the region. It is also vital to the creation of a Central American integration law, which would reinforce regional interdependence and regional cohesion. Currently there is no integration law binding the states because the governments have avoided compromising sovereignty in the building of regional arrangements (Gallard 1999). Article 22 of the Tegucigalpa Protocol establishes the prevalence of the national law of the states over regional decisions. This has created a sense of scepticism and insecurity regarding the longevity of most regional arrangements. This sense of insecurity about its legal fabric constitutes a major weakness of Central American regionalism. Salvadorian regional policy aims to reinforce legal security (legitimacy of regional agreements) in order to consolidate the region's trade regime. A proposal presented by the Salvadorian Minister of Economics Miguel Lacayo in 2000 made this clear. Lacayo exhorted the region to adopt a mechanism of solving trade differences within the existing integration treaties, without reforming existing treaties and protocols such as the Tegucigalpa Protocol (El Diario de Hoy 2000). This is also the main reason why

El Salvador supports the Central American Court of Justice as the system for resolving trade disputes within the CACM.

Both the government and business interests have favoured improving the competitiveness of the Salvadorian economy and integrating it more successfully into the world economy. In its 1996 Manifesto the Association of Private Businesses (ANEP) argued that 'Central American integration must not be an inward process, but a strategy to negotiate in bloc the insertion of the region in the new economy in the fashion of sub-regional agreements' (ANEP 1996, 64). Most measures adopted by the government during the 1990s were directed at this purpose. Thus, El Salvador pursues integration both to substitute and to complement national policies.

In the 1990s, attracting FDI and improving the international competitiveness of the economy became a priority of the government. Emphasis was put on keeping macroeconomic stability and the external openness of the economy as well as creating specific legislation to favour foreign investment. Although by 1997 El Salvador was opened to FDI in most sectors of the economy, it had been behind in the region in terms of legislation to attract FDI. Foreign Investment legislation was updated in 1999. Non-traditional exports, especially maquila, have been the most dynamic sector promoting economic growth in the 1990s. However the model of export promotion followed by El Salvador is not based on monetary and fiscal subsidies to exporters.

El Salvador has traditionally rejected subsidising exports. Instead, the competitiveness of Salvadorian exports is based on macroeconomic stability, productivity, and low wages. The state does not employ direct export subsidises with the same generosity as other states. Although 'it offers a six per cent rebate to exporters of non-traditional goods on the FOB value of the exports, the exporters have found it very difficult to collect' (Department of State 1997). Nor has the exchange rate been used as an instrument to favour exporters. It remained fixed since 1986, when a new rate was established at 8.50 colones per dollar. In April 2001 the exchange rate was increased to 8.75 colones per dollar. President Francisco Flores refused further devaluation of the currency to favour exporters arguing that 'competition cannot be based on stealing the acquisitive power from the people, but on productivity' (La Prensa Gráfica 2000a). A swift move by the Francisco Flores' government to adopt the US dollar in parallel with the colón had the purpose of deepening macroeconomic stability and increasing the competitiveness of the economy. The assumption was, that with this measure, the interest rates of the country, already the lowest in the region, would become even lower, favouring new investment and exports.

El Salvador is already at the forefront of the region in terms of macroeconomic stability, external openness, and competitiveness. As a result of the structural changes made during the 1990s, the government has developed a pragmatic view of integration. Regional integration is seen as a platform to increase the attractiveness and competitiveness of the economy not only within the CACM, but also in the global market. This will be the result of breaking down border barriers to intra-regional trade. In turn, this will encourage private investors to reallocate their resources in El Salvador. The attraction will not be the local market, but the enlarged regional one made up of about forty million people with a GDP of around $50 billion.[7]

In the attempt to make the Salvadorian economy competitive in the region and the global markets, the government seeks to take advantage of the country's potential as a growing market. The country qualifies as a potential market on the following grounds: a) the comparatively low labour costs, b) the discipline of its labour force, c) its macroeconomic stability and d) last but not least, the advance in building democracy and political stability.[8] These four aspects combined, according to Peña, place El Salvador in a better competitive position within the CACM in relation to the other states. Three factors can be said to underlie the Salvadorian quest for leadership in the region. First, there is the backing of social forces, particularly big businesses, political parties, the army, and public opinion. These forces share the ideal of integration and their support allows the government to act purposefully in the Central American negotiations. Second, as José Francisco González argues, there is the impact of the economic reform and the end of the civil war.

> 'El Salvador has created a high sense of political and macroeconomic stability, which favours its economic expansion in the region. In addition, because of its demographic situation El Salvador needs space. For this reason, El Salvador is interested in promoting the free movement of labour and has led the cause for factors' integration within the CACM'.[9]

Lastly, integration allows the state to diffuse or negotiate its vulnerability. This vulnerability is highlighted by the strong dependence of the Salvadorian economy on the CACM. About half of its exports go to the CACM and the government continues to see the CACM as a safety valve for the state's growing population. Because of this dependence on the CACM, the Salvadorian government has repeatedly attempted to expand the North Triangle free-trade regime to include all the states of the region. This would provide some guarantees against protectionist measures in the other states against Salvadorian exports and open the way to the movement of factors. In line with this interest, El Salvador has repeatedly defended the free-trade regime within the CACM. It has done so despite opposition from domestic and regional pressure groups, such as rice growers and industrialists grouped in the Central American Federation of Industrialists (FECAICA), which demand protectionism.

President Flores' response to these demands was uncompromising. During the 2000 Independence celebration Flores defended the policy of economic openness calling it a new independence. In his view the future of the country does not depend on closing the borders to international trade or in maintaining short-term privileges, but in a strategy of long-term openness (La Prensa Gráfica 2000b). Thus, although El Salvador puts considerable effort into Central American integration, the government has increasingly tended to see integration as part of its global strategy of integration to the world economy.

INTERESTS AND PREFERENCES OF COSTA RICA

Costa Rica is sometimes seen as the awkward partner of Central American integration. In 1966 the former Salvadorian Economics Minister Jorge Sol Castellanos directly blamed the Costa Rican government, under Mario Echandi, for obstructing integration by signing but not ratifying the integration treaties (Sol Castellanos 1972). However, for El Salvador, Costa Rica, though awkward, operates intelligently and responsibly. In Peña's words:

> 'Costa Rica is a partner hard to work with. Costa Rica's government does not like silliness and wasting time. But when Costa Rica makes a commitment to integration it takes it seriously. This differentiates Costa Rica from other awkward partners in the region such as Nicaragua, who pay lip-service to integration, but in fact are obstructionist and do not follow the rules'.[10]

So, what accounts for the reluctant but ultimately co-operative role that Costa Rica has played in the process of Central American integration? There are four fundamental reasons: the fear of political integration; the likely economic cost; the elimination of borders and the effects of asymmetry of trade.

There is a reluctance, especially in the parliament, to compromise sovereignty. In general, Costa Rican politicians feel that political union would work as a transmission belt through which all the malaise and instability of the other states would be transferred to Costa Rica. This in turn constrains the capacity of the government to strike far-reaching compromises with the region. The fear of political union goes as back as far as the time of the federation in the nineteenth century. As a result Costa Rica has refused to play a leading role in the region whenever political union is at stake.

It is precisely because of the fear of political integration that the Costa Rican constitution (Article 121) makes no direct reference to Central American integration, although it does not discount the possibility of transferring some power to a regional arrangement. The voting system, however, is rigid in this respect requiring two-thirds of the parliamentary votes.[11] In spite of the political change that occurred in Central America during the 1990s, these kinds of fears still trouble the Costa Rican government. When the presidents met in Managua on September 02, 1997 to discuss the political integration of the region, President José Figueres Olsen surprised the other governments when he agreed to political integration. But as Rodrigo Carreras argues, his approval was highly conditional:

> Figueres' answer was yes, we want full integration, we want a single treaty of integration, we want a single Secretariat in SICA, and we want to make San Salvador the Brussels of Central America. But he added a set of preconditions before going along with political integration: these included, the 'full submission of the armies to the civilian authorities, the reduction of the military budgets, and improvements in the conditions of living of the population of the other states to catch up with the Costa Rican high standards'.[12]

In fact the conditions set by Figueres constituted a diplomatic way of saying no to political integration. Nevertheless, the government was willing to reach some kind of compromise. In his inaugural speech in May 1994, Figueres announced that he intended to strengthen Costa Rican co-operation with the states of the region (La Nación 1994). This, to a certain extent, explains why Figueres managed to get both the Tegucigalpa and Guatemalan protocols approved by the parliament, which was remarkable after the failure of the previous administrations to do so. He recognised the importance of organising the region as a bloc and was, therefore, more willing than his predecessor to commit Costa Rica to integration and to related issues such as institutional reform. During the Panama summit of June 1997, Figueres was at the forefront leading the process.[13] However, integration remains a divisive issue in Costa Rica. The conservative forces grouped in the Social Christian Party and other right wing organisations prefer the anti-integrationist tradition.

A second issue emerged at the end of the 1950s which still remains a powerful reason for rejecting full integration, the high economic cost that integration represents for Costa Rica. Integration entails costs and benefits to all the states, but those governments and domestic groups that feel disadvantaged by policy co-ordination are likely either to offer a limited commitment or to oppose regional co-operation (Moravcsik 1993a). Since the onset of the process of integration the Costa Rican conservatives have not seen integration as beneficial overall and when in power refuse to embrace full co-operation. The Economics Minister Jorge Borbón wrote in 1961 that because most of the Central American population was concentrated in the north of the region, and because of the low wages in these states compared to Costa Rica, the industrial development and most FDI would concentrate on these states. Consequently, the government believed that Costa Rica would lose competitiveness as a result of integration (La República 1961, 7; Cochrane 1965, 335). That was one of the main reasons why the

Echandi administration avoided committing Costa Rica to the process of integration under the common market in 1960.

The issue of lower production costs in the other states together with the higher level of protection, not only in the sense of social security, but also in terms of economic protectionism, still prevents the full participation of Costa Rica in the integration process. Interviews with officials in Costa Rica reveal that, because of the high dependence of the state on customs duties, the government is uneasy about embracing the attempt by the CA-4 (Guatemala, El Salvador, Honduras and Nicaragua) governments to transform the CACM into a customs union or a common market. This is so, despite pressures from industrialists, especially those who rely on the CACM. If the government were to commit the country to integration, the result would be a considerable loss of revenues.[14] 50 per cent of the state's revenues come from taxation, including customs duties, so eliminating the borders as fiscal entities, as would be required with a customs union, would have a strong impact on the state's finances.

Third, the elimination of the borders as a means of political control would clear the way for the open migration of Central Americans, attracted by the better standards of living in Costa Rica. This is something that the Costa Rican government wishes to avoid. For this reason, Costa Rica has resisted the expansion of integration beyond the exchange of goods. Costa Rica, thus, favours some kind of controlled interdependence where the government performs a gatekeeper role, rather than complex interdependence or supranationality where intra-regional forces could undermine the authority of the state and its external and internal sovereignty.

The fourth aspect preventing Costa Rica from moving towards deeper integration is the asymmetry of its trade relationship within the region. Despite the fact that Costa Rica's trade with the region increased remarkably during the 1990s, exports to the region were declining when compared with the overall performance of the country's total exports. In 1996, for instance, its exports to the region accounted for about 14.3 per cent of its total exports. By 1999 the ratio dropped to 9.5 per cent and has remained roughly at that level since. It is important to note that despite the fall in the ratio of Costa Rica's exports to the region, in nominal terms its exports have been growing since 1996. In 1999 they reached about $573.7 million and by 2005 the figure was $1.199 billion (Comex 2008). If we compare these exports with its total exports we will find that Costa Rica does actually have a very dynamic trade relationship with Central America. But the ratio of its regional exports tells us that, despite the expansion of trade with the region, in global terms the trend is downward or remains stagnant. In other words, in the 1990s, Costa Rica appears to have become increasingly less export-dependent within the CACM. Recent figures however, reveal that this situation is changing as the region is gradually becoming more important for Costa Rican exports, overtaking the EU as the second largest destination of its exports.

Likewise, the success of the country in attracting FDI, where it is the leader in the region, does not seem to be influenced significantly by its membership of the CACM. Most investment in the 1990s came from outside the region, especially the USA, and went to sectors exporting to third markets. The major attraction for FDI is a combination of political and social stability, legal protection of foreign investment and the relatively high level of education and skill endowment of the labour force. In other words, in Costa Rica, a successful exports and investment programme does not depend on membership of the CACM. This explains the country's ambivalence to integration. As Mattli argues (1999, 13) 'economically successful leaders may not see the need to pursue deeper integration because their expected marginal benefit from further integration in terms of retaining political power is minimal and thus not worth the cost of integration'. Instead, the Costa Rican government favours a strategy of global integration based on clear rules for the free movement of goods.

Economic reform implemented by the government since the early 1980s influenced Costa Rica's view of integration in the 1990s. In 1982 the country began seriously to move away from the model of import-substitution which had prevailed since 1948. The new paradigm of development began to take shape when President Carazo floated the colón in September 1980 to counteract economic destabilisation (Rovira Más 1988). This later involved expanding the incentives granted to industries exporting to third markets. Thereafter this policy shift involved the adoption of a 'strong stabilisation programme followed, in subsequent years, by further movements towards privatisation and other liberalisation measures' (Buttari 1992, 180, 183) which allowed the state to get back on the track of positive economic growth as early as 1983.

The state, domestic and transnational forces, co-operate to secure the implementation of neo-liberalism and to preserve the export support programmes in public policy. Thus, the success of the new model has relied heavily on the willing co-operation of the state, domestic interest groups and external actors in order to promote a 'strategic liberalisation designed to improve and protect Costa Rican exports of non-traditional goods' (Grugel 1998, 228).

Two important consequences follow as a result of the economic policies implemented since the 1980s in Costa Rica. First, there is the unleashing of economic forces which have become the backbone of the strategy of export promotion. A new generation of industrialists grouped in CADEXCO (Costa Rican Exporting Chamber) and bankers became the main private recipients of US aid during the 1980s. The natural market for this new generation of entrepreneurs is the US market under the Caribbean Basin Initiative (CBI), which was launched by President Reagan in 1984. CADEXCO, supported by the American Chamber of Commerce, has been a major pressure group lobbying the government for further liberalisation and for the development of the exporting regime.

But this is a policy that the government has followed since 1982 anyway, regardless of domestic pressure groups. The government has pursued the policy of export promotion despite opposition from domestic forces (especially trade unions) and has used external support as a leverage to implement unpopular economic reforms, despite strong resistance to economic liberalisation.

The second consequence is the creation since 1983 of a broad conservative consensus around neo-liberalism and the policy of export promotion. The two major political parties, the National Liberation Party and the Social Christian Party, once in government, have instigated policies designed to consolidate the export bias. This not only involves eliminating internal obstacles to exports, but also strengthening the system of incentives in the way of tax credits, financial, monetary and institutional facilities. Non-traditional exports to third countries reacted 'strongly and favourably' to the myriad of incentives granted by the government (Buttari 1992, 203).

As a result of these political and economic changes since 1983, Costa Rica has gradually been transformed into an exporting nation, relying heavily on international trade for its economic development. Although the country faces a problem of market concentration with the US and the EU, it has the most diversified economy and the most diversified and dynamic exports. Economic growth in the 1990s was largely determined by the performance of non-traditional exports, which include not only goods but also services such as tourism. In 1999, for instance, the economy grew between 7.5 to 8.5 per cent. About 5 per cent of this growth was accounted for by exports from the free trade zones. The remainder came from other sectors of the economy (La Nación 1999).

Costa Rica's attitude towards integration has changed significantly with the success of the strategy of promoting non-traditional exports to third markets. In practice, the export bias has tended to counter support for integration. In the 1990s, all governments tended to favour integration, but with different levels of intensity. Although economic growth in Costa Rica is not determined by the CACM, the development of a Central American trade regime is important for Costa Rica because a large sector of its industry depends on the CACM for its survival. Data from CADEXCO in 2000 revealed that only 7 to 10 percent of the industrial establishment of the country exports outside the CACM. The remaining 90 to 93 per cent of the industrial sector produces either for the local, or for the Central American, market (Barquero S 2000).

Despite this, Costa Rica's policy towards the CACM does not depend on its view of integration, but rather is part of its policy of export promotion. In the 1990s Costa Rica's integration into the world economy has been pursued at every level. As Pacheco argues:

> The commercial policy of Costa Rica seeks the insertion of the country in the world economy at every geographical level: the world, the

> hemispheric, the region and at the level of bilateral relations. Thus, Central America is an important part and it does not contradict the general policy of global integration. In other words, Central American integration cannot run in opposition to the efforts at global integration. I believe that no government attempts to do this. All countries are looking to harness the advantages and experiences that they have learned in their international negotiations in order to improve the quality of the Central American trade regime.[15]

Thus, within the economic foreign policy pursued by the government, regional integration is important, but it cannot contradict the efforts made by the government to integrate the country into the global economy. The so-called Central American preference, therefore, is less important and at all costs should not hinder the global integration of the Costa Rican economy.

Rather than grounding Costa Rican foreign trade policy within the rules of the CACM, the government increasingly takes the rules of the Word Trade Organisation (WTO) as the point of reference. Costa Rica's government believes that the experience gained in the external negotiations, the GATT-WTO included, should be used to 'update the CACM and to transform it into a market of clear rules, transparency, and higher disciplines'.[16] The increase in trade with the CACM during the 1990s has not generated pressures on Costa Rica for a closer integration with the region, nor does the government regard it a condition for deeper integration. In Echeverría's words:

> 'Increased trade with the region does not necessarily mean deeper integration. What is required is clear rules of transparency, the homogenisation (but not integration) of the trade laws throughout the region, and the abolishing of obstacles to trade'.[17]

Thus, Costa Rica's image for the region is that of one integrated for the purpose of expanding trade relations at every level: the CACM, the hemisphere and the world. For this purpose, the region needs clear rules to deal with trade disputes, unfair trade practices and lack of compliance with regional agreements rather than institutional development. The lack of compliance is in Costa Rica's view one of the main problems facing the Central American integration. In the words of Pacheco:

> In this moment, the main obstacle for deeper integration and regional development is the lack of compliance with regional agreements. When the borders are closed arbitrarily without resorting to the processes that the governments have agreed to deal with extraordinary situations. When regional arrangements have to succumb due to pressures from organised groups pressuring for decisions to be taken in one or

> another direction, but against regional agreements, that is the principal obstacle facing integration today.[18]

Accordingly, since 1998, Costa Rica has pressed the other governments for the adoption of a liberal treaty on trade disputes, which in its view should be managed as a specific instrument for solving trade conflicts among the states. Costa Rica opposed the adoption of the treaty on trade disputes under integration. The government opposed the attempt by Nicaragua, Honduras and El Salvador to bring the issue of trade disputes under the Central American Court of Justice (CCJ). The liberal-Morazanist states [19] argue that trade disputes should be dealt with within integration and that the accord on trade disputes should be used to strengthen the region's institutions. Therefore, in their view, the CCJ, which is located in Nicaragua, is the appropriate regional body to deal with trade disputes. Article 35 of the Tegucigalpa Protocol provides the basis for this interpretation. According to it, every controversy regarding the interpretation and implementation of the Protocol and other regional instruments 'must be submitted to the CCJ'. Costa Rica, although a signatory of the Tegucigalpa Protocol, has refused to ratify the statute of the CCJ, therefore it does not admit the Court as the right body for dealing with the issue of trade disputes.

Apart from the issue of sovereignty, which is a strong reason for not accepting the CCJ, the Costa Rican government believes that keeping trade disputes outside regional institutions will serve integration better by easing the way to resolving trade conflicts in accordance with international standards. Costa Rica's view of the mechanism on trade disputes is as follows:

> 'The authority dealing with trade disputes (the CCJ excluded) should be a technical, specific and specialised entity capable of producing expeditious solutions to the states. It should be an ad-hoc body instead of an existing institution, for instance, a panel of experts, free from the vagaries of the political processes. Article 35 of the GP should be reformed in order to exclude trade disputes out of the competence of the CCJ because it does not serve the purpose of expanding intra-regional trade. The mechanism adopted in the negotiation with Mexico and the Dominican Republic which the five governments have signed should be taken as the model for resolving trade conflicts within the CACM'.[20]

Costa Rica, therefore, favours the systems of trade disputes accepted by the governments in their negotiations with extra-regional partners and the WTO. In Costa Rica's view, dealing with trade disputes within the context of foreign trade instead of integration would guarantee that intra-regional trade would not be severely affected as a result of trade and political conflicts between states. The opposite would happen if trade disputes were to be dealt with under integration because of the prospect of long-term disputes and the possibility that governments could block institutions and co-operation when an issue under their review ran against their interests. Thus, after strong bargaining with Costa Rica, but especially given the impact of the negotiations of a free trade agreement between Central America and the US (CAFTA), the governments finally agreed and ratified the accord on trade disputes on November 30, 2002. The need to face trade negotiations with the US as a bloc forced the other states to accept the pragmatic view of Costa Rica. Thus, the Costa Rican vision prevailed on this matter. The agreement reflects the weakness of integration in the face of powerful external pressures.

Costa Rica favours a model of integration based on transparency in the conduct of the foreign trade of the states, joint internal and external actions, but without a commitment to union, be it economic or political. The agreement on trade disputes follows this pattern. The Costa Rican view of integration is limited to trade integration and co-operation in developing regional projects such as creating a stock market on electricity, developing Central American roads or improving customs' infrastructure across the region. Integration is viewed as a component of the state's foreign trade policy that cannot run against the interest of the government. Neither can it constrain the freedom of the government to negotiate trade accords unilaterally with potential trading partners such as Panama, Canada and so on. Despite these limitations Costa Rica is prepared to co-operate with the other states in turning the CACM into a free-trade area where the country can commercially expand and extract resources for its own economic development.

CONCLUDING REMARKS

The comparative analysis of Costa Rica and El Salvador reveals that there are as many differences as similarities between the interests and preferences of these two states regarding integration. In El Salvador, the constitution commands the government to pursue a far-reaching integration involving the creation of political union. The political elite and the public are committed to this kind of integration. Through integration the government seeks to overcome domestic constraints (size of the market, population density, lack of natural resources) which reduce the prospect for economic growth and political stability.

Integration is also a way of diffusing the country's dependence on the CACM, while at the same time using the CACM to improve the efficiency of the national economy and propel it into integration with the global market. In the 1990s El Salvador increasingly used the CACM as a means to ease the external integration of its economy. Increased regional interdependence is viewed as a way of asserting Salvadorian influence on Central American affairs. Asserting regional interdependence signifies the consolidation of regional institutions and engaging the other states in a myriad of economic, political and social relations with El Salvador. SICA has become the institutional fabric of Central American interdependence and El Salvador has pursued its consolidation as a system of integration.

Costa Rica in contrast has traditionally been reluctant to commit to political and economic union in the terms put forward by El Salvador and its partners of the CA-4 area. Structural factors such as highly developed social and political institutions, the dependence of industries on state subsidies, the strong dependence of the state on customs duties, and the traditional external orientation of its economy have prevented Costa Rica from embracing the far-reaching programme of integration favoured by the other states. In the 1990s economic and political convergence between Costa Rica and the other states increased considerably, creating the basis for cooperation to rebuild the CACM. But, in many ways, the political priorities and national interests of Costa Rica and the other states are different. Although all the states are engaged in promoting exports to third markets, only Costa Rica has been successful in doing so. Its external success in non-traditional exports following the economic reforms of the 1980s has conditioned Costa Rica's view of integration. Although Costa Rica does support economic integration, in general it is favourable to any policies that expand opportunities for export promotion. Nevertheless, the government has been reluctant to commit to political union and to full economic integration. It is only recently that Costa Rica has made a commitment to integrate its custom unions with the attempts by the other states, but still the government favours a gradual process instead of the quick and far-reaching one of the other states of the region (Barquero S 2004).

Costa Rica is committed to the international integration of the country's economy. The CACM is only one piece of this policy. It is important to the extent that it complements this effort and also because a sizeable sector of Costa Rican industry depends on the Central America for its survival. But the engine of Costa Rica's economic growth is not the CACM, but non-traditional exports to third markets.

To the extent that both El Salvador and Costa Rica are engaged in policies of promoting their external integration, it is possible to argue that there is a similarity in their strategies and views of the CACM. Both governments consider Central American integration as a means to improve the external competitiveness of their economies, embracing, therefore, regional initiatives aimed at achieving such a goal. But Costa Rica, which is less dependent on the CACM, rejects supranationality. For this reason, the Costa Rican government opposed initiatives that would place the management of trade conflicts in the hands of regional institutions. The Costa Rican government believes that applying international standards on trade disputes would favour integration and encourage intra-regional trade, while protecting national interests.

Deepening integration in Central America, therefore, depends on three factors. First, it depends on the possibility of a compromise between Costa

Rica, El Salvador and the other states on the issue of trade disputes, which is vital for the regular functioning of the CACM. This has been largely overcome with the adoption of the accord of trade disputes where the Costa Rican view prevailed. Second, it depends on the capacity of El Salvador and the other states to create negative externalities which would force Costa Rica to compromise with integration at some point of the level of regionness sought by the former. Finally, it depends on pressures stemming from the external environment, for instance, the preference of other states and economic blocs to consider the region as a bloc or the need of the governments to act as a bloc to increase their bargaining position (e.g. CAFTA, the Free Trade Agreement for the Americans, and the EU). The final outcome will, therefore, reflect the combination of regional and external pressures.

3 The Establishing of the Central American Common Market (CACM)

This chapter traces the building up of the Central American Common Market back to its inception in the late 1950s. The central contention here is that the CACM was the result of strong bargaining and asymmetric co-operation among leading governments through which they pursued the realisation of their own political and economic interests. Integration was a means of strengthening the governments' political control vis-à-vis domestic forces, building supportive coalitions to underpin their policies, particularly, the emerging industrial class. This perspective challenges the traditional arguments that explain Central American integration in terms of American hegemony, technocratic leadership, or structural determinants. These explanations assign no active role to the governments of the region except that of pawns following others' dictates.

Integration is understood as a state programme designed to modernise the Central American economies through the development of the industrial sector and by linking the Central American markets through a process of policy co-ordination and market liberalisation. The final end pursued through integration was the industrialisation of the region through a policy of import substitution which in turn was expected to increase the bargaining power of the governments in their external relations and reduce the vulnerability of the states from the world economy. It was expected that through the CACM the governments would overcome some structural factors which impeded economic development and would open up opportunities for creating some strategic alliances between the states, the nascent industrialists and foreign investors.

TRADITIONAL VIEWS REGARDING THE FORMATION OF THE CACM

Despite the salience of conflict among the states, in the 1950s it was possible to make headway in integrating the economies of Central America. While political and territorial conflicts were still unresolved, the governments found common ground for launching a programme of economic integration centred on trade liberalisation. It looked as though the governments had made a distinction between the economic and the political realms quite in line with the theoretical distinction made by Hoffmann between high and low politics. The former focuses on the uncompromising security and vital political interests of the states, whereas the latter emphasises economic and welfare co-operation (Hoffmann 1965; 1966).

The main reason for going ahead with economic integration despite high politics differences among the states was the fact that at the beginning integration was not perceived to contradict the foreign policy of the governments, neither did it compromise sovereignty. The Ministers of Economics had been integrated as part of the structure of ODECA and so were all regional institutions managing the economic integration. Their function consisted of 'planning, co-ordinating and implementing the region's economic integration' (ODECA 1962: articles 17,18). Integration, thus, did not become a controversial issue-area in domestic politics.[1] In other words, it impinged very little on the foreign and security interests of the states. Domestic actors viewed it as an appendage of the local markets with few external consequences other than expanding and complementing the domestic economies (SIECA 1973).

Another reason for supporting integration was a sense of ideological convergence among the governments sparked off by the wave of political change that was taking place in the region and by the economic change that was blossoming in Latin America. When conflicts developed during the negotiations to set out the CACM, it was diffused by co-operation and hard bargaining among leading governments impelled both by the fear of non-agreement and by the fear of exclusion from integration. The process of integration was, thus, guided by the logic of the lowest common denominator reflecting the power asymmetry and bargaining capabilities of the governments. This manner of viewing integration in Central America has not been used because of the preference of most analysts for structural explanations informed by political sociology, technocratic functionalism, economics and realism. They all tended to over-emphasise the role of variables other than the governments making political decisions.

SOCIOLOGICAL VIEW OF INTEGRATION

The sociological analysis has been one of the predominant ways of interpreting Central American integration. The main concern of sociology has been the role of social forces (classes) competing for political control and domination over society and the state. Politics (and government) is subordinated to the role of mere aggregate structures and forces, which operate outside the political realm. Thus, in this view, political theory 'ceases to have a major role as an independent social science' (Ball 1977, 10). At the core of this interpretation is a disregard for the functionality of the state as an organising and political structure. This is because the state is considered to be too weak to provide leadership or because it serves the interests of powerful social forces, for instance, the oligarchies or US interests (Monteforte Toledo, 1972). Hence, sociologists tend to explain integration in terms of the struggle for power and domination among social forces both internal and external to the region. These forces act in pursuit of their own self-interest, normally viewed as class interests or the construction of hegemony. The actors are considered to be domestic industrialists, transnational businesses, intellectuals, and the US government co-acting in order to submit the economies of the region to the voracity of international capitalism (Monteforte Toledo 1972; Bodenheimer 1974).

Sociologists tend to see the politics of regional integration in developing areas as a neo-colonial or imperialist project with the consequence of not only retarding the development of the regions concerned, but also keeping them isolated from the world economy. This thesis was originated by Baran who argued that the 'main task of imperialism was to slow down and to control the economic development of underdeveloped countries' (cited in Evans 1979, 19). In Baran's thesis, then, the alliance between foreign investors with local capitalists is a conspiracy to prevent development in the periphery.

Most Central American analysts adopted this mode of analysis to explain integration. They were strong defenders of the principle of balanced development and expected that this principle be incorporated into the process of building common markets. As this did not occur, they questioned the rationale for integration. In their view, Central American integration became a process stolen by the Americans in order to maintain the pattern of uneven development and defend US political and economic interests in the region. This involved the organisation of economic integration in accordance with the market's determinants, neglecting the real developmental needs and interests of the countries of the region (Monteforte Toledo 1972; Bodenheimer 1974). The CACM, thus, became an economic space to be exploited by American firms where neither the governments nor local businesses exercised control of the process. The region's governments, therefore, acted as the executive board of big businesses and the US companies. At best they are viewed as prisoners of the struggle for power by domestic and external forces. Consequently, the programme of integration is seen to have had few implications for industrial development, job creation and social participation. Above all, it reinforced the authoritarian and oligarchic pattern of political and economic development (Torres Rivas 1975).

FUNCTIONALIST VIEW

Contrary to the sociological interpretation, the technocratic view centres on the enlightened role played by the Economic Commission for Latin

America and the Caribbean (ECLAC) and the dynamic leadership played by the region's technocracy, especially those at the Ministries of Economics. This functionalist approach sees the process of Central American integration as a technical issue directed by ECLAC in alliance with governments' bureaucrats to promote a rapid process of industrialisation within a concept of balanced development.

The success in the negotiations for the establishment of the CACM is seen as a consequence of the active role played by a newcomer generation of technocrats (mainly economists) working under the aegis of ECLAC. According to Fuentes Mohr, the negotiations to establish the CACM were carried out 'by a group of professionals pursuing their own professional success. It was not led by the interests and actions of nascent industrialists who lacked a class project, neither was it led by the interests of the US, or by the interests and actions of self-conscious governments' (Fuentes Mohr 1973, 79–80).

In this account, the Ministries of Economics and their close assistants were the leading forces behind the process of economic integration in the region. Their leadership, it is said, was deliberately facilitated in order to develop a particular concept of economic integration, 'a scientific- led one which at the same time brought to fruition their own professional success' (Dada Hirezi 1980, 735). The role of other governmental agencies and officials is ignored or minimised in order to keep the process of integration a discrete area of concern of the Ministries of Economics.

ECLAC and its regional associates (the technocratic elite) viewed both underdevelopment and dependence as having an external origin: the uneven terms of trade between peripheral and central regions of the world economy. In this case, regional integration is a variable to modify the hierarchical nature (structure) of the international economic system and to bring about greater autonomy as well as development to peripheral regions.

ECLAC, thus, developed a structural view of underdevelopment in Latin America. Contrary to sociologists who viewed underdevelopment in the periphery as a political design by imperial powers, ECLAC took the terms of trade and the adverse consequences of the technological progress as the main variables explaining underdevelopment. For Prebisch, one of the main exponents of ECLAC's analysis, the exclusion of the periphery from the process of industrial development was not intended. Peripheral countries were left outside the process of industrialisation, 'not as a result of a deliberate design to exclude them, but as a consequence of the dynamics of the process itself' (Prebisch 1985, 50).

Import substitution and integration were perceived not only as the way of supplying the region with industrial goods, but also as the way forward to secure the industrial development of the region, especially in small states as in Central America. It was considered that import substitution alone would not reduce the external dependence of the region. Because of the size of the Central American economies, integration was seen as the viable way forward which 'would avoid high costs and the duplication of inefficient plants' (Bulmer-Thomas 1997, 1).

This was the rationale underlying ECLAC's intellectual support to the process of integration in Central America. ECLAC provided intellectual and technical assistance for the process by the means of carrying out specialised studies and facilitating the ground for international co-operation. The main difficulty that the programme of integration faced under ECLAC's paradigm was how to make it viable given the level of fragmentation of the Central American markets. When the process began in 1951 the region did not have consolidated national markets, but rather fragmented local ones with poor means of communication because of the lack of infrastructure and inadequate means of transportation. Intra-regional trade was insignificant as a result, just $11 million, accounting for 4 per cent of total regional trade. Underdevelopment and fragmentation characterised all the economies of the region, even the more developed ones.

Therefore, the problem was how to turn integration into a viable strategy for equitable development that could attract the interest of all the governments. The solution envisioned was a limited integration consisting of creating an imperfect economic space ranging between a free-trade area (FTA) and a customs union (CU) for the transaction of agro-industrial goods. It was imperfect because the CACM was not opened to all goods produced in the region. In addition, it did not eliminate most obstacles to free trade among the member states as would have been expected from a FTA, neither did it evolve fully into a CU. On the other hand, a far-reaching integration such as the setting up of a common market (CM) and an economic union (EU) was deliberately avoided. A common market implies free trade in goods and services as well as the free mobility of factors of production (labour and capital) while an EU involves harmonisation of policies in areas such as taxation, investment, social security, and institutional development, etc (Lizano 1979). This would not have been feasible in Central America because of the fragmentation of the markets and the lack of political entanglement and mistrust among the governments. Thus, the process of integration would be limited, based on the principles of reciprocity and co-operation.

By reciprocity was understood the political location of so-called integration industries in each country to which the governments had not only to agree, but also guarantee markets for. This meant free trade and a commitment not to close national markets to regionally produced goods. This kind of reciprocity based on national and regional planning was regarded as essential for the success of integration in developing areas (Wionczek 1968). It was understood that a market-led integration would deepen the economic differences among the countries of the region with most new investment going to the most developed states. Thus, ECLAC took integration as a strategy to promote balanced development in the region. But, it did not follow a radical conceptualisation of it. It was seen as a process of economic growth from which all the countries benefit regardless of their comparative position both in terms of the level of rates of growth and in their reciprocal balance of payments' (ECLAC 1974, 24). For this reason Bodenheimer (1974, 65) accuses ECLAC's technocrats of having become 'agents of the status quo'. This view of balanced development might find explanation in the fact that by necessity, technocrats and international organisations operate within the range of an intergovernmental win-set, following as Moravcsik argues (1998, 53), 'the path of least resistance', avoiding controversial issues in order to gain political support from governments and their domestic constituencies. This lack of recognition of the dependence of integration on governments' interests and political power seems a considerable shortcoming of this technocratic-structural approach to integration.

HEGEMONIAL VIEW

This refers to the central role played by the US in forging integration in Central America in accordance with its own geopolitical interests and liberal values. The US, the hegemonic power in the region, showed outright opposition to the ECLAC paradigm of integration and industrial development in Central America. Since the end of the Second World War the US had been working to set up an international economic order based on free trade and the free mobility of capital. This would largely favour the expansion of the American multinationals and open up markets for American industrial as well as agricultural products. ECLAC's policies of industrial protection and the principles informing such policies were at odds with the American policies of free trade and investment. Opposition to ECLAC's way of integration came from both government departments (e.g. the Justice and the State departments) and private corporations (Wionczek 1966). For these reasons the American government not only opposed ECLAC's policies, but also the creation of the institution itself because it regarded it as an intellectual challenge or a 'counter culture' to its hegemony in Latin America (Nef 1994, 404).

Traditionally, the US has been prone to neglect Central America. The region has only had the attention of the US when it faced a political crisis or when there was the danger of revolutionary change with great political consequences for Central America and the Caribbean (Daly Hayes 1982; Bell 1984). These are events that the US government regards as damaging to the US national interest. It is only when the US government perceives these kinds of dangers in terms of challenges to its national security or its hegemony that aid is granted to the region in large quantities in order to alienate any move towards social mobilisation. Guatemala after the coup against Arbenz, was an example, in which the US tried 'to make a showplace for democracy' (Cohen Orantes 1972, 28). So was El Salvador during the decade of 1980. The assumption is that economic aid will restore political stability and would encourage some social-controlled reforms (Huntington 1968). This was the logic behind the Alliance for Progress in 1963, which coincided with the launch of the CACM.

Prior to the signing of the so-called Tegucigalpa treaties in 1958, [2] the Eisenhower administration showed no interest in Central America's integration (Fuentes Mohr 1973). Previous uninterest and even distrust for integration seems to be explained, first, by the American preference for free market arrangements; second, by the fear that a far-reaching economic co-operation with Latin America 'would have diminished the United States' control over its economic relations with the region' (Wagner 1970, 18). Because of this the Eisenhower administration showed an uncompromising attitude and even disdain towards Latin American demands for aid and support to the region's developmental policies. The US response to such demands was that Latin America should follow 'a positive self-help and a genuine mobilisation of efforts, as prior conditions for economic co-operation' (Wagner 1970, 21, 32), and there was no readiness to provide funds on favourable conditions. As with the CACM, they were sceptical about the feasibility of the programme, but they also mistrusted ECLAC's patronage of the governments because of their dislike of protectionism. But increasing discontent and rising anti-US feelings in the region may have forced a re-evaluation of the original mistrust and lack of co-operation.[3] Thereafter, the US, especially during the Kennedy administration, looked at integration more sympathetically and even promoted it, granting aid to the governments of the region.

The US official position on Central American integration was presented by Undersecretary of State Douglas Dillon during a meeting of the Organisation of American States (OAS) held in Washington in February 1959. In its six points [4] it reaffirmed the US liberal stance regarding the process of integration in Latin America. Getting the economic integration in line with its view was the quid pro quo for American support to such processes.

This position was a counterattack to ECLAC's strategy for Latin American integration. Under ECLAC's strategy the US viewed itself as a loser for the following reasons:

1. Trade diverting effect. ECLAC's model of integration would rely heavily on the establishment of a high common external tariff (CET), which would produce a trade diversion effect. This would have affected US trade with Central America which accounted for about 75 per cent of the region's total imports in the 1950s. It was feared that because of the CET Central American consumers would be forced to replace high quality US goods with poor quality and more expensive regionally produced ones. It was, therefore, in the interest of the US that the CACM remained open to US corporate investors and to international trade. The assumption is that free market integration would be good

for Central America because of the welfare and efficiency gains associated with international trade. A common market is judged to be efficient in orthodox theory of integration 'only if trade creation is greater than trade diversion' (McClelland 1972, 105). It is the welfare gain associated with trade creation which led economists reluctantly to accept the utility of customs unions in international economic relations (Lipsey 1960; El-Agraa 1996).

2. Restrictions on FDI. About 90 percent of FDI in Central America came from the United States. The US government, therefore, feared that under ECLAC's paradigm of integration, American investment in the region would be affected because of the Central American regime of industrial protection. In 1958 ECLAC presented to the governments the proposed convention for the Regime of Integration Industries (RII) which gave a monopolist position in the market to industries of the region. Plants from the region, with the capacity to supply at least 50 per cent of the region's demand and use a high level of regional inputs, were entitled to receive the benefits granted by the regime. The regime also required Central American investors to have a predominant position in such industries, between 50 and 60 per cent of the investment. The US saw themselves in a disadvantageous position because of the RII and their efforts to undermine it accounts to a large extent for its failure.

The US government remained concerned about the long-term implications of ECLAC's model on FDI and capital movement. As ECLAC perceived the role of FDI within a short-term perspective, long- term American investment could be at risk. ECLAC's rationale was that foreign capital was not only desirable but also indispensable to put the import-substituting model into motion, but in the longer term Latin American countries should reduce their dependence on foreign investment by taking over new investments themselves (Prebisch 1962; Caputo and Pizarro 1982). In addition, ECLAC had a preference for multilateral loans rather than private capital which contradicted the nature of American international economic expansion since 1945, based on FDI. For the US, capital should be able to move freely without any political restriction, wherever it was economically cost effective.

As with the previous approaches, this focus on American hegemony as the main independent variable explaining integration or disintegration in Central America leaves many things unaccounted for. It assumes that the governments of the regions are inevitable pawns of the US imperialism and, therefore, ignores the host of domestic impulses and pressures which can better explain Central American integration. The formulation of a more dynamic approach based on the interest of the governments of the region, their strategic interactions and co-operation and on the coalitions supporting them, both domestically and externally is needed.

THE CACM AS AN INTERGOVERNMENTAL BARGAIN.

Moravcsik's assertion (1993a, 473) that European integration 'has developed through a series of celebrated intergovernmental bargains, each of which set the agenda for an intervening period of consolidation' can be restated in Central America. Since it inception, integration in this region has been the result of bargaining and political compromises among incumbent governments through which they have set out both the speed and the reach of the process. As such, the interests and preferences of the larger states (Costa Rica, El Salvador and Guatemala) have determined it.

The sociological and functionalist theses about Central American integration have tended to ignore this power politics aspect of the decision-making process. They tend to see the governments as proxies or the troublemakers instead of sources of explanation. Because of this, when the process of integration suffered setbacks they blamed some egotist governments for it (Bodehheimer 1974; 1981), but they did not provide a political explanation of why a government should be made responsible. The reason for this is, as Moravcsik argues (1993a), the lack of attention to the decision-making process by both neo-functionalists and sociologists. In other words, they do not properly explain how governments make decisions and how domestic forces may influence the decision process.

The belief that modernisation overrides everything, for instance, led neo-functionalists to identify the Central American Ministers of Economics as self-interested technocrats rather than politicians pursuing the interests of their states and those of the governments. Their obsession with welfare and balanced development led them to see integration as a mere technical issue which can be carried forward by means of applying technocratic expertise and scientific knowledge. They therefore, ignored politics and the necessary link between integration and foreign policy, especially the economic foreign policy of the states.

That the Ministers of Economics were at the forefront of the negotiations to achieve integration was not determined by technocratic imperatives. 'It had to do with the fact that the efforts at integration in the 1950s and 1960s were limited to the areas of trade and market liberalisation'.[5] As domestic actors, beginning with the governments, viewed this effort at integration as the continuation of their domestic economic policies, it had little implication in terms of the foreign policy of the states. Functionally they fell under the reach of the Ministers of Economics. This was reinforced by the fact that regardless of the high politics differences among the states, trade relations and economic co-operation have consistently been protected and allowed to flourish, especially since the 1950s (Fuentes Mohr 1973). This seems to be a fact of life of Central American politics which is explained by the separation between high and low politics emphasised by Hoffmann (1965; 1966) and Nye (1967) which put the burden of the integration process quite discretely in the hands of the Ministers of Economics. The perception that economic co-operation impinges little on the foreign and defence policies of the states is the explanation for economic relations normally surviving despite the mistrust and enmity that from time to time plagues Central American relations. It is this residual space for economic interactions granted by the 'security complex' [6] of the region which allows the Ministers of Economics to play a leading role in fostering economic integration. This consistently tells us that as long as integration is restricted to the economic sphere it is possible to proceed ahead with a far-reaching agenda. But as Hoffmann rightly argues (1966), if the functional method touches the security and political interests of the states, that is, if integration becomes too intrusive in domestic politics the governments, may then find it in their own interest to set limits on it in order to preserve the states' sovereignty and their power.

The Ministers of Economics may therefore be seen as technocrats, but their actions are in line with the policies and interests of the governments they served, not their personal interests as some analysts suppose. Their centrality in fostering the economic co-operation in the region, particularly before the 1990s, was the result of the increasing interest devoted by the governments to economic modernisation. Hence, contrary to the explanation that sees the success of the Ministers of Economics regarding integration as a result of lack of interest on the part of the governments, the opposite is likely to have been the case. It is plausible, as Wynia asserts (1970, 328), that 'integration was not ignored because it represented economic change but was actually supported by governing elite who saw it as a viable alternative to such change'.

Integration was viewed by some governments as a means to modernise the economies while relaxing or at least tempering distributional conflicts domestically (Lizano and Willmore 1975). This was clear in countries such as El Salvador where integration appears to have provided a temporary way out from domestic pressures for political, social and economic reforms. Integration allowed the government to reaffirm its political control over domestic politics through relaxing the social conflict and weakening the political opposition. Integration had the advantage that it could be pursued at a relative low cost by pooling resources and by using international finance. By pooling their markets the governments could overcome some limitations of their domestic economies. This in turn offered to the nascent industrial class the advantage of having an enlarged market. Politically the success of economic integration would reinforce the power of the governments vis-à-vis domestic forces, while they would avoid the transfer of sovereignty to regional institutions. This is the political payoff from integration and the basis for the governments' support.

Keeping the power of decision-making under governmental control would prevent the opposition to integration by domestic power holders such as the army and the landed gentry (Nye 1967; Bulmer-Thomas 1987).

In addition, emphasising a limited economic integration would open up market opportunities for active economic actors which would be wooed and co-opted by the governments, therefore, strengthening their political power domestically and their influence regionally. This provided a strong incentive for the governments to co-operate. Governments feel encouraged to co-operate where policy co-ordination 'increases their control over domestic policy outcomes, permitting them to achieve goals that would not otherwise be possible' (Moravcsik 1993a, 485). They could control the process by agreeing a rigid system of decision making as well as by adjusting such systems to the constitutional frameworks of the states. This is a practice that the governments have been following since the formation of ODECA in 1951 (Padelford 1957).

In the 1950s the economic policies of the governments tended to converge around the issue of modernisation. In the 1940s, supported by the urban bourgeoisie, the middle classes and progressive sectors of the armed forces, a generation of modernising leaders replaced long lasting dictatorships. In Nicaragua the Somoza regime survived the tide of political change by repressing as well as skilfully co-opting the opposition through political and welfare concessions, weakening the prospect for an anti-dictatorial challenge (Dunkerley 1988).

The new ruling elite claimed a technocratic and progressive view of the developmental process. They all shared some integrationist beliefs, and therefore, aspired to expand their influence to their neighbours. Guatemala under Arévalo and Arbenz governments (1944–1954), Castañeda and Osorio in El Salvador (1945–1954), and José Figueres in Costa Rica in 1948 through the so-called "Caribbean Pact" purported to depose the dictators of the region and re-institute the Central American Republic (Schifter 1986).

Some of the new leaders (José Figueres and Oscar Osorio) had been exiled in Mexico where they came into contact with the new developmental doctrine then blossoming in Latin America, especially as a result of the creation of ECLAC in 1948. These modernising governments began to pursue policies designed to modernise not only the traditional export sector, but also the industrial sector through embracing ECLAC's notion of 'national industry of transformation' (Menjivar 1982). El Salvador and Costa Rica were in the forefront in the region enacting legislation to promote industrialisation in 1952 and 1959, respectively. This consolidated domestic coalitions (industrialists, the Army, the middle class and labour unions) which became their main constituency, hugely benefiting from the processes of industrialisation and regional integration.

It was believed that industrialisation would foster the economic self-reliance of the region. The governments thought that 'if the region could gradually develop its own manufacturing capacity, then increased Central American production for the domestic market would diminish its dependence on the export sector for economic growth' (Hansen 1967,

14). The traditional exporters could constrain the governments' policies of industrialisation by exercising the 'option of voice', complaining and opposing such policies as to some extent they did, particularly in Costa Rica (Araya Pochet 1982). But, the fact that they could not substantially exercise the "option of exit" because their ownership was largely fixed, rather than mobile, forced them into a compromise with the modernising elite (Hirschman 1978). After all, they could benefit from integration through the creation of new business opportunities in trade, finance and new developments in infrastructure. Needless to say, integration as a way of 'superimposed development' as ECLAC terms it (1986, 16–17), did not threaten the status quo. Therefore, their economic and social interests were not in danger.

The conflict between the traditional exporters and the new modernising interests did not take a Manichean form. It was not a conflict between modes of capitalist or non-capitalist development. As Cueva argues (1985) the contradiction between the traditional sector and the nascent industrialists was not about abolishing the former but about the appropriation of the surplus generated by it. The traditional sector would remain the motor of economic growth and this would leave the process of industrialisation in a situation of dependence on this sector. Moreover, the social cost of industrialisation could be transferred, especially in El Salvador, to the consumer through indirect taxation and through a reduction in the cost of factors of production (Dada Hirezi 1983; Guidos Béjar 1988).

The way to pursue the industrial development was through the integration of the markets through a programme of policy co-ordination where governmental officials would perform the role of gatekeepers or guarantors of the states' sovereignty. Although this programme of policy co-ordination began to take place through the negotiation of trade agreements between pairs of countries, it reached a higher organisational form through the multilateral process undertaken through the Central American Committee for Economic Co-operation (CEC) set up in 1952 with the support of ECLAC.

THE BILATERAL TREATIES: THE STRATEGIC ROLE OF EL SALVADOR IN FORGING INTEGRATION

Central American integration began in the North of the region and has remained fundamentally a northern concern, even though it has gradually been expanded to Costa Rica and Panama and countries such as Belize and to a lesser extent to the Dominican Republic. The force behind this process was El Salvador. As early as 1918 El Salvador had signed a bilateral trade agreement with Honduras, which remained binding until 1954 when it was subject to revision and re-negotiation. The agreement was renegotiated in 1956–57 at the request of Honduras which felt in a disadvantageous position in the face of the advance of the industry of transformation in El Salvador (Fuentes Mohr 1973).

In the first half of the 1950s El Salvador displayed active economic diplomacy in the region leading to the negotiation of trade agreements with all its neighbours. By 1955, El Salvador had successfully created a fragmented trade regime in Central America. To the original accord with Honduras and its amendments of 1954–1957 were added the treaties with Nicaragua and Guatemala in 1951 and with Costa Rica in October 1953. The explanation for this Salvadorian leadership on integration is found, on the one hand, in the structural conditions of Salvadorian society and economy, patterns of trade dependence which constrained economic growth. On the other hand, there was the political interest of the government to use integration as a way of enhancing its domestic position through the enlargement of the market and the creation of links with other integrationist forces of the region. The government, thus, aggregated these interests in its economic and foreign policies and integration with its neighbours became an outlet for these pressures.

This move reflected the impact of the successful consolidation of market economics in this country. El Salvador consolidated economic liberalism in the period 1880–1920. This implied the abolition of communal land and the take over of land from Indians and peasants to develop a new exporting dynamic economy centred on the intense cultivation of coffee (Menjivar 1982; Dada Hirezi 1983). Later on in the 1940s was added strong state intervention in the way of public investment, particularly in the industrial sector and infrastructure. This intervention by the state was required to reverse the decline and stagnation of private investment. A strong public investment created the basis for the modernisation of capitalism in the 1940s and 1950s and gave rise to the emergence of a dynamic private sector. The Salvadorian oligarchy became as Torres Rivas observes (1975) the most capitalised and the most entrepreneurial of the region. It became the backbone of the most successful exporting economy of the region with 'most Central American exports to the world market coming from El Salvador' (Halperin cited in Cueva 1985, 44).

Since the 1940s the building of a modernised infrastructure further expanded the economic basis of the country both in the traditional and the industrial sectors. Soon the country became the land of trade and industry with powerful economic groups capable of expanding their influence to the other states. By the time the move towards integration began in the 1950s, El Salvador was already in a process of expansion in the region not only commercially, but also financially with financial assets in other states of the region (Monteforte Toledo 1972).

Despite all this, by the 1950s capitalist accumulation in El Salvador was reaching its limit. The domestic market was entering into a stage of exhaustion. A sizeable amount of the surpluses generated by the export sector was leaving the country because of the geographical limitation of the state, which prevented the expansion of export agriculture. At the same time the investment of the surpluses generated by the traditional sector into the industrial sector was quite risky because the inequalities in income distribution placed an objective constraint on the expansion of the local market. This limited industrial development. Only 20 per cent of income per family was spent on industrial goods in the 1950s. As a result, in the period 1945–50 the country experienced a quite serious outflow of capital accounting for about 11.2 per cent of the earnings from coffee, and the situation worsened in the subsequent period (Guidos Béjar 1988).

There was, therefore, a paradox between external success and domestic exhaustion. In 1948 the government was forced to intervene in economic development in order to reverse the trend of capital flight and to encourage the investment of new resources in the industrial sector and infrastructure. These efforts included negotiations leading to the establishment of the CACM with the other states. Integration was, thus, a rational course of action undertaken by the state in response to domestic political and economic interests. The integration of the region in the terms proposed by El Salvador would, it was thought, alleviate the social problems of the country with the possibility of exporting industrial goods as well as labour to the other states. This was important because the dissatisfied population was rallying together with the opposition parties, especially the Christian Democrats whose popularity expanded very quickly in the 1960s (Caldera T undated). Regional integration was therefore a political response of the Salvadoran government to pressures emerging from its political economy, including structural difficulties (political and economic) faced by the state. It was also an interest shared by most governments of the region, with the possible exception of Costa Rica in the period (1958–1961), that regarded integration necessary to support their strategies of industrial development and economic modernisation and stability. Thus, far from being an external imposition on the governments, it was a demand rooted in the domestic political economy of the states. However, given their external dependence, external factors were ineluctable components of the process of states' preferences in the region.

ASYMMETRIC INTEGRATION

Asymmetries in power and in economic development play an important role in fostering integration allowing stronger states to influence their neighbours' policies into supporting a process of policy co-operation. But asymmetries, if not dealt with properly, as will be seen below, could give rise to conflicts and disintegration.

The process was led by El Salvador because, during the 1950s and 60s, that country possessed the most advanced economic structure of the region, which included more integrated internal markets and a fairly developed physical infrastructure. The road system of El Salvador not only connected most of its regions and domestic markets, but also facilitated the access to the markets of the other states. Its maritime infrastructure was advanced and the country had also the most advanced airline system with the national airline TACA accounting for 60 per cent of the region's services (OECEI 1968). This gave El Salvador a competitive industrial and trade advantage and political leverage over its regional competitors, which explains the government's preference for free trade and market integration and its salience in the region's negotiations. For Honduras, for instance, with fragmented internal markets isolated from one another because of the lack of infrastructure and underdevelopment, it was easier to access the Salvadorian market than its own one. The Honduran market, thus, was an appendage of the Salvadorian one. This largely explains the asymmetrical trade relationship between these two countries and the Salvadorian ability to exercise influence on the Hondurans. This Salvadorian influence over the Honduras was reinforced by the federalist ideology shared by both states. A similar situation happened with Guatemala. Owing to its scarce industrial development, in spite of being the largest economy of the region (Poitevin 1977), Guatemala relied on El Salvador as a supplier of industrial goods and capital as well as outlet for its exports. Thus both Honduras and Guatemala were susceptible to the trade policies undertaken by El Salvador.

In general, lack of industrial development was a common feature of the Central American economies, which was, to a large extent, due to the way these states were integrated into the world economy as suppliers of agricultural goods. The outward model of development heavily conditioned the growth of industrial activities in the region, placing industrialisation in a subordinate position on the performance of Export Agriculture (EXA) and heavily dependent on extraregional imports (Bulmer-Thomas 1987). El Salvador and Costa Rica were the only states, which had managed to make substantial moves towards industrialisation early in the 1950s as a result of both structural conditions and government policy preferences.

Guatemala not only responded to Salvadorian commercial diplomacy but also followed its own as a counterbalancing manoeuvre, negotiating trade agreements with Costa Rica in December 1955 and with Honduras in 1956. The other states followed the same pattern of negotiations as El Salvador and Guatemala in order to secure their own economic interests. As a result, by 1956 there were five trade zones in the region all of them pursuing a modest liberalisation of trade where limited lists of products enjoyed free trade while others were granted preferential treatment (Fuentes Mohr 1973).

Therefore, the impulse for creating a fragmented economic space in the region through bilateral arrangements is found, primarily in domestic pressures faced by the states, especially El Salvador, due to the expansion of industrial development and a fast growing population. This may have been the only possible way of approaching integration at the beginning of the 1950s owing to the high politics risk [7] or political mistrust among governments.

Integration began between Honduras and El Salvador because of the existence of an asymmetrical interdependence between the two states and a consequent reduction of the high politics risk between them. Honduras was a "natural partner" for Salvadorian industrial goods, while El Salvador was the main regional market for Honduran industrial and agricultural production.[8] Together these two states accounted for nearly 50 per cent of total intra-regional trade in 1950, $3.9 million out of a total of $8.3 million for the region. Politically the two states reached high levels of understanding during the 1950s, which favoured their economic co-operation. But the Honduras market was no longer sufficient for the increasing Salvadoran industrial production and Honduras was already complaining about the asymmetrical relationship with El Salvador, pressing for the revision of the bilateral treaty of 1918. As a result a new treaty was adopted in February 1957 which replaced 'a nearly perfect free trade zone for products originated in the two countries for a system of lists of items and preferential tariffs' which largely restricted bilateral trade (Fuentes Mohr 1973, 42, 47–48). The Salvadoran search for new markets became a structural necessity of survival owing to its limited natural resources and its growing population which largely set the conditions for its potential for development (Sol Castellanos 1972).

As with the practice followed during British hegemony in Europe [9], the trade negotiations between El Salvador and Honduras set the standard for the gradual liberalisation of trade in Central America. El Salvador and Honduras initiated the practice of limited trade based on lists of products and preferential treatment as the way to expand trade relations in the region. Among the preferences was the so-called 'Central American clause' which excludes from the 'most-favoured-nation clause' the reciprocal preferences granted by the countries of the region themselves (Cepal 1975, 31). Amending the original treaties via protocols, which required parliamentary approval, was the path to expanded trade relations. This is a practice still favoured in Central America as reflected in the cases of SICA and the reform to the General Treaty of Economic Integration in 1993.

That was very much the Salvadorian way of dealing with treaty reform, which made the processes unnecessarily long and tedious and added a degree of uncertainty because of the requirement of parliamentary approval. El Salvador may have used this practice as leverage either to prevent the reform of treaties or to increase its position in the negotiations by calling up the rigidity of domestic approval as a bargaining chip. Guatemala followed a more flexible path of dealing with treaty reform because the alteration of bilateral treaties could be done through the simple exchange of notes between the foreign secretaries concerned (Fuentes Mohr 1973). However, the Salvadoran practice has prevailed in the region giving rise to conflicts because of the lack of flexibility in the processes of ratification, affecting therefore the implementation of regionally agreed policies.

A second force behind the creation of a fragmented free trade area in the 1950s was the elusive external environment. Two factors are especially relevant in this respect. Firstly, there was the increase in export earnings experienced by the Central American states triggered by the Korean War. The strong performance of exports produced surpluses in the current account of the balance of payments of the states. This fact reveals a situation which is characteristic of Central American industrialisation and integration, that is, their dependence on the traditional export sector and on favourable world market conditions for primary products. Secondly, there was the unwillingness of the US to guarantee a price stability regime to protect Latin American export earnings after the war. This forced the governments to embark on some level of integration to protect existing economic gains.

Therefore, the external environment constitutes an independent variable which, together with government attempts, explain integration. This seems to be true for Central America as it is for other regions. The exclusive focus on endogenous variables, such as spillover or upgrading common interests, constituted a shortcoming of earlier analyses of regional integration. The concerns about the economic security of the region (its dependence on the world market for economic growth and financial stability) prompted the governments to embrace the process of integration in the 1950s. The rationale was to use the surpluses created by the good international prices of the region's primary exports to finance industrialisation and integration (Sol Castellanos 1972; Fuentes Mohr 1973). There was the belief that integration would work as a cushion against future external crises. Thus, contrary to what happened in South America, Central American industrialisation took place in a period of fast growth in the traditional sector (Furtado 1970; Inotai 1971). In South America the process of industrialisation in the 1920s was as a reaction to stagnation and economic decline. In Central America it was based on the 'steady liquid assets in the fifties and on the increased stock of foreign currency in the central banks' (Inotai 1971, 41). The uncertainty about US co-operation on price stability further encouraged the governments to support integration. This feeling of uncertainty may have forced even as reluctant a state as Costa Rica to lend credible commitment to integration, particularly on trade and financial issues.

Through the negotiation of bilateral trade accords, the governments gradually began to construct the Central American trade regime based on the free movement of industrial goods and services and increasing economic interdependence. Before the decade of the 1950s the economies of the region showed very few interactions. There was no real sense of regionness as verified by regional interdependence and patterns of trade relations. This was due both to high politics differences among the states as well as the success of the outward model of development. As a result, the states were more solidly connected with the outside world than with themselves (Furtado 1970). Intra regional trade began to prosper following trade accords, soaring from $8.6 million to $13.7 million between 1950–56. About 65 per cent of the increase was 'accounted by Honduras and this consisted almost entirely of additional trade with El Salvador' (Bulmer-Thomas 1987, 172). Therefore, the move from an anarchical society, based on rivalry and high politics, towards a form of regional community based on rudimentary elements of policy co-operation and elite assimilation, began to take shape in Central America with the Salvadorian policy of trade integration with its neighbours. This was a change enabled both by the domestic political economy of the states as well as by the impact of their external dependence on the global economy.

THE MULTILATERAL PROCESS OF POLICY CO-ORDINATION AS A RESULT OF INTERSTATE BARGAINING

As has been argued, the process of Central American integration in the 1950s and 1960s advanced as a result of intergovernmental bargaining through which leading governments put forward their interests and preferences. This challenges the traditional approaches, which emphasise economic forces, technocratic leadership and hegemony as major explanations. From the outset, the process of integration was an intergovernmental affair defined by a political logic based on bargaining rather than a mechanistic logic (spill-over) or external imposition. The pace of the process since 1958 has been determined by the weight of the counteractive strategies by governments through which they pursue the realisation of the national interest of the states as well as their own political short-term interests. In this process the role of external forces is not discounted, but they did not determine the process of integration. At best they acted as catalysts in the process facilitating interstate bargaining and providing resources to the governments to sustain regional co-operation. This is a better way of looking at both the US and ECLAC's role in the process of integration, as provider of 'willpower to leap from the brink to the other side rather than allow spill-back' (Nye 1965, 882).

THE CATALYST ROLE OF ECLAC

The technical assistance and intellectual support of ECLAC, for instance, was accepted and even requested [10] by the governments of the region because, as Hansen asserts, its doctrine of economic integration 'seemed to offer both an explanation of their economic difficulties and a prescription for economic development'. It also appeared 'as an indigenous solution to the problem of growth' (Hansen 1967, 17). However, although

ECLAC's technical support was an important variable accounting for integration it would be misleading to focus too much attention upon it, disregarding the central role of the governments. International organisations (regional or general) are accountable to governments. The interests, expectations and support by governments condition the effectiveness of these organisations. As Moravcsik argues (1998) governments determine the level of institutional structuring of integration as a result of inter-states bargaining. That institutions can influence governments' policies is not denied. Their ability to do so largely depends on their capacity to provide leverage to realise the governments' foreign policy objectives and on whether they follow the path of least resistance. This would imply, for example, advancing proposals, mediating compromises or providing technocratic expertise, increasing, therefore the returns to the governments (Pentland 1991; Moravcsik 1993a).

The real significance of ECLAC to Central American integration falls in the realm of international co-operation rather than in determining integration and development. The institution did succeed in fostering intergovernmental co-operation, which in turn provided the basis for further bargaining and negotiations among the states. According to former Salvadorian Economic Minister Sol Castellanos, previous to the catalytic role of ECLAC the relationship between the countries of the region was cool and sporadic. They viewed each other as 'powers' rather than friends. As a result, it was not feasible, for political and security, rather than technical reasons, to commend a group of Central American experts to carry out studies leading to economic integration. ECLAC became, therefore, an appropriate vehicle for cementing mutual trust and co-operation among the governments (Sol Castellanos 1972). It was because of this original mistrust among the governments that most studies related to the region's integration were assigned to ECLAC. As a result, ECLAC enjoyed strong political support from the governments, which largely explains its success. The studies carried out by ECLAC advanced the understanding of underdevelopment in the region and provided the blueprint for drafting the programme of integration as a developmental strategy.

As with the bilateral trade arrangements, El Salvador was the main force behind the multilateral diplomacy in the region. El Salvador proposed to ECLAC the unification of the Central American markets as early as 1949. By 1951 El Salvador had already rallied the support of the other states, especially Guatemala and Nicaragua, in order to make a joint proposal to ECLAC to begin the process of integration (Monteforte Toledo 1972; Sol Castellano 1972). Governments favour multilateral solutions when unilateral solutions become unavailable or are too expensive to carry out. In Moravcsik's words, 'when it is no longer possible to realise producer interests unilaterally' (Moravcsik 1998, 38). Some reasons for going multilateral can be mentioned:

1. A reduction of the high politics risk. There were some gains in trust among the governments.
2. The desire of some governments (largely El Salvador and Guatemala) to strengthen trade relations beyond the limited reach of the bilateral treaties.
3. The need to avert political opposition to free trade from traditional exporters, industrialists, and other social organised interests which favoured protectionism.
4. Lastly, there was the fear of some governments that they would be excluded from integration, therefore, participation in the process could be seen as Moravcsik (1998, 9) hypothesises, as the result of the interests of governments to 'constrain and control one another'. All this happened in a context of rising co-operation among the governments.

Co-operation was encouraged by the experience of the bilateral treaties themselves as well as by a reduction of territorial and high politics conflicts among some governments. These conflicts largely concerned the territorial disputes between Honduras and Nicaragua and political rivalry and hatred between the governments of Costa Rica and the latter since 1948. The rivalry between Costa Rica and Nicaragua was diminished, if not ended, on February 21, 1949 when both governments signed a "friendship pact" under the auspices of the Organisation of American States (OAS). Likewise, the territorial conflict between Honduras and Nicaragua was resolved through a resolution by the International Court of Justice which both governments accepted, enhancing, therefore, the prospect for co-operation in the region. The reduction of these conflicts facilitated the catalytic role of ECLAC in drawing proposals and mediating distributional conflicts among the states.

Regarding the bilateral treaties, although they had served the cause of expanding trade relations and enhancing regional interactions they were already reaching their limits and had given rise to domestic complaints about asymmetric gains. According to Fuentes Mohr (1973) there were intense pressures from industrialists throughout the region against Salvadorian goods arguing that their competitiveness was based on cheap labour and overexploitation. They argued that El Salvador would reduce the other states to the neo-colonial status of supplying primary products and raw materials. This complaint was made especially in those states that lacked a sufficient industrial basis and where the developmental needs were more acute.

Turning the bilateral accords into a regime of common rules and policy-co-ordination, despite asymmetries between the states, would to some extent overcome these domestic concerns. Integration, thus, would be used to weaken the opposition by domestic forces to economic and trade liberalisation and policy co-ordination. As a result of this the markets of all the states would be open to regionally produced goods, creating opportunities for the least developed states to expand their exports, and making some strategic alliances with the most developed ones. As Castillo Argues (1966, 148), 'being near a manufacturing centre and having other products and services to trade for its output may be as advantageous or even more advantageous than having such a centre'. In addition, the process of co-ordination would provide the opportunity for small states to make linkages, where support to integration could be linked, for instance, to infrastructure development or getting preferential treatment on some issues. Furthermore, as well as the benefit of having decisional power, small states could be granted side-payments, for example, a larger share in the regionally allocated financial resources.

THE INTERSTATE BARGAINING PROCESS

There is plenty of evidence of hard bargaining that took place among states, particularly Guatemala and Nicaragua, to avoid being excluded from the process. Under ECLAC mediation, in 1958 the governments signed the Tegucigalpa treaties.[11] However, Costa Rica and Honduras failed to complete the ratification process, the former because the conservative government of Mario Echandi utterly opposed integration. There was the perception in the Costa Rican government that integration, because of differences in the structure of costs and other geo-economic factors, would not improve the welfare of the country. The Economic Minister of this country, Jorge Borbón, played the role of gatekeeper, following a very nationalistic stance. He identified integration as a danger to the Costa Rican welfare system and to Costa Rican competitiveness (La República 1961, 7; Cochrane 1965, 335).

Two reasons explain Echandi's government's reluctance to commit Costa Rica to the integration programme. First, its national conservative ideology. This was based on the traditional stance shown earlier in the nineteenth Century by President Braulio Carrillo when Costa Rica opposed rebuilding the Central American Federation. In the same fashion, the Mario Echandi government opposed any attempt at integration which would involve compromising national sovereignty. Second, the Echandi administration represented the traditional exporters and the oligarchy. Therefore, the government was wary about the biases of integration in favour of industrialists and the middle class. In Costa Rican politics these sectors, particularly the middle class, have been very strong and more enlightened than in the other states (Bell 1971; Solano Orfila 1982). Since 1948 they have been intrinsically linked to the National Liberation Party (PLN) and became the backbone for the consolidation of the social democratic model of development put forward by this party. After 1948 the PLN became the largest party holding the executive power and enjoyed a substantial majority in Parliament. The PLN gathered the support of progressive forces which were committed to economic modernisation and regional integration. Integration would have strengthened the political position of the

PLN within the national politics as well as regionally. Because of this fear as well as concerns about loosing sovereignty to regional institutions, the Echandi's government did not submit the Tegucigalpa treaties to the Congress for ratification. In Honduras, by contrast, the main difficulty was that the territorial conflict was not resolved and the government refused to participate in a programme of integration alongside Nicaragua (Fuentes Mohr 1973).

It was disillusionment with the failure on the part of Costa Rica and Honduras to ratify the agreements as well as dissatisfaction with the Regime of Integration Industries, which neither El Salvador nor Guatemala favoured, that forced El Salvador into a change of direction. As a result, the Salvadorian government purported to consolidate its economic relations with Honduras through the establishment of a customs union between the two states. An alliance was formed in 1959 between these two states and the US attempted to increase the credibility of the alternative route of integration. El Salvador requested US support during a visit by President Lemus to the United States in 1959. The Honduran President Villeda Morales fully supported the talks between presidents Lemus and Eisenhower regarding the establishing of a customs union (with US financial backing) between his country and El Salvador (Fuentes Mohr 1973).

The US government not only supported the alliance between these two states politically but also was ready to commit resources to make it work. There is no doubt about the role played by the US in the process of integration in terms of pressing for liberal arrangements in accordance with its liberal hegemony, although this policy was already favoured by El Salvador and supported by Guatemala. El Salvador needed not only to open markets to allocate its industrial surplus but also a safety valve to lessen the social impact of its growing population. This forced its government to pursue policies which guaranteed the free movement of goods, services and factors of production (labour and capital) in the region. The main role played by the US government, therefore, was that of facilitator of resources and political backing, which increased the credibility of the strategy followed by the Salvadorian government.

The main function of this arrangement was to be used as a bargaining chip to force the other states to agree to a speedier and more far-reaching integration than the one put forward by ECLAC. Guatemala was the first state that redefined its position in relation to this nascent bloc in the North. President Ydígoras favoured the integration of all the states of the region. This was in line with the traditional geopolitical interest of Guatemala, which has always tried to lead the region. In January 10, 1960 Ydígoras attempted to do this by inviting the other presidents to a summit at Esquipulas in order to discuss the way of advancing the process of integration. However, he did not succeed and the other presidents did not attend. This left Guatemala's bid for leadership in serious doubts. President Echandi of Costa Rica used a labour strike in the banana plantation in the South Coast as pretext for not attending (La Nación 1960, 30). President Somoza did not attend as a protest because rebel forces opposed to his regime were launching sporadic attacks on his territory from Honduras. Honduras would not tolerate meeting the Nicaraguan President and El Salvador avoided annoying the Hondurans by meeting Somoza (La República 1960, 8).

This failure of leadership forced President Ydígoras to come to terms with the Salvadorian project of integration. Guatemala considered that its exclusion from the Salvadoran plan would be prejudicial to its political and economic interests. Moreover, the size of its economy, being the largest market of the region, gives the Guatemalan government a bargaining power on integration even if the state does not attempt to lead it. Therefore, it proposed that 'if the integration of all the states was not possible, the Salvadorian-Honduran programme should be transformed into a tripartite arrangement with Guatemala participating' as a main partner (Fuentes Mohr 1973, 183). After all, these three states were the most interdependent of the region and there were already historical records of them getting together, as when in 1921 they attempted to create a federation from which both Nicaragua and Costa Rica were excluded. Talks for a tripartite alliance began in La Palma, El Salvador in July 1959 between the Economic Cabinets of the three states. The alliance was consolidated in successive talks during 1959, which took place in Esquipulas (Guatemala), July, Cerro Verde (El Salvador), October, and Tegucigalpa (Honduras), October.

In Tegucigalpa, the Guatemalans who had been pressing for a compromise between the Salvadoran interest in faster integration and ECLAC's incremental programme, lined up with the Salvadorian policy. Guatemala accepted that the best way to accelerate economic integration was through the consolidation of the bloc with El Salvador and Honduras (Fuentes Mohr 1973). After the failed attempt to gather the other presidents in Esquipulas in January 1960, Ydígoras had no choice but to sign with El Salvador and Honduras. In January 9, 1960, Presidents Ydígoras and Villeda Morales travelled together from Honduras to El Poy, El Salvador, in order to meet President Lemus where they signed a joint declaration. They then committed themselves to work for the economic association of the three states calling for the full integration of their economies.

The Treaty of Economic Association (known as the Tripartite treaty) was formally signed in Guatemala on February 6, 1960, which in Article 1 guarantees the free circulation of persons, goods, and capital between their territories. It purported to consolidate a customs union in five years through the equalisation of their tariffs system and the adoption of a common external tariff. The Treaty had four aspects, which largely accounted for the Honduran support and participation despite the fact that it wiped out the Regime of Integration Industries altogether:

1. According to Article IX it granted immediate free trade not only for industrial goods but also 'natural products' from the member states which would favour Honduras as well as Guatemala's non-industrial

exports. The treaty was a bold step in terms of the expansion of trade among the participants. The shift was from a so-called *positive list* of goods agreed under the Multilateral Treaty of Economic Integration of 1958 to a *negative list* which was more far-reaching than the former. The Multilateral Treaty granted free trade to just 20 per cent of items and established a period of ten years for the full liberalisation of trade. The Tripartite, on the other hand, guaranteed immediate free trade to a wide range of items.

2. The Treaty excluded from free trade industrial goods that were only assembled in the region. Honduras repeatedly complained that most of its manufactured imports were largely assembled rather than totally constructed in the other states, to the detriment of its own industrial interest. The Hondurans felt they were subsidising production in the other states. Thus, the exclusion of items with very little regional value added appeared to have satisfied the Honduran government.
3. The Treaty set out a Development and Assistance Fund, which would largely favour Honduras' development (Article XIX). It appears that Honduras took the fund as a substitute for the Regime of Integration Industries. The fund would be settled with quotas from the governments as well as financial co-operation, especially from the US government.
4. The Tripartite excluded Nicaragua, which was a major incentive for Honduras to go ahead with El Salvador and Guatemala. The Salvadorians realised that the inclusion of Nicaragua would have jeopardised the agreement not only because of the rivalry between the governments of Honduras and Nicaragua but also because of the latter's original aversion to a market-led integration. El Salvador and Nicaragua were also facing some political tensions following the assassination of President Anastasio Somoza in September 1956 (Parker 1964).

JUMPING ON THE BANDWAGON

It is clear that the process of building Central American integration shows a combination of co-operation and power politics, in the sense of bargaining power. The states outside the original bloc carrying the banner of integration redefined their position and felt compelled to embrace integration in order to avoid being left out or becoming absolute losers. From a systemic position, that is, taking into account the impact of integration on the capability and security of the states outside the original bloc (the so-called external effects), these states can either react by embracing the new situation, exploiting their own bargaining power, or build alternative alliances 'creating their own regional group' (Mattli 1999, 61). These kinds of behaviours were clearly observable in Central America.

If the aim of the treaty was to reopen the negotiations as well as to strengthen the cause for the expansion of free trade after a period of stalemate, it was very successful in redefining the interest of the other states, especially, Nicaragua, but also Costa Rica. Nicaragua, one of the enthusiastic integrationist states, felt threatened with virtual exclusion from the northern bloc. The government regarded the Tripartite treaty as an act of economic aggression against Nicaragua and diplomatic protests were delivered before the northern states and the US government (Sol Castellanos 1972; Fuentes Mohr 1973). Clarifications by the Salvadorian government regarding the reach of the treaty and its compatibility with the general movement towards integration, including the willingness to extend the treaty to the other states, did not satisfy the southern states (Memoria 1959–60). They, therefore, sought to pursue an alternative course of action by attempting to establish a southern bloc. Costa Rica and Panama started negotiations for a bilateral treaty which Nicaragua unconditionally offered to join (La República 1961, 4).

A Southern bloc, however, would not be an alternative option to the Tripartite, not only because the trade relations of these states were meagre, but also because their productive structures were heterogeneous. Panama, for instance, was a service economy with few trade relations with Central America. Because of this, among other reasons, Panama was not fully involved in the Central American negotiations. In addition, Panama was sympathetic to the Tripartite agreement and viewed with a degree of disapproval the attitudes adopted by Nicaragua and Costa Rica in relation to it (Fuentes Mohr 1973).

It was these issues together, along with the fear of exclusion from the main current of intra-regional trade, which forced Nicaragua to look for a compromise with the northern states. Nicaragua and Costa Rica had been assiduous opponents to the thesis of fast and unlimited trade integration and enthusiastic defenders of the principle of balanced development and of the Regime of Integration Industries. The realignment with the North implied a major defeat for the Nicaraguan theses. The option for Nicaragua was, as Enrique Delgado recognises (former Nicaraguan Economics Minister), 'either to get excluded from the programme of integration or to accept the terms that the other states had decided to give to the process' (Delgado 1981, 74). Both, the lack of an alternative credible option and the fact that the exclusion from the Tripartite zone would hurt fundamental economic interests of the state meant that the Nicaraguan government's co-operation was the rational course of action to follow.

With the intention of preventing the Northern states from granting each other preferential treatment from which Nicaragua would be excluded as well as the desire for rapprochement, the Nicaraguan Minister of Economy suggested the abolition of the Tripartite in order to embrace a more radical and far-reaching process of integration. This was mere diplomatic juggling full of inconsistency given Nicaragua's preference for a limited integration based on balanced development. However, the Nicaraguan Minister was constrained by the unwillingness of the tripartite governments to go beyond the reach of the tripartite agreement. The bargain was limited to extending the Tripartite benefits to Nicaragua, including the right to be an active member in exchange for its support to a far-reaching integration. This paved the way for expanding integration region-wide. Thus, Nicaragua agreed to the terms and conditions under which the integration would be carried out, while at the same time having decision making capacity in the negotiations. The Tripartite would be the framework for further negotiations and reform of the existing integration agreements.

The fact that Nicaragua adapted to the northern states' interests, while Costa Rica remained indifferent, facilitated the adoption of Resolution 101 by the CEC [12] which enabled ECLAC to develop a new integration treaty which took into account the interest of the Northern states and Nicaragua. The General Treaty of Economic Integration (GEI) signed in Managua on December 1960 was therefore to a large extent a reformed version of the Tripartite treaty. El Salvador, Guatemala and Nicaragua viewed themselves as the winners with the new treaty and they soon completed the ratification process, while Honduras delayed the ratification until 1961. Nicaragua's acceptance of the ruling by the International Court of Justice in November 1960 in the territorial dispute with Honduras much favoured the latter's participation in the Managua treaties. The Managua treaties included the General Treaty of Economic Integration (GEI) and the treaty creating the Central American Bank for Economic Integration (CABEI).

Costa Rica remained outside the negotiations but it was granted the benefit of later incorporation according to Article XXXIII of the Treaty. In 1963, as a result of the takeover by a new government favourable to integration as well as regional pressures, Costa Rica ratified the General Treaty.[13] Opting out was against the country's long-term interests because the government would have deprived itself of the capacity to influence decisions with a potential effect, not only on the integrated states, but also on Costa Rica (negative externalities). The Costa Rican government was further encouraged by the 'expression by the U.S. government of its willingness to extend special economic assistance to help solve the problems of transition if the five governments were to establish regional free trade' (McClelland 1972, 193). The US offered financial support for the establishment of CABEI, which was very much in the interest of Costa Rica. In this respect, the US acted as catalyst for integration. But CABEI was to a certain extent a Costa Rican brainchild. It was ex-president Otilio Ulate who suggested to the Americans the creation of CABEI in June 1960 during a trip to Miami and Guatemala (Parker 1964, 88). The PLN was a supporter of integration since the very beginning of the process. Therefore, President Francisco Orlich did not hesitate to sign the Managua treaties in 1962.

In the GEI, the logic of fast trade integration prevailed. 74 per cent of the industrial items were immediately granted free trade and by 1965, 94 per cent of items were moving freely within the region (Delgado 1981; Bulmer-Thomas 1997). Intra-regional trade expanded very quickly as a result, and the region became a major recipient of FDI, which expanded very fast during the 1960s favoured by the increasing trade liberalisation and development of physical infrastructure. Integration, hence, reflected the inner logic of asymmetric interdependence, interstate bargaining and patterns of trade dependence. External factors, including the role of external actors worked as catalysts, but their function was not more important than the domestic determinants of integration.

CONCLUDING REMARKS

It is very clear that the logic of integration leading to the formation of the CACM in the 1960s conforms to intergovernmentalist hypotheses, which explain integration asymmetrically in terms of governments' preferences, policy convergence, trade dependence and intergovernmental bargaining. The formation of the CACM was achieved as a result of the interests and preferences of the leading governments, especially those of El Salvador and Guatemala. El Salvador instigated the process of integration to mitigate the impact of domestic constraints and external conditions. These constraints included the size of the market, the expansion of the industrial elite, the danger of economic decline and the pursuit of power both domestically and regionally. External support stemming from the US and ECLAC was used to invest the Salvadorian strategy of integration with credibility and legitimacy which would temper opposition to it by regional rent-seeking forces clinging to protectionism. Policy convergence, especially the embracing of integration by the governments seeking to reinforce their programmes of modernisation and industrial development, was a major factor in bringing them to support policy co-ordination.

Integration as "negotiated policy co-ordination" as Moravcsik calls it (1993a, 474) was favoured by most governments because it would enhance their power and credibility vis-à-vis domestic forces while at the same time increasing their bargaining power regionally and in their relations with the outside world. In addition, integration was originally perceived as a cost-effective process with relatively low political and economic implications. It did not involve a major social or economic restructuring, neither did it imply the surrender of sovereignty to regional institutions. Pressures from rent seekers (domestic groups adversely affected by integration) were averted, to some extent through intergovernmental co-operation and through the promise of benefits arising from integration, including financial advantages. The fact that some states also played the role of rent seekers increased the space for asymmetrical bargaining among the governments.

Integration was carried out within market principles rather than the orthodoxy of balanced development, as demanded by some governments; this is explained by the preferences of the leading states. The creation of the CACM therefore was an asymmetrical process, one through which leading governments sought to manipulate high politics differences in order to secure economic co-operation and the expansion of intra-regional trade. Grounding integration within market principles was also a condition for securing US support and that from foreign investors. Preferential access to regional financial arrangements and support for infrastructure development was given to the least developed states in order to secure their support for integration, while the threat of exclusion from integration was used against reluctant governments. This included preferential access to credits from CABEI to Honduras and Nicaragua. Furthermore, longer adjustment periods were permitted for these states to allow them to comply with regionally agreed policies. In Costa Rica CABEI was used both as an incentive to encourage its participation in the process of integration and as a threat of exclusion. Costa Rican access to credits from CABEI was conditional on membership of the CACM. In turn, participation in the CACM was also a condition to receive US aid both from regionally based institutions and the Alliance for Progress. This linkage of aid to integration was intended to force reluctant states to support integration.

In sum, alliances, side-payments and the threat of exclusion were used by the leading governments to force the adaptation of policies in the other states. Evidence of this intergovernmentalist logic of integration is observed in the actions and strategic interactions of the states. It is also found in the abundant works on Central American integration produced in the 1960s and 1970s. However, the preference for structural and economic explanations precluded most analysts from viewing the process in terms of governments' preferences and intergovernmental bargaining. This intergovernmental way of viewing integration provides a better framework for understanding the patterns of conflict and co-operation in the region during the 1950s and 1960s. It also provides the framework for understanding the conditions accounting for disintegration and the disruption of the process of policy co-ordination throughout the 1970s and 1980s.

4 Growth and Instability in the CACM

This chapter analyses the contribution of the CACM to economic change in the region, and the circumstances that prompted the crisis and disruption within it by the end of the 1960s. Historically the CACM has been seen as an engine for economic growth in Central America. Economic analyses have predominated in explaining economic growth, making the case for economic integration under the common market. The traditional argument is that integration is good for the states in that it promotes free trade within the region. Disintegration and unilateral actions, on the other hand, are undesirable or counterproductive for economic development given some levels of interdependence between states. The selfishness of the governments has been invoked to explain disintegration. Little attention, however, has been dedicated to understanding the impact of distributional conflicts and the central role of high politics in explaining instability and setbacks on integration. Likewise, the impact of the external environment in the process of integration was largely neglected in earlier studies. Intergovernmentalism provides an explanation for these crises and will attempt to address some of the shortcomings of the traditional views of integration. The case will be made for the connection between the domestic political economy of the states with the greater picture of the global political economy. Two theses are advanced here.

1. Integration gave rise to economic change in the region, which favoured the expansion of trade and industrial development in all the states.
2. That paradoxically, the crisis faced by integration in the 1960s and 1970s was the result, on the one hand, of its stunning success in promoting trade and industrial growth and, on the other, due to political and institutional failures to deal with distributional conflicts. As a result, a crisis of expectation and a subsequent questioning of the rationale of integration supplanted the original optimism of some governments.

In the end, the process of integration became a casualty of its own intricate decision-making system because of governments' competition and the unwillingness to compromise state sovereignty. As a result, the CACM suffered a crisis, which can be termed 'system overload' where decisions are taken but scarcely implemented. It proved difficult to turn the states' inputs into regional outputs and to enact the feeding process that would have enriched integration and fostered the development of a security community based on the rule of law and the development of wider social and economic interactions. This compromised the expectations of political and economic actors, and gave rise to distributional conflicts between the states. Co-operation was, therefore, superseded by conflict. Some governments began to pursue strategies designed to increase their gains from integration and even made the accruing of gains the quid pro quo for participation in the CACM. External factors were also determinant variables in the unfolding of the crisis. However, the blame cannot be placed exclusively on such factors ignoring the internal contradiction created by the CACM itself.

THE CACM AS ENGINE FOR ECONOMIC CHANGE

Although there is no clear-cut agreement regarding the extent of the contribution of the CACM to the economic growth of the region, there is no doubt that it was positive for growth. This has been rated between 0.6 per cent, 0.7 per cent, and 1.6 per cent of the region's GDP, comprising between 10 per cent and 25 per cent of the economic growth of the region (McClelland 1972; SIECA 1973; Nugent 1974; Lizano and Willmore 1975). However, the main contribution of the CACM to the economic development of the region had probably to do with the diversification of the economies, the improvement of infrastructure, the development of industry and trade, and the utilisation of otherwise idle resources. In other words, integration re-balanced economic development within each state, even though it may have exacerbated imbalances among them (Castillo 1966). Before integration, the economies of the region remained largely agricultural and the economic growth was highly dependent on the performance of export agriculture to the world market. With integration the industrial development of the states expanded at a fast pace. The share of industry in the GDP rose from 'approximately 10 per cent in 1950 to nearly 20 per cent in 1970' (Bulmer-Thomas 1997, 7). Most of this growth took place during the 1960s and 1970s.

Integration also prompted some important changes in industry. There was a move, although slow, from basic or traditional industries towards new and higher tech industries. Prior to the signing of the General Treaty of Economic Integration (GEI) in 1960, 'traditional industries accounted for 87 per cent of industrial production. By 1964 it had dropped to 82 per cent, while new industries in intermediate goods increased their participation from 9 per cent to 13 per cent during the same period' (Hansen 1967, 38).

Integration not only allowed traditional industries (textile, foodstuff, shoes and light chemicals) to expand but also brought about new intermediate goods industries (petrochemicals, paper, tyres and metal-mechanic). Of these, the chemical industry (fertilisers, insecticides, detergents) was the most important, accounting for over 50 per cent (Hansen 1967; Cline 1978; SIECA 1982; García 1988). All the countries gained experience in industrial development although some performed better than others, depending on their original position and internal conditions, as can be seen in Table 4.1. All showed an appreciable leap in the annual rates of industrial growth during the decade of the 1960s, although this was less impressive but also less unstable in Honduras as shown in Table 4.1. Integration not only had a positive impact in terms of promoting industrialisation, it also widened the production frontier and strengthened the traditional exporter sector. For instance, cotton production acquired an enormous importance in the 1960s encouraged not only by an increased external demand but also by integration, which sparked off the creation of a regional network of road systems, allowing the expansion of production.

Table 4.1 Central America: Indicators of Industrial Development, 1950 to 1973b/. (percentages)

Years	*CA.*	*Guatemala*	*El Salvador*	*Honduras*	*Nicaragua*	*Costa Rica*
	A. Annual growth rates of industrial GDP.					
1950–60	6.0	4.6	5.5	7.0	7.3	8.0
1960–67	9.3	7.7	10.5	7.1	12.8	8.9
1967–70	6.3	7.4	3.0	6.1	7.2	8.7
1960–70	8.4	7.7	8.2	6.8	11.1	3.8
1970–73b/	5.6	5.5	5.6	6.3	4.2	6.2
	B. Degree of Industrialisation.					
1950	12.2	11.8	13.5	8.1	13.3	15.0
1960	13.9	12.8	14.6	11.2	16.0	16.2
1967	17.0	15.1	18.6	12.8	20.7	18.8
1970	17.6	15.5	18.4	13.6	22.9	19.6
1973a/	18.3	15.7	19.6	15.4	22.9	20.8

Source: ECLAC (Economic Commission for Latin America and the Caribbean) (1974, 31).
a/ In Central American Pesos=US$. A= at factors cost. B= at market prices.
b/ 1973, preliminary.

Development in infrastructure, particularly roads, was probably the largest long-term gain from integration after the gains in industrial development and trade, with most of the investment in roads concentrated largely in the least developed states. By 1960 only El Salvador and to some extent Costa Rica, had made headway in terms of expanding their road systems.

Road infrastructure in the region was normally concentrated on the capitals of the countries with outlets to the sea in response to the needs of the outward model of development, which had prevailed since the nineteenth century. Most internal regions, involving clusters of communities, and in some cases main cities, remained largely isolated because of the lack of infrastructure. The lack of road networks also kept the countries isolated accounting for the development of strong nationalist attitudes in the region (SIECA 1973).

As a result of improvements of the road systems under integration, overland transportation (lorries) became the main way of mobilising intra-regional trade. Other means of transportation such as shipping and railways were discontinued. 94 per cent of total intra-regional trade was transported through the road system in 1970. Physical infrastructure together with other additional actions such as tariffs reduction, fiscal incentives, the enlargement of the market, payments and monetary co-operation, and the good performance of traditional exports had a creative impact on intra-regional trade and FDI. More than 98 per cent of items enjoyed free trade by 1969. Intra-regional trade expanded at a fast pace from $32.7 million in 1960 to nearly $300 million in 1970, growing at an annual rate of 25 per cent (SIECA 1972; Nugent 1974).

Likewise, FDI doubled in the 1960s from $388 million in 1959 to $755 million in 1969.[1] About 30 per cent of FDI in 1969 went to the manufacturing sector compared to 3.8 per cent in 1959. Guatemala and El Salvador were the main recipients of the FDI allocated in the industrial sector, while Honduras was the least favoured (SIECA 1973; Rosenthal 1975). Honduras experienced mainly an expansion of traditional exports destined for outside the CACM. In the period 1961–1968 Honduras' exports to third countries showed the highest annual rate of growth in the region, 9.7 per cent, compared to 1.2 per cent in the previous decade (Willmore 1975a). The equivalents for Guatemala and El Salvador were remarkably low, 1.4 per cent and 1.1 per cent, respectively. In fact, the annual rates of growth of Guatemala and El Salvador in the traditional export sector declined from 1951, whereas those of Honduras, Nicaragua and Costa Rica showed a continual upward trend (Lizano and Willmore 1975, Table II). This suggests that the CACM encouraged some degree of specialisation in the economies of the region where losses in one sector may have been compensated with gains in another sector.

The extent to which FDI dominated the industrial development of the region has always been disputed. McClelland (1972), for instance, argues that about 85 per cent to 90 per cent of fixed capital formation in manufacturing was of Central American origin, while most analysts tend to see the CACM as a neo-colonial instrument designed to satisfy the economic appetite of US corporate interests. The increasing FDI in the 1960s was a direct result of the economic growth and integration, including the improvement in infrastructure. FDI tends to follow economic growth, not the other way round (Bergsman and Shen 1995). This is why FDI largely concentrates on industrialised countries, and in the case of the CACM, it went to the most developed and "safe" states of the region (García 1988, 95). This was something not properly understood in Central America during the 1960s and 1970s. This explains the strong opposition to FDI, especially from intellectuals and sociologists inspired by dependency theory that in the decades of 1960 and 1970 had a strong influence in the studies of Latin American development.[2] Intellectuals tended to view integration as a symptom of underdevelopment and therefore felt disappointed and withdrew their support for the CACM (Lizano and Willmore 1975). This opposition may have precluded the states from taking full advantage of foreign investment not only in the industrial but also in other economic sectors.

All countries benefited from the expansion of intra-regional trade, although the distribution of the gains was uneven with the lion's share going to the largest economies, especially Guatemala, as can be seen in Table 4.2. This table reveals that a distributive trend in the patterns of trade among the states took place in the 1960s. In the 1950s trade relations were highly concentrated between El Salvador and Honduras. In the 1960s this trend was reversed in favour of the other states with Guatemala and Costa Rica showing the best performance. In the first case exports to the region leaped from 6 per cent to nearly 31 per cent, while in the second it soared from 1.2 per cent to 14.5 per cent in the period 1950–1967.

Table 4.2 Central America:Intra-Regional Trade, 1950–1967. (Millions of US dollars)

	Exports		*Percentages*		*Imports*		*Percentages*	
	1950	1967	1950	1967	1950	1967	1950	1967
CA: Total	8.6	213.6	100.0	100.0	8.6	213.6	100.0	100.0
Guatemala	0.5	65.6	5.8	30.7	1.8	41.8	20.9	19.6
El Salvador	4.0	74.9	46.5	35.1	2.9	54.4	33.7	25.5
Honduras	2.8	23.5	32.6	11.0	2.5	40.8	29.1	19.1
Nicaragua	1.1	18.6	12.8	8.7	0.4	42.4	4.7	19.8
Costa Rica	0.1	31.0	1.2	14.5	1.0	34.2	11.6	16.0

Source: Adapted from Castillo Zeledón 1970, 34.

Integration had some impact as well in terms of reducing the external dependence of the states. According to Nugent (1974), in the 1960s the trade dependence on the United States declined from about two-thirds of total trade to about one-third. Central American states also lowered their dependence on traditional exports (coffee and bananas) from about 80 per cent in 1953 to just over 40 per cent in 1968–69, while manufactures increased their participation in the region's exports from less than 1 per cent to more than 20 per cent. The increased share of manufactures since the 1950s contrasted with the decline of agriculture which fell from 37.9 per cent of GDP in 1953 to 28.7 per cent in 1968. However this decline may not be attributable entirely to industrialisation but to a fall in the prices of extra-regional exports, especially the price of coffee since the end of the 1950s and cotton in the second half of the 1960s (Bulmer-Thomas 1987; Thielen 1989).

According to Reynolds, the fast industrial growth was not detrimental to agriculture, since it was accompanied by a parallel expansion in the agricultural sector. He argues that this parallel growth was the major reason for the 15 years of relatively rapid growth in both output and productivity. Thus, the economic growth of the CACM 'was achieved with productivity gains in all major sectors' (Reynolds 1978, 212–213). Integration also gave rise to a slight diversification of the sources of FDI. In 1959, 90.2 per cent of total FDI came from the US. Ten years later US FDI represented 81.3 per cent of the total accrued to the region. More importantly, during the 1960s FDI spread more evenly among the countries of the region. Although Guatemala still enjoyed the largest amount of FDI, it had the lowest rate of growth in the region with the higher rate of growth of foreign investment going to the other states, especially, Nicaragua, El Salvador, and Costa Rica (Poitevin 1977).

Nonetheless, the core question is, did the CACM reduce external dependence? While the region did successfully reduce its dependence on export agriculture (EXA) for a time and managed to increase its industrial base, it became highly dependent on imports of intermediate and capital goods which were needed to sustain industrial development. Despite a high proportion of goods circulating in the region in 1970, a large proportion of the value was made up of imported materials (McClelland 1972). According to Bulmer-Thomas (1987), almost 100 per cent of capital goods imports came from outside the region, and in 1970 extra-regional imports for industry accounted for nearly 60 per cent of all extra-regional imports, which consumed about two-thirds of earnings from extra-regional exports.

The consequence of this heavy reliance on imports to sustain the industrial development was a strong dependence on EXA in the 1970s and a subsequent aggravation of the fiscal and trade deficits of the states, which became unbearable for most governments. This led the governments in 1968 to adopt some remedial measures through the so-called San José Protocol, which raised the Common External Tariff (CET) by 30 per cent and re-imposed additional restrictions on regionally produced goods (McClelland 1972). The measures, however, did not resolve the underlying conflicts, which in the 1970s heavily disrupted intra-regional trade and intergovernmental co-operation. In sum, the CACM led to a relocation of the sources of dependence rather than its overall reduction.

ENTRENCHED INTERGOVERNMENTALISM AND REGIONAL CRISIS[3]

The decision-making system adopted within Central American integration accounts to a large extent for the crises faced by the CACM by the end of the 1960s. Motivated by concerns about political control and sovereignty, the governments had favoured decision making through unanimity, and imposed constitutional restrictions on every regional agreement. In other words, the governments favoured a trend of state-led interdependence, where the states set up and observed the rules of the co-operation game. This method of state-led interdependence differs substantially from that exercised in Europe, whereby the diffusion of power and the development of transnational relations led to a joint management of integration through 'international institutions, the pooling of sovereignties, and the co-ordination of policies and goals' (Hoffman 1978, 131–132). In Central America entrenched intergovernmentalism was the style of decision-making set out in 1951 for the Organisation of Central American States (ODECA), which was thereafter adopted by the governments in every regional agreement. Co-operation around ODECA 'was made possible only by avoiding debate upon the issues of sovereignty and political control that would be involved in establishing anything approaching a federation and by steering away from political and defence questions' (Padelford 1957, 43).

The nation-state was both the departure and end point of integration. Integration was, therefore, perceived not as a way of downgrading but of strengthening the nation-state. Provided integration is restricted to the area of welfare, that is to say, that it does not touch high politics issues, as Hoffmann argues, the governments would find grounds for co-operation. But if welfare issues gain notoriety as to overlap with high politics matters, they will be 'infected by the disharmony, which reigns in the latter' (Hoffmann 1966, 882). Co-operation could therefore be questioned because of the centrality of political and security concerns. In underdeveloped regions such as Central America co-operation is further complicated by the process Nye (1965, 872) called 'premature over-politicisation', which means that the dividing line between high politics and welfare is less visible. Welfare is always politicised, and the procurement of welfare is quickly turned into the politics of welfare ordained along side class conflicts and the struggle for political control and domination of society through the use of state power.

This rationale seems to explain the development of the process of integration in Central America. Rather than pursuing the old agenda of federation, the governments engaged in a policy of co-operation aimed at promoting industrialisation and economic growth. Some level of economic interdependence was favoured in order to boost the modernisation of the economies and the integration of the markets of the region. However, complex interdependence viewed as lack of hierarchy, vulnerability and mutual sensitivity among the economies and politics of the states was seen as something to be avoided by most governments (Cooper 1972; Keohane and Nye, 1989). Complex interdependence would have increased the dependence and vulnerability of the economies of the region and substantially eroded the power of the governments. The concern with political control and sovereignty did not favour this kind of development.

Indeed, it was the desire to avert the implications of complex interdependence which led the governments to strengthen the decision-making machinery by concentrating the decisional power on the two main political organs created by the General Treaty of Economic Integration (GEI). These are, the Central American Economic Council (CAEC) integrated by the Ministers of Economics, and the Executive Council (EC) made up also of governments' representatives (Lizano 1976). They are both intergovernmental bodies. The CAEC is the main decision-making body within the CACM, especially regarding the politics of integration. As such, it operates as an instrument of last resort when the EC, which has the primary responsibility to implement the programme of integration and making daily decisions, fails to get agreement.

It was this desire to maintain the process of integration under political control which led the governments to deprive regional institutions of political power, including financial deprivation and external representation (no delegation of sovereignty) (Lizano 1976). The intergovernmental bargaining took place in the Councils where state officials acted as gatekeepers and defenders of national sovereignty. Through it the governments avoided potential spill-over effects of integration on their domestic politics. Concerns with the premature over-politicisation of integration may have reinforced the rigidity of the decision-making system.

The Permanent Secretariat of the CACM (SIECA), as well as a multitude of functional institutions created by the governments in the 1950s and 1960s, were entrusted with the function of safeguarding and ensuring the implementation of all treaties and agreements. They were also entrusted with the task of providing information and carrying out technical studies. But, politically, they were deprived of decision-making power subordinated to the Councils. Supranationality was consistently avoided (Fonseca and Ramírez 1970). The only embryonic attempt at creating a supranational body, according to Sancho was the establishment in 1972 of the so-called 'Comision Normalizadora' (Normalising Commission) of the CACM where the governments of Costa Rica, El Salvador, Guatemala and Nicaragua agreed to be legally bound by its decisions (Sancho 1979). But this was conceived as a temporary mechanism and did not succeed in its attempts because of the lack of final agreement among the governments.

The decision-making system followed by the CACM became a source of disintegration and conflict because it did not leave room for flexible manoeuvring. Unanimity or consensus became the rule, preventing the governments from reaching decisions by majority voting (pooling sovereignty). Even when agreements were reached in the councils, constitutional obstacles in the form of ratification procedures were imposed by the states (Padelford 1957; Ramsett 1969). Integration arrangements, thus, mean that the governments can veto a Central American accord whenever it does not fit their interests. The resort to veto in the CACM has taken place at four levels.

1. At the level of the Ministers of Economics. When they meet both at the ECLAC sponsored Council for Central American Economic Cooperation and in the CAEC, the Ministers of Economics can veto agreements that endanger the national interest of their states. The Modus Operandi [4] and Central American Social and Economic Community (CASEC) are the most outstanding examples of initiatives vetoed by El Salvador and Guatemala in 1970 and 1976, respectively, which prevented the reform of the CACM to promote the pattern of balanced development.
2. The Executive Level. The Presidents can directly reject any agreement or avoid submitting it to the national assemblies for ratification. One example of this was Costa Rica in 1958, when President Echandi refused to submit the Tegucigalpa Treaties [5] to the Parliament. This was in effect an Executive veto (Soto Acosta 1990).
3. The Legislative Level. A veto may take place when the Legislative bodies of the states do not approve (ratify) any agreement. While all the states have done this, Honduras is the state which has persistently delayed or avoided the ratification of most Central American treaties on the grounds that they were not based on the notion of balanced development (Delgado 1981).[6] Honduras had made balanced development a fundamental principle of its Central American economic diplomacy and its very lack of flexibility constituted an obstacle to integration.
4. The equality of states promoted by ECLAC through its principles of reciprocity and balanced development. This became in effect a camouflaged way of vetoing regional accords, particularly within the Regime of Integration Industries (RII). Under this regime no country could receive a second integration industry until each was designated one (Wionczek 1966; Ramsett 1969). This became a major discouragement for the implementation of the regime in question as the governments that possessed industrial power and location advantages

> would not willingly surrender them in favour of less developed states. Instead the governments chose not to co-operate with the regional industrial programme by pursuing their own industrial policies based on lavish incentives to foreign investors.[7]

From 1958 to 1964 the principle that industries would not be replicated by each state prevailed, which greatly discouraged the governments from making applications for new plants and gave rise to political conflicts. One of the most notorious conflicts was Costa Rica's application for a tyre industry in 1962. This was opposed by Guatemala, which had already been granted the authority for a tyre industry (GINSA) in accordance with the RII. Thus, Costa Rica was defying the regime (Ramsett 1969; Guerra Borges 1979).

The policy of non-co-operation which prevailed until 1964 was replaced thereafter by fierce competition and resentment following a reinterpretation of the RII which eliminated the requirement of not replicating industries. The result was that SIECA and the CAEC were inundated with applications well beyond their capacity to cope. Competition gave rise to the concentration of the new industrial activities in the better-endowed states. Out of 16 new industries approved up to 1970, 7 went to El Salvador, 4 to Guatemala, 3 to Costa Rica and 2 to Honduras (Nuhn 1991). Owing to the inability of the CACM to curtail competition and the concentration, the governments pursued industrialisation under their own national programmes (Ramsett 1969). The financial crisis faced by most Central American industries contributed to the fact that most FDI took the form of taking over existing industries or 'investment by absorption' (Guerra Borges 1979, 13). Thus, rather than being the victim of a highly protective CET and the exhaustion of the market because of its small size,[8] the CACM became a prisoner of the entrenched intergovernmentalism, giving rise to a protracted conflict of interests among the states, largely serving the interests of foreign corporations. It was these conflicts of interests among the states rather than the impact of corporate interests alone, which largely accounts for the failure of the RII.

THE IMPACT OF DISTRIBUTIVE CONFLICTS ON INTEGRATION

The expectation of gains is a major stimulus for states to integrate. These gains could take the form of economic efficiency (enhancing the economic achievements of the governments) or relative power (increasing their bargaining power both internationally and in the domestic arena).[9] But if the gains are uneven among the states, this can give rise to a 'crisis of expectation' in the sense that those governments, which feel they gain too little from integration, could feel disappointed and resent that they are exploited by the larger states. The resulting disapproval amongst the population could reach intolerable levels, and therefore, governments could question their participation in the process. If the costs of integration outweigh the benefits those governments could turn reluctantly to co-operate. Co-operation, as Keohane asserts (1984), does not always succeed, despite some similarities in the interests of the states. The uneven distribution of gains as well as changes of preferences in some member states may bring co-operation into question.

In Central America all the states expected to gain from integration, but as explained earlier, the lion's share of the gain went to the most advanced states which possessed advantages of location and political leadership. These two factors, structural advantages and leadership acted as catalysts for the attraction of FDI, particularly in the industrial sector. The distribution of benefits, thus, does not happen by default neither is it a neutral process. It is intrinsically related to power differentials among the states and to patterns of asymmetrical interdependence. (Bull 1977; Moravcisk 1998).

This situation was clearly understood in Central America. But an attempt was made within the ECLAC paradigm of integration based on balanced development to reverse it in order to avoid conflicts. Preoccupation with the principle of equality of the states and with the condition of underdevelopment prompted ECLAC to suggest reciprocity, gradualism, and balanced development as the principles that should guide integration in Central America. Although all governments paid lip service to such principles, it soon became apparent that the concept of balanced development entailed some ambiguities, which disguised relative costs. In addition, each government could interpret it in line with its own interests and preferences (Lizano 1979). However, little attention was paid to distributional conflicts and to the need to devise a mechanism to deal with such conflicts (Hernández Alcerro 1976). Without a proper system of dealing with distributional conflicts the programme of integration would not be sustainable in the long run. This neglect of conflict resolution in the CACM was a direct consequence, on the one hand, of the rigidity of the intergovernmental process of decision making, and on the other, the influence of neo-functional theory, which had caught the attention of ECLAC's technocrats.

In the first case, the governments kept the decisional power in their hands depriving regional institutions, particularly the CEC and SIECA, of any substantive power and therefore highly influencing their effectiveness to deal with regional problems. They avoided delegating sovereignty in any issue, which involved policy-making and settling disputes. It is possible to assert that the CACM did not properly take the form of an international regime. Regimes, according to Young, 'form a horizontal rather than a vertical or hierarchical system of public order. The result is a complex pattern of decentralised authority' (Young 1999, 6–7). In the CACM the pattern of institutional decentralisation was (quantitatively) high but in terms of authority (qualitatively) it was unquestionably low, as the governments remained the decision-makers in the central bodies.

Conflict resolution was an issue to be dealt with first by the EC and if this failed by the CAEC where the Ministers of Economics could make a final decision (GEI: Arts.XXI and XXVI). Although Art. XXVI of the General Treaty of Economic Integration contemplates international arbitration as a last resort; the process is complex and not necessarily free of governmental interference. In practice the governments played the double function, of being both the judge and the accused, in any controversy. This could only result in failure and the aggravation of regional tensions. The lack of an efficient system of conflict resolution has been a major weakness of the CACM. Even when decisions were taken, the institutions were unable to implement them, not only because of their lack of resources but because of overload. SIECA and the CAEC were paralysed by the number of demands they had to deal with (Castillo Zeledón 1970). Most of these were complaints by Honduras and Nicaragua of unfair trade practices (dumping) against which they had no right to take action unilaterally.

These problems were worsened by the time taken to ratify and the time span of the implementation of agreements. In some cases the implementation of regional agreements could take between two and three years and in others could take up to seven years owing to political obstructions (Nuhn 1991). In most cases this delay was due to tortuous ratification procedures as well as tactical holding of the instruments by the governments. The Convention on Fiscal Incentives for Industrial Development was one example of an instrument, agreed by the governments in 1962, that the Honduran government consciously delayed ratification of until 1969 because it did not satisfy the government's concept of balanced development (Delgado 1981).

As far as the technocratic view is concerned, the lack of attention to conflict resolution was ingrained, on the one hand, in ECLAC's homogeneous perception of underdevelopment in the region. On the other hand, there was the overestimation of the ability of the technocrats in isolating and controlling conflicts by means of upgrading the common interests (Schmitter 1970a). Regarding the first, ECLAC's view was that the states of the region all shared the same developmental problems. They were all least developed states by Latin American standards. Although it was recognised that Honduras was the most backward of all, they all shared the condition of backwardness (ECLAC 1974). It was believed that integration could only be a good thing for all the states. Provided they all followed the integration agenda based on reciprocity they all would enjoy net gains from co-operation. Distribution would be the result of growth. Conflicts would rather produce a creative effect reinforcing integration. This was a belief that both ECLAC and SIECA shared, influenced by neo-functional theory (ECLAC 1974; Delgado 1981).

Because of this thinking as well as the competitive interests of the states, the GEI did not make any distinction among the levels of development of the states, therefore, no preferential treatment to the least developed states (LDS) was acknowledged. Neither was there any institutional machinery set out to compensate deficit states from the vagaries of intra-regional trade. In this regard, the CACM fell far behind the other integration arrangements in Latin America where preferential treatment was granted to the LDS. The logic of diversity, not only in the high politics sense advanced by Hoffmann (1966), but also in terms of the economic policy preferences favoured by the governments, was ignored. Sooner rather than later the governments learned that, as Cohen Orantes asserts (1998, 11), 'the hypothesis that the sacrifices would be compensated with the benefits brought about by integration was not a sufficient condition to move forward the process' or stop the ambitions of member states. The outbreak of crises did not bring about creative opportunities as expected, but 'rather a process of continual attrition' (Lizano and Willmore 1975, 302). As a result of the crisis as well as pressures by LDS, some readjustment was made by granting preferential treatment to Honduras and Nicaragua as integration went on, but this did not stop the conflicts that were troubling the CACM. Distributional conflicts rose to the realm of high politics, severely disrupting the functioning of the process of integration in the 1970s.

EXPLAINING HONDURAS' QUARRELS WITH INTEGRATION

The poor performance of Honduras within the CACM is not due entirely to adverse effects of integration on its economic development, although a programme of integration based on market determinants is bound to work overwhelmingly in favour of the most advanced states. This, however, does not mean that LDS are left worse off by integration (Nye 1987). But they will not be able to take on the new opportunities brought about by integration with the same dexterity and rapidity as the most advanced states, deepening, as a result, the gap in the levels of development among the states. Feeling a loser within integration, a government can voice its dissatisfaction or show its unwillingness to support policy co-ordination or may make demands aimed at redressing the balance of gains. The latter could involve using its veto power in order to satisfy such demands (voice option) [10] (Hirschman 1970). The possibility that such a state could succeed in persuading its partners will largely depend on its bargaining power which in turn will be determined by its political and economic weight, including its level of engagement with the regional market. On the other hand, failure on the part of the most advanced states to satisfy such demands may force a dissatisfied government to rethink its position and, if an attractive alternative option exists, it could withdraw its support for integration (exit option) (Hirschman 1970; Moravcsik 1993a). The final outcome could well be a stalemate and worse yet, a halt to the process of integration. This appears to have been the case in the CACM.

One major structural failure of the CACM, which prompted distributional conflicts, was the inability of states to adapt to external competition. External competition here is understood both at the intra-regional level and the extra-regional one. At the regional level the main difficulty was that some states, particularly Honduras, had failed to catch up with the level of industrial development and competitiveness of the other states. Although the CACM created opportunities for all the states, Honduras was the only one that failed to take full advantage of the programme despite particular concessions granted to it (Nye 1987).[11] Twenty years after the signing of the GEI the country was far behind the other states in terms of economic modernisation. Table 4.3 shows the disparities in the accruing of gains from the CACM in terms of share of the region GDP and per capita GDP.

Table 4.3 Central America: GDP at Cost of Factors. 1950 and 1960 till 1973.

	1950	*1960*	*1965*	*1970*	*1973*	*Annual Rates of Growth* *1950–60*	*1960–65*	*1965–70*	*1970–73*
			Per capita GDP (US dollars of 1960)						
Central America	220.0	258.0	302.0	337.0	352.0	1.6	3.2	2.2	1.9
Guatemala	243.0	268.0	301.0	346.0	383.0	1.0	2.3	2.8	3.4
El Salvador	210.0	253.0	301.0	315.0	324.0	1.9	3.5	0.8	0.9
Honduras	176.0	181.0	193.0	213.0	215.0	0.3	1.3	2.0	0.3
Nicaragua	178.0	224.0	316.0	335.0	344.0	2.3	7.1	1.2	0.9
Costa Rica	285.0	394.0	452.0	544.0	569.0	3.3	2.9	3.8	1.5

	1950	*1960*	*1965*	*1970*	*1973*
		B. Share of the GDP per countries (percentages)			
Central America	100.0	100.0	100.0	100.0	100.0
Guatemala	40.2	37.2	35.3	36.0	37.5
El Salvador	22.1	22.3	22.8	21.7	21.2
Honduras	13.4	11.8	10.9	10.7	10.3
Nicaragua	10.0	11.5	13.7	13.0	12.7
Costa Rica	13.5	17.2	17.3	18.6	18.2

Source: ECLAC (Economic Commission for Latin America and the Caribbean) (1974, 30).

Three factors largely explain Honduras's failure to match the other states in extracting benefits from integration: a) lack of leadership, b) economic geography, and c) lack of industrial development. With regards the first factor, Honduras unlike the other states did not have an entrepreneurial class. In the other states of the region, especially in El Salvador, Guatemala and Costa Rica, an entrepreneurial elite was formed around the cultivation and trade of coffee. The nation-building had been linked to the production and trade of coffee, which remained largely under national control. In contrast, in Honduras geological and climatic factors (unsuitable soil) prevented the creation of a coffee oligarchy which in turn hindered the development of a physical and financial infrastructure which would have been required for strengthening the economic development (Cáceres 1980).

While the other states not only controlled the production and trade of coffee but also had a banking system to provide financial resources, the Hondurans did not. Instead, 'the banana plantations which were American owned, geographically isolated from the rest of the country, became states within the state' (Schulz and Sundloff Schulz 1994, 9). As a result, Honduras became a rent-seeking state. The political elite has been vulnerable to pressures and bribes from the banana companies while the economic elite felt discouraged to get involved in production, becoming instead a 'comprador' or importing class (Cáceres 1980; Schulz and Sundloff Schulz 1994;). Consequently, Honduras remained severely underdeveloped even by Central American standards.

Honduras lacked physical and financial infrastructure. While the other states began to consolidate a banking system as early as the end of the 19th century and developed physical infrastructure (roads, electricity,) in the 1950s and 1960s, Honduras only began to undertake these tasks after 1974. According to Cáceres (1980), by 1971 the main road connecting the capital (Tegucigalpa) with the rich Atlantic coast (banana plantations and San Pedro Sulas) was still unpaved. By 1955 Honduras only had twenty-four miles of paved road, and the Inter-American Highway, 'the only east-west highway crossing the country, traversed only the narrow southern tip of Honduras, a distance of only 95 miles' (Checchini et al 1959, 29). Not only its main urban centres faced isolation, but most of the country remained inaccessible by land, relying 'almost entirely on aeroplanes for both incoming supplies and outgoing produce' (Checchini et al 1959, 36).

Because of the banana plantations, Honduras's development was concentrated on the Atlantic coast where San Pedro Sulas, the second city of the country, became more developed and industrialised than Tegucigalpa (Villagrán Kramer 1967, 271). Deprived of access to the Pacific coast because of its own geographical location, Honduras became more a Caribbean state largely divorced from the main stream of development in Central America. This economic fragmentation and the lack of leadership largely accounts for Honduras' limited involvement with Central America, which ultimately prevented it from making higher gains from integration. Because of its internal disintegration it was easier to supply large regions of the country, Tegucigalpa and San Pedro Sulas included, from El Salvador and Guatemala (Checchini et al 1959).

Yet, with the exception of trade, it does not seem that participation in the CACM added more calamities to the backward condition of Honduras, as the government repeatedly complained. On balance all the states drew gains from integration and the Hondurans realised this as both politicians and entrepreneurs admitted that the CACM brought them more benefits than costs (Willmore 1975a; Facussé 1976). The economic underachievement of Honduras predates the establishing of the CACM. Its share of the region's GDP as shown in table 3 was in a downward trend since 1950, falling from 13.4 per cent in that year to 11.8 per cent in 1960; both figures predate integration under the CACM. In this regard Honduras was not alone because Guatemala also faced a drop in its performance in the same period. But Honduras' share of the region's GDP continued deteriorating throughout the 1960s and even during the first half of the 1970s when Honduras no longer was a member of the CACM.

It is interesting that while Honduras' performance considerably deteriorated, those of Nicaragua and Costa Rica improved quite dramatically with the CACM. With a worse position than that of Honduras both in 1950 and 1960, Nicaragua overtook Honduras from the very beginning of the CACM, not only in terms of the share of the region's GDP but also in terms of per capita GDP. In 1950 Honduras and Nicaragua were roughly at the same level in terms of per capita GDP, as can be seen in Table 4.3, but by 1960 Nicaragua was catching up with the other states while Honduras remained virtually static. By 1965 Nicaragua had doubled its per capita GDP while Honduras showed no great level of improvement. The following question therefore arises. If the CACM was the cause of Honduras' malaise, why did it not have the same effect in Nicaragua? The answer to this question is that the CACM, as Lizano and Willmore (1975) have asserted, did not account for the whole level of growth experienced by the region in the 1960s. The major stimulus for economic growth during that decade came from the expansion of the traditional agro export model of development, in response to an improvement in the demand not only in terms of volume but also in value.

Costa Rica, Guatemala, El Salvador, and Nicaragua widened their export opportunities through intensive cultivation of cotton, sugar cane and livestock. Nicaragua, for instance, became 'the number one Latin American beef supplier to the US during the 1970s' (Karliner 1989, 791), while cotton became the first source of foreign exchange for this country and the second for Guatemala and El Salvador (Rouquié 1994). Agro-exports reinforced the industrial development of these states. But most of the new export-led activities concentrated on the Pacific side of the region, leaving Honduras outside of the new wave of growth.

As a result of failure to catch up with the other states, the Honduras government became increasingly dissatisfied with the CACM and increased its pressure to reform it. Although the government did not ignore the country's responsibility for the low industrial development, President Oswaldo López Arellano placed a large share of the blame on the CACM. He maintained firmly that 'the explanation for the unbalance affecting our country could be found as well in the terms of the integration treaties because they do not take full account of the principle of balanced development' (cited in Delgado 1981, 103–104). The notion that integration is not a substitute for a good domestic economic and industrial policy (Robson 1998, 7) was not followed seriously by the Honduran government. Instead of trying to close the gap by enacting a consistent policy of industrial development, Honduras sought to force the adjustment at the level of the CACM. When this strategy showed little sign of paying off, the government then turned to nationalism, blaming not only the CACM but also the Salvadorians for their malaise. A deterioration in the relations with El Salvador thus followed, ending in the so-called "football war" (Cable 1969).

The war between Honduras and El Salvador was not entirely due to integration, but the CACM aggravated the trade deficit of some member states, giving rise to nationalist resentments in deficit states. It thus contributed to the tensions leading to war. Honduras' policy of close co-operation with El Salvador [12] was replaced by non-co-operation, rivalry and hostility during the military governments of López Arellano (1963, 1965–1970). As both the Honduran and Salvadorian governments failed to adjust their policies an escalation of the conflict between the two became inevitable. It ended in the short war of July 1969, when the Salvadorian Army occupied a large chunk of Honduras' territory.

The government of López Arellano linked its domestic problems with the country's performance in the CACM. Honduras' trade deficit with the region deteriorated very fast from 1965 when López Arellano came back to power. The deficit rose from $5 million in 1965 to $14 million in 1966. By 1968 the trade deficit with El Salvador alone reached $9 million and $5 million in the year of the war, and some of the country's intellectuals as well as the press began talking of the 'imperialism of the colón', the Salvadorian currency (Rowles 1980; Greiner 1991). The deterioration of the deficit, not just with El Salvador but with the region as a whole, was due to the inability of Honduras to improve the quality and content of its exports. The country basically exported agriculture or agro-industrial goods scarcely processed while its imports from El Salvador and the other states were highly processed. Honduras, however, by no means represented the worst situation in intra regional trade. Nicaragua was running a deficit of $24 million in 1967, Costa Rica a larger in 1968 of $43 million which resulted in the enactment of protectionist measures by the governments of these states, particularly after 1968 (Greiner 1991).

El Salvador was not free of costs stemming from its participation in the CACM either. Although the industrial sector increased its share of the GDP from 15.4 per cent in 1961 to 18.1 per cent in 1966, the CACM also increased the dependence and vulnerability of the Salvadorian economy in the way of increased extra-regional imports of intermediate and capital goods (Cáceres 1980). By 1967 the Salvadorian economy was reaching stagnation and was facing balance of payments difficulties and the government joined its regional counterparts in enacting protectionist measures against imports from the other member states (Jiménez 1974). By 1969 the CACM was collapsing even without the war between Honduras and El Salvador. Nicaragua asked in 1969 for a preferential treatment similar to the one granted to Honduras three years before and even threatened to disrupt the CACM. Somoza followed the tactic of the empty chair in the CAEC and 'slapped an import surcharge on Central American goods in manifest violation of the General Treaty' (Schmitter 1970b, 27). It is interesting that although it was clear that by 1969 the CACM was on the threshold of a deep crisis of disintegration because of the clashes of the national interests of some states, Schmitter failed to recognise that trend. Instead, he categorised the problem as spill-around, an intermediate situation between spill-over and self-encapsulation; a situation which in his neo-functional theory, is "naturally expansionist", but without the element of automaticity or the degree of predictability of the spill-over syndrome (Schmitter 1970b, 39–40).

THE COST OF NON-CO-OPERATION

Following the war, Honduras and El Salvador failed to reach a compromise. Their national interests and policies were not convergent. The governments stopped viewing their decisions within the CACM as interdependent and their negotiations became a zero-sum game where a gain for one side implied a loss for the other. Honduras sought to inflict damage on the Salvadorian economy. This included denying access to the Inter-American highway, seizing Salvadorian assets, especially bank accounts in Honduras, and a massive deportation of the about 300,000 Salvadorians living in Honduras. These measures were as damaging to El Salvador as to Honduras as industrialists from the interior of the country not only depended on the Salvadorian market, but also transported their products to Guatemala through Salvadorian roads (Facussé 1976). It also affected Honduras' agricultural development as the breaking of trade relations with El Salvador meant losing the main market for Honduras's agricultural and agro-industrial goods which was El Salvador, while the Guatemalan market, the second major market, faced disruption as well. The result was that Honduras became a net importer of basic grains by 1975, a situation aggravated by the devastating effect of such natural disasters as hurricanes and droughts

(Bulmer-Thomas 1987). The boomerang effect of the measures enacted by Honduras against El Salvador clearly reflected the degree not only of economic, but also strategic interdependence of both states. According to this logic Honduras could not hurt El Salvador without hurting itself. Its economic goals in the region would also flounder without co-operation from El Salvador. As Hoffmann (1978, 123) argues, 'An actor's hostile or aggressively competitive use of economic power may well backfire at home'.

Both Honduras and El Salvador desperately needed the CACM and attempted ways of bringing it into working order again, but they pursued diametrically opposed policies and they tied themselves with inflexible policies, which prevented an early solution to their bilateral problems.[13] This in turn prevented the normalisation of the CACM, which remained disrupted for two decades.

Believing that El Salvador was on its knees Honduras pursued an uncompromising policy of reforming the CACM. Its proposed version of a 'Modus Operandi' [14] not only emphasised planning and protectionism, but also passing the costs of improving the situation of deficit states on to surplus states, as well as extending preferential treatment to LDS. But, such policy was matched by the unwillingness of El Salvador and Guatemala to sign up to a package that contradicted the principle of free trade. A mediating proposal presented by Costa Rica, Guatemala and Nicaragua, which looked for a restructuring of the CACM without rolling back the existing achievements in terms of free trade and policy co-ordination, was rejected by Honduras' negotiators, terming such a proposal 'insufficient, inadequate and disappointing' (Mariscal 1989, 100). The essential problem was, as Delgado asserts (1981, 111) that 'Honduras wanted more than partial concessions but a highly preferential status' close to the condition of free rider. This was a situation that both the Central American Committee for Economic Co-operation and the other governments wanted to avoid because it would have been highly disruptive for the CACM.

THE COST OF BEING AN OUTSIDER

Failing to adjust its policy to the interests of the other states, Honduras decided to leave the CACM in December 1970, through the adoption of decree 97 by the parliament, and retreated to bilateralism, negotiating bilateral trade accords with the other states. This was a high politics move designed to regain control of the country's economic sovereignty. It reflects how high politics and clashing national interests impinge on integration. It also shows how a government may be willing to sacrifice economic gains in its attempt to secure political control and its political objectives. This could happen when there is the illusion of an alternative option, which may be perceived to be economically and politically less expensive, such as the gaining of access to regional markets through bilateral negotiations.

Honduras's withdrawal may have been as a result of misperception. It could have been based on the belief that the country could exploit the CACM without the cost of policy co-ordination and without compromising sovereignty. But, by withdrawing from the CACM, Honduras gained the reputation of failing to behave in accordance with recognised international practices regarding the abrogation of international treaties (SIECA 1975). It also exposed its own exports in the CACM and economic development, in general, to a permanent risk because of discriminatory treatment by the other states. The bilateral treaties reopened the Central American markets to Honduras but these markets were highly restricted. Honduran products faced countless obstacles, especially costly tariffs and administrative measures in the other states, which not only made its exports more expensive than those from the other states, but also put them and its industrial production in an unstable situation (Facussé 1976). The strategy of exploiting the market without paying the cost did not succeed as expected; Honduras became a state with restricted markets within the region.

Leaving the CACM gave Honduras the opportunity to implement its own industrial policy for the first time, but made Honduras unattractive to real as well as potential investors who would not feel encouraged to risk their resources in a very restricted national as well as regional market. The CACM was a major attraction of FDI for Honduras despite the fact that the country was lagging far behind the other states. Between 1961 and 1965 the country received $200 million in FDI, mostly from US investors which were eager to take advantage of the enlarged regional market (Schulz and Sundloff Schulz 1994).

THE IMPACT OF THE EXTERNAL ENVIRONMENT

The external environment impinges on integration. However, earlier studies of regional integration tended to limit the analysis to endogenous factors, like pressure groups, underdevelopment or tariff reduction, out of which integration would follow in a more or less incremental way. Joseph Nye has made the point that external factors can act as catalysts for integration as well as disintegration. According to Nye (1965, 683) 'Even European integration was helped by its initiation in an environment in which Europe had (as a result of war) undergone a drastic change from autonomous actor to pawn in a bipolar power struggle'. Thus, the interests of external powers as well as changes in the international economy could impact on the process of integration in one way or another.

External factors further aggravated the crisis of the CACM in the 1970s. The main external sources of conflict were the fall in earnings of the traditional exporter sector and the world economic recession, which were internalised in the way of fiscal and balance of payments deficits, and inflation. As the CACM remained an appendage of the traditional agro-exporter sector, a financial crisis in this sector shook the willingness of the governments to co-operate on regional integration. The governments increasingly tended to view the deterioration in terms of trade in correlation with the gains derived out of their participation in the CACM. Thus, negative trade balances reinforced their beliefs that they were losers in the CACM and, therefore, increased their unwillingness to co-operate in regional matters and they increasingly defected from their obligations (SIECA 1973).

The strengthening of the agro-exporter model, likewise, brought about disfunctionality in the process of development of the region. The modernisation of the production structures, both in the traditional exporter sector and the industrial sector, ran counter to the need for social and sustainable development. The expansion of EXA was made at the expense of agriculture for domestic consumption (ADC) which threw the great majority of the population of the region, especially peasant families, into poverty (Bulmer-Thomas 1987). The expansion of EXA with the intense cultivation of cotton, sugar cane and livestock gave rise to an irreversible cycle of environmental degradation in the region. This was as a result of the indiscriminate use of pesticides, deforestation, and the intensive use of the soil, which led to further deterioration in the conditions of living of the poor (Karliner 1989).

Exasperation in the countryside gave rise to internal and external migrations and social mobilisation, increasing the demand for social justice, but also the need for political control. Governments responded to social demands with repression, particularly in Guatemala, El Salvador and Nicaragua, leading to civil war and in the case of El Salvador and Honduras to external war. With the exception of Honduras and Costa Rica (Baloyra-Herp 1983), agrarian reform was avoided in Central America because of the outright opposition of the oligarchy. In El Salvador, for instance, the Molina government (1972–1977) was forced to abandon its timid reformist programme owing to the violent opposition of the oligarchy (Dunkerley 1982). In Guatemala there was a concerted action between the conservative forces of the region and the US government in 1954 to overthrow the Arbenz government in order to stop an agrarian reform. In Nicaragua the land problem was not so acute as in El Salvador and Guatemala. However, a consistent programme of land reform only ensued after the revolution of 1979.

Although both the CACM and the development in the agro exporter sector produced a modernising effect in the Central American economies, they did not bring about development in the real sense. In the first case, as Bulmer-Thomas asserts (1987, 194), 'the result was a distorted form of industrialisation, very capital-intensive, heavily dependent on imports and offering little opportunity for backward linkages because of the preference for assembly of imported components over the manufacture and processing of local raw materials'. This militated against integration. In the second case, because the economic growth was based on intensive social exclusion, dilapidation of natural resources and political repression, it strengthened the military regimes and the oligarchic order.

CONCLUDING REMARKS

It is clear that the CACM had some positive impact in terms of modernising the productive structure of the region. The level of industrial development attained by the region since 1960 was due to the intra-regional openness to trade following the formation of the CACM. Intergovernmental co-operation under the CACM produced a positive impact in expanding trade in industrial goods across the region. But the crisis faced by integration at the end of the 1960s clearly revealed intergovernmentalists' predictions. That is, the political dependence of co-operation and the centrality of high politics and the issue of distribution which brought into question the neo-functionalist theses of self-sustainability and automaticity which were assumed would boost integration.

The intrusion of high politics and the conflictive nature of distribution were neglected by the traditional theory of integration. It was believed that integration was a self-sustained process. As such, the logic of the spillover would create pressure for further integration, deepening economic interdependence and forging new community bonds, which the governments would find hard to avoid. The concentration on community building and on absolute gains brought about by integration led analysts to ignore distributional conflicts and their impact on the domestic politics of the states, which at the end would turn integration into a high politics issue. The self-sustainability and technocratic theses led analysts to believe that integration would be unaffected by domestic politics or by high politics differences between the governments, for instance, change of governments or lack of diplomatic relations among some of them (Fuentes Morh 1973; Lizano 1979).

Even though neo-functionalists did not ignore the possibility that conflict would emerge, they did not think it could turn into high politics. According to Schmitter (1969, 164) conflicts would be resolved 'by expanding the scope (new issues) or the level (authority) of central institutions'. The politicisation variable which in the neo-functional theory would produce integrative effects proved to have a reversed effect in developing countries, as in Central America, because of the early politicisation of welfare issues. As Moravcsik argues (1993a, 487), 'powerful groups disadvantaged by co-operation will seek to obstruct government policy, even where such policies generate net gains for society as a whole'.

Clearly this logic explains the disruption of the CACM before and after the war of July 1969 between Honduras and El Salvador. Even though the CACM brought about gains to all the states, the uneven distribution of benefits (relative gains) generated domestic pressures in deficit states, bringing those governments to question the asymmetrical nature of integration. Honduras and Nicaragua, feeling losers under integration, exerted pressure in order to reform the CACM in line with their preference for balanced development, which in their view would redress the balance of gains out of integration. They used techniques such as the empty chair, the delay in ratifying regional agreements, even the threat of not approving them, in order to achieve their aims. The governments in deficit countries (Honduras and Nicaragua), in order to support their policies and circumvent regional rules regarding the preservation of the free-trade regime under the GEI, exploited nationalism. The regional normative was itself a sort of conflict because of its own rigidity. It did not allow deficit countries to enact countervailing measures in order to protect themselves against trade imbalances. The lack of flexibility of the decision-making process reinforced the durability of distributional conflicts, which in turn led to disintegration.

The conflicts of the 1960s and 1970s also revealed the importance of the external environment in the process of integration. The impact of the external environment was a variable ignored in the original neo-functional analyses of regional integration. Haas acknowledged in the second edition of the "Uniting of Europe" that they have overlooked the external environment by concentrating exclusively on domestic politics (Haas 1968). Integration was thought to be led by a technical and political spill-over which in both cases was taken as automatic and internal to the region. The external environment impacts heavily on Central American economies because of their extreme openness and dependence on EXA and external earnings (Bulmer-Thomas 1988). Thus, a fall in the prices of the region's external exports gave rise to financial instability and economic depression, which in turn made governments wary about supporting regional co-operation. The uneasy external environment was therefore a major variable accounting for disintegration and the return to national ways of dealing with economic conflicts in the 1970s. The recognition of these factors provided the rationale for reforming Central American integration in the 1990s. This has involved greater integration of the decision-making process by linking both economic and foreign policy, turning integration into a flexible arrangement and greater concern with the need of economic convergence, something which has been favoured by the embracing of neo-liberal economics by the governments. Accepting neo-liberal economics in the 1990s, itself a conflictive process, has reinforced the need for economic convergence, while at the same time downgrading the ideological conflict regarding balanced development.

5 War and Disintegration in the CACM in the 1980s

During the 1980s the CACM went into further disruption as a result of the impact of the world recession on the economies, civil wars and foreign intervention in Nicaragua and El Salvador. The first half of the decade was dominated by political conflict, which prevented the reconstruction of the CACM. Most political efforts concentrated on the avoidance of direct military intervention by the US and the prevention of a military success of the left-wing guerrillas over the government in El Salvador.

The aim of this chapter is to highlight the intergovernmental bargaining around the Esquipulas process of negotiation, which focused on both peace and integration. The main contentions are:

1. That the Central American integration could not be reconstructed until the internal and external causes of the conflicts were properly addressed by means of negotiation. This required opening the political systems to the social forces, which were advocating and even fighting for a broader political participation, something that both the US and the rightist groups of the region had traditionally rejected.

2. That the reconstruction of the CACM, although very important for the region's development, required the restoration of the territorial and political capabilities of the states as well as sorting out high politics differences among the governments. The Arias peace plan was important in this respect, allowing for political and economic convergence.

3. That the outcome of the negotiations reflected the preferences and relative power of leading governments. Thus, the Arias plan became an arena for political bargaining between the governments. The success of the process of negotiation relied heavily on the mutual recognition of national interest of the states and the legitimacy of the governments. The political negotiations for peace facilitated the emergence of an integration agenda.

REGIONAL CRISIS AND DISINTEGRATION

Disintegration was what characterised the CACM in the 1980s. This was the manifestation of a long-term trend of decline since the second half of the 1960s, although temporally alleviated in 1975–1977 because of a 400 per cent increase in the price of coffee, sparked off by a frost in Brazil (Rouquié 1994). The crisis worsened with the increase in the price of oil from 1973, which severely hit the monetary reserves, deepened the fiscal deficits and accelerated inflationary pressures in all the states of the region. Trade conflicts widened as a result, badly disrupting the CACM throughout the 1970s and 1980s.

Intra-regional trade continued growing in nominal terms during the 1970s despite trade conflicts, reaching over $1 billion in 1980 compared to $300 million in 1970. However, in real terms intra-regional trade was in a quite sharp decline (Willmore 1989; Guerra Borges 1990). By this time, largely owing to the crisis in the CACM, exports to outside the region were taking the lion's share of the region's industrial outputs. Trade diversion rather than trade creation began to characterise intra-regional trade, particularly after 1978, with extra-regional imports taking the lead in all the states (Fuentes K 1989).

The rise or fall pattern of intra-regional trade, however, does not represent the best way of measuring integration. Intra-regional trade may well be simply the effect of a more enduring process of policy co-ordination and co-operation among the governments. What matters is the willingness of the governments to continue regulating their relations, including trade, within a framework of co-operation, which to a large extent constrains their national behaviour. In this sense, the CACM had been severely disrupted by the war between El Salvador and Honduras in 1969. In the face of burgeoning economic and political crises the government began to adopt unilateral action to economic problems to the detriment of regional policy co-ordination and interdependence (INTAL 1982; Gerardi 1986).

During the 1970s and 1980s, policy co-ordination was declining as the governments refused to harmonise or adjust their economic and trade policies or reform the CACM. Although between 1979 and 1982 intra-regional trade showed a high increase this was not because of recovery of the CACM, but as a result of an increase of imports by Nicaragua under its reconstruction program following the 1979 revolution. As soon as the import capacity of Nicaragua was exhausted, the dynamism of intra-regional trade was over. By 1985 'the dollar value of intra-regional exports had fallen by more than half accounting for just 15.5 per cent of the region's total trade' (Bulmer-Tomas 1997, 12). Trade disputes and protectionism intensified by the 1980s. By 1982, trade relations among Central American countries resembled a trade war with retaliations being pervasive (INTAL 1982; Cline 1986). The adoption of export promotion policies to third markets by some states based on currency devaluation and state subsidisation further increased the level of divergence among the economies, eliciting disintegration pressures.

The Nicaraguan revolution and the subsequent civil wars in the region created havoc with the integration process. The Nicaraguan revolution made the region ideologically more diverse and exacerbated the security dilemma [1] experienced by member states. It thus raised further barriers to integration as fear and mistrust plagued Central American relations. Pressed by U.S. foreign policy, the governments of Costa Rica, El Salvador and Honduras pursued policies designed to isolate Nicaragua. The Contra war in Nicaragua and the civil wars in El Salvador and Guatemala also negatively affected integration. First, it forced the states to divert resources from normal economic production to security. Security became the main recipient of the national budgets, taking up 50 per cent in Nicaragua, 25 per cent in El Salvador and 15 per cent in Guatemala (Benítez Manaut 1992). Resources that otherwise would have been dedicated to peaceful production, which would have favoured development and integration, were wasted waging wars against guerrillas forces.

The other direct effect of the civil wars was the loss of security for the export of goods as a result of damage to regional infrastructure and political division among and within the states. Lorries transporting Central American goods were vandalised both by the official armies and the guerrillas. In Honduras the Contras became a state within the state terrorising the host population and disrupting economic relations and every sort of communication along the Nicaraguan border (Jonas 1988a). Contra operations in northern Costa Rica also disrupted relations between this country and Nicaragua, and in El Salvador the Farabundo Marti Liberation Guerrilla (FMLN) disrupted intra-regional trade by burning vehicles and damaging the physical infrastructure of the country (Pelupessy 1991).

As damaging as the civil wars, was President Reagan's foreign policy. In order to contain the rise of the left in El Salvador and isolate and reverse the Nicaraguan revolution, the Reagan administration targeted the CACM. Contrary to President Carter, who had been ready to accept that instability was rooted in social structures of the region, and was willing to tolerate 'progressive regimes, provided they were not communist' (Dunkerley 1982, 110), the Reagan administration saw all instability as communist-inspired. Therefore, it favoured a military response to the problems of the region. Reagan blamed the Soviets as 'the true authors of every disagreeable challenge to the status quo' (quoted in Farer 1980, 161). There was the belief, strongly influence by Jeane Kirkpatrick [2] that traditional autocrats, such as Somoza in Nicaragua and the Shah in Iran, whose fall Carter failed to prevent, were preferable because they were friendly to the US. They did not challenge the status quo despite the poverty of their population. Kirkpatrick also suggested they were likely to be democratised gradually by American influence (Kirkpatrick 1979).

The preference for a military response to Central American troubles, and to Third World nationalism generally, led the Reagan administration to increase the military budget to well over $1 trillion, which was as large as the combined military spending by Nixon, Ford, and Carter (Trubowitz 1998). Aid to the governments of Central America was accordingly increased, reaching about $6.514 billion in the period 1980–1988. More than 65 per cent of such aid was allotted to increase the military capability of the armies and to fund the operations of the Contras against Nicaragua (Fagen cited in Benítez Manaut 1992). Even the military capability of Costa Rica was increased, despite the fact that this state does not have an army, doubling the number of its police force from 5,500 men in 1980 to 12,600 in 1985 (Rouquié 1994).

Supporting Central American integration was incompatible with Reagan's other foreign policy objectives. Rather than supporting the reconstruction of the CACM the Reagan administration, backed by the International Monetary Fund (IMF) and the World Bank (WB), pursued a policy designed to enforce economic liberalism in the region and the integration of the economies to the global market. This increased the dependence of the economies of the region on the US market and strengthened their external vulnerability. The Caribbean Basin Initiative (CBI) launched by Reagan in 1984, allowing duty free access to Central American and Caribbean exports to the US market together with the implementation of structural adjustment policies, were the two instruments used by the US government to fulfil such purpose.

Because of the lack of support for the reconstruction of the CACM, particularly on the issues of trade and payment differences, intra-regional trade showed a sharp decline from 1982. It fell to $530 million in 1986. As a result of the fear of not being paid, surplus states (especially Costa Rica) reduced their trade with the region, favouring instead extra-regional trade (Cáceres and Irvin 1989). By 1984, for instance, Nicaragua (debtor) and Costa Rica (creditor) were supplying their industrial needs with extra-regional imports owing to payments difficulties. Nicaragua, for instance, increased her imports from other Latin American as well as socialist states, which were prepared to tolerate trade debts or accept compensatory trade. Costa Rica, likewise, increased her trade relations with states outside the region, which were able to pay. In some sectors such as the textile industry, supply from the US increased by more than 50 per cent to the detriment of intra-regional trade (Fuentes K 1989).

The National Bipartisan Commission on Central America [3] recommended to the Reagan administration the rebuilding of the CACM and the implementation of flexible policies of structural adjustment as part of a strategy of recovery. Economic recovery and increased economic aid were thought to be the antidote to social rebellion. However, this approach was rejected by those within the administration who favoured neo-liberal policies and the integration of the region into the global economy. As a result of bureaucratic pressures, but also out of conviction that free markets were good for development, the US government rejected the rebuilding of the CACM and the funding of intra-region debts (Rosa 1989). Unsettled trade debts reached $723 million in 1986. Attempts at settling the region's payments system produced little impact in terms of reconstructing the CACM. It was clear that the CACM could not be reconstructed until the predominant security concerns (civil wars and American intervention) were settled.

Policy co-ordination is a precondition for carrying out the process of integration and this could not be ensured while the governments remained divided and the region was politically unstable. Attempts by the Contadora Group[4] to find an all-encompassing solution to the political problems, which would inhibit both development and integration in Central America, failed to materialise in the form of a regional agreement. Its 'Act on Peace and Co-operation' presented to the Central American governments in September 1984 was rejected by Costa Rica, Honduras and El Salvador because of pressures by the US government (Fagen 1987). The failure of Contadora, however, prompted the governments to search for their own solution under the Esquipulas peace process aimed at regaining some level of autonomy in the conduct of the internal and external affairs of the states.

GUATEMALA'S FRUSTRATED ATTEMPTS AT REGIONAL LEADERSHIP

After 1986 the Central American process of negotiation aimed at pacification and integration became increasingly a regionally based process in which Guatemala and Costa Rica competed for regional leadership. Disenchantment and the lack of credibility of Contadora's initiative led these governments to put forward a regionally driven alternative for a peaceful settlement based on intergovernmental bargaining. Their bids for leadership were the result of the desire of each state to lead the region, to rebuild their external credibility and to solve the conflicts.

The so-called Esquipulas process began in Guatemala during a presidential summit convened by President Vinicio Cerezo on May 25, 1986. Cerezo was interested in filling the vacuum left by the failure of Contadora to secure peace and to re-assert Guatemala's leadership in the region. Cerezo was also attempting to shore up the civilian regime by winning externally validated prestige. There was also the fact that the disruption undergone by the CACM was severely affecting Guatemalan industrial exports, which were aimed mainly at the rest of Central America. Because of this vulnerability Guatemala was the member state which showed less readiness to implement discriminatory practices against intra-regional imports (Fuentes K 1989). In 1980 Guatemala exported to the CACM $404 million. But by 1986, as a result of the payments crisis, protectionist measures and the fall of the economic growth in the other states, its exports to the region fell sharply to $192 million (Guerra Borges 1991). Cerezo's initiative was, therefore, not only driven by the desire to regain stature in world politics, particularly the region's affairs, also by the need to reverse the impact of the disruption of CACM on the economy. Cerezo's initiative infuriated not so much the Reagan administration, but members of the Contadora Group, particularly Panama and to some extent Colombia, who resented being replaced by 'a purely Central American endeavour dominated by countries amenable to US influence'.[5]

Cerezo took office on 14 January 1986 as the first civilian democratically elected president of Guatemala. One of the central objectives of his foreign policy was to try to reduce the financial and diplomatic isolation faced by Guatemala owing to the abuses of human rights, military coups, electoral frauds and economic mismanagement committed by the previous military regime. The Foreign Affairs Minister, Mario Quiñones Amézquita, argued that Guatemala had been isolated because it did not have world wide foreign policy objectives (Quiñones Amézquita 1986). Its foreign policy did not go beyond Central and Latin America, the Belize question with Britain and the acceptance of US leadership. The Cerezo's government intended to change this situation. In order to carry out a more active foreign policy, the Cerezo government redefined Guatemalan neutrality. The previous military governments of General Rios Montt and Mejía Victores had claimed to follow a policy of neutrality. For Cerezo's government, Guatemalan neutrality should be "active neutrality" which meant not only remaining impartial but also providing leadership in the quest for a diplomatic solution to the conflicts of the region (Quiñones Amézquita 1986, 52).

Cerezo first tried to revive Contadora, a decision which led to the Caraballeda meeting (Venezuela) of the foreign ministers of Contadora and Central America on January 11 and 12, 1986. After the failure of the meeting, Cerezo proposed to the other presidents a summit, to discuss ways to move forward the negotiation process. At their May 25th summit in Esquipulas, the presidents adopted the Esquipulas Declaration in which they expressed their unequivocal support to Contadora and their willingness to sign Contadora's Act on Peace and Co-operation.[6]

The first presidential summit known as 'Esquipulas I' was important for Central America not only in terms of its pacification rhetoric. It was also a watershed in the pursuit of the region's political and economic integration because it was the first attempt to revive the moribund process of integration in the 1980s. Intra-Central American relations, as mentioned, had been badly affected by the conflict. Since the fall of Somoza in 1979 there had been only one regional meeting at the presidential level.[7] In its pursuit of regional leadership the Cerezo government also attempted to revive the integration agenda where Guatemala expected to recover her historical place as the General Captaincy of an integrated Central America.

As a result of Guatemala's diplomacy, in Esquipulas the presidents institutionalised the presidential summit as the main mechanism to move the process of integration and Central American negotiations forward. It was also an expression, in the words of Rouquié (1994, 283) 'of the willingness to reintegrate Nicaragua both politically and economically to the region' and a manifestation of the willingness of the Sandinistas to compromise politically with the rest of the region. In addition, the Presidents agreed on the creation of the Central American Parliament (PARLACEN), an ill-conceived project, which was at the heart of Guatemala's plan of integration. The political agreement on PARLACEN represented a milestone in the intention to resume the integration agenda. The regional Parliament would not only be located in Guatemala, but would also form the new political core of the Central American integration process, performing some supranational functions as well as vesting itself with some level of legitimacy. The latter aspect would be realised through the election of Central American deputies in equal number by each state and through integrating the Presidents and Vice-Presidents into the system as the higher decision-makers. PARLACEN was intended in the original Guatemalan proposal to be less than a real parliament but a system of integration aimed at restructuring the whole integration system of the region with Guatemala as its core.[8]

In the Esquipulas declaration the Presidents restated the Guatemalan push for integration and expressed their support for the revision and revitalisation of the institutions of integration. They also expressed their conviction that peace in Central America 'could only be the fruit of an authentic democratic process'.[9] Cerezo's government, thus, stressed democracy and integration as the way to attain peace in Central America with Guatemala at the core providing leadership to the region.

Despite severe human right violations in Guatemala, Cerezo enjoyed some credibility in the region. One factor was the size of the Guatemalan economy, the largest of the region as well as its historical salience since colonial times. In addition, Cerezo had the possibility of persuading a new generation of Presidents such as Oscar Arias of Costa Rica, and José Azcona in Honduras to go along with his regional plan because they shared concerns regarding the US foreign policy. These two presidents had expressed their dissatisfaction with the US intervention in the region and their wish to recover the territorial integrity of their states abused by the US in its counterrevolutionary war against Nicaragua.

Cerezo was also able to persuade President Ortega in Nicaragua because of Guatemala's policy of neutrality, which allowed his country to maintain normal friendly relations with Nicaragua. He had influence with President Duarte in El Salvador because both states had co-operated on security matters against the FMLN (Dunkerley 1982). In addition, the economic relations between the two states had traditionally been strong showing a high degree of interdependence. More importantly, both governments shared the Christian Democratic ideology. Thus, there was a clear Guatemalan-Salvadorian axis in the area of regional integration. The Christian Democratic parties have traditionally been strong supporters of Central American integration (Villagrán Kramer 1967). Last but not least, the fact that Guatemala managed to keep its neutrality virtually intact brought some external recognition, especially from regional powers such as Mexico and Venezuela, which in the face of Contadora's failure to attain peace were willing to support a Guatemalan leadership.

However, Cerezo was not in a position to lead the region into a comprehensive process of restructuring of integration and to lead the region out of its political difficulties. Guatemala was unable to provide the enduring leadership that the region required. Because of the lack of democratic credentials and an appalling record on human rights violations, Guatemala lacked the moral qualifications to lead the region. This largely disabled Cerezo's bid for leadership. Moreover, Guatemala had been involved in a prolonged civil war since the 1960s. Democracy in Guatemala was still uncertain and the extreme right anti-democratic factions of the army were still very strong. Cerezo is said to have acknowledged that 'the elections of 1986 gave him the presidency but not the power' (Rouquié 1994, 245). Consequently Costa Rica, not Guatemala, assumed the regional leadership through a strategic alliance with Guatemala.

COSTA RICA'S SUCCESS UNDER THE ARIAS PLAN

Esquipulas I was a clear indication that Central America was entering a new stage in the process of negotiation and political development. But Guatemala proved unsuitable to provide an enduring leadership. Costa Rican leadership because of its democratic and economic stability was more likely. Without major domestic conflict and with the economy in a quite good shape, Costa Rica was less vulnerable than its neighbours. The government of Oscar Arias (1986–1990) wanted to pursue an independent foreign policy towards the region. Its democratic and human rights credentials meant that Costa Rica's foreign policy was externally legitimate and the internal cost (political and economic) of co-operating with the other states was minimal.

By the mid-1980s Costa Rica was recovering from the economic crisis and negative rates of growth at the beginning of the decade. It was successfully turning into an exporting economy. However, during Luis Alberto Monge's government (1982–1986), despite the adoption of a policy of neutrality in 1983,[10] the country had not been able to avoid becoming involved in the US policy of destabilisation of Nicaragua. Costa Rica was perceived externally as being fully engaged with the American foreign policy and played its part in hindering the Contadora process by lining up with Honduras and El Salvador. As Fernández asserts (1986, 223), 'Costa Rica was no longer seen in some Latin American Foreign Offices as the weak and unarmed country, but as an ally of the US which proclaimed its neutrality, while sympathising with the cause of the Contras'.

The problem of Costa Rica was dependence on US economic aid through the worst economic crisis of its history. This forced the Monge government to overlook the activities of the Contras and the CIA in the North of the country. US economic assistance to Costa Rica reached about $634 million in the first three years of Monge's government and the US backing was vital in reopening the IMF-World Bank financial assistance to the country (Rovira Más 1988). US aid and the CBI were used to transform the Costa Rican economy and to move the country away from the CACM by reorienting its economy towards an outward model of development based on exports promotion to the world market (Clark 1995; 1997). The economic recovery of the Costa Rican economy and its successful adoption of free market principles was central to Reagan's counterinsurgency strategy in Central America. This was important not only in terms of defeating the left in the region but also because of the American neo-liberal crusade against protectionism and the developmental state. Immersed in an acute economic crisis, Costa Rica became the testing ground for the implementation of neo-liberal economic policies where the US created parallel institutions to the state designed to weaken the state.[11]

OSCAR ARIAS' FOREIGN POLICY

It was against this background that Oscar Arias developed a new foreign policy. The pursuit of a negotiated solution to the conflicts of the region became the main issue of his policy. This was considered to be central to Costa Rica's national interest. There was the conviction that the pacification of the region was vital for 'keeping the political stability of Costa Rica, its economic and social development, and even its political autonomy' (Rojas Aravena 1990a, 48). In other words, considerations of strategic interdependence convinced the Arias government that regional co-operation was crucial for peace and that Costa Rica, by virtue of her internal and external conditions, was the country best placed to promote it. Peace was also a necessary condition for the realisation of Arias' programme for the country, which intended to create thousands of new jobs and houses and to expand the export programme with clear goals for 1990. Costa Rica had paid a hard price as a result of instability in the region. It suffered heavy losses in capital flight of about $5.644 billion according to some accounts (Hernández 1994) and thousands of Central Americans fled to Costa Rica in search of refuge which aggravated the social difficulties and created some security concerns in this country. Thus, a negotiated settlement to the conflicts of the region was central to reverse these trends.

The main worry of the Arias government was the use of Costa Rica by the US to destabilise Nicaragua, which had increased tensions with its neighbour and strongly discredited Costa Rica abroad. Thus, launching a foreign policy based on neutrality and the search for peace was a deliberate attempt by the Arias government to avoid the 'honduranisation' of Costa Rica [12] (Soto Acosta 1991), and to clean up the image of the country at the same time. Arias reversed Monge's policy of 'benign tolerance' with the US in order to avoid Honduras' experience. It was a deliberate attempt at reasserting Costa Rica's independence and sovereignty and re-building the Costa Rican external credibility. Besides, there was great concern regarding the impact of the flood of refugees on the Costa Rican economic and political stability. The end of the conflict would therefore mean the end of the refugee crisis.

Arias' foreign policy was also a reflection of a major disagreement with Reagan's policy towards Nicaragua. Although both shared the principle of defeating the left and the Sandinistas they differed in the method. For Reagan the use of force was a necessary condition to elicit a democratic change in Nicaragua. Secretary of State George Shultz had stated that 'diplomacy is unlikely to work unless there is effective resistance' (cited in Jonas 1988b, 221). The Contras were therefore the solution in the American view to force the Sandinistas to negotiate with the opposition and to democratise Nicaragua or even to depose the Sandinistas altogether. Arias, on the other hand, regarded economic destabilisation and military aid to the Contras as wrong and ill-considered. To him the Contras were the 'problem rather than the solution' to the Nicaraguan conflict.[13] Arias made this criticism to Vice-President George Bush during a visit to Washington in early 1986 when he also mentioned his intention to launch a peace plan for Central America.

Before launching his own peace initiative, Arias embarked on a policy of regaining the external credibility and prestige of Costa Rica. Several steps were taken to rebuild the external image of Costa Rica as a bastion to enhance Arias' leadership. These included paying lip services to Contadora. Oscar Arias was determined to ensure effective compliance with Costa Rica's neutrality (Arias Sánchez 1986). Under his government Costa Rica would follow an "active policy of neutrality" similar to the one adopted by President Cerezo in Guatemala. 'It was not sufficient to say that Costa Rica was a neutral state-he argued-, it was necessary to search for peace in an active manner' (Arias Sánchez 1997, 207). This commitment to an active role of Costa Rican neutrality brought Arias close to Cerezo.

In line with his goal, Arias rejected pressures from the US to allow the use of the Costa Rican territory by the Contras.[14] He closed clandestine airports and training camps in the North of the country used to supply the Contras (Rouquié 1994). He also banned members of the Nicaraguan opposition, exiled in Costa Rica, from getting engaged in military activities against Nicaragua because that would violate the country's neutrality. Those who did not comply with this prohibition were asked to leave the country immediately (Memoria 1986–1987). Furthermore, Arias removed Costa Rica from the so-called 'Tegucigalpa Group',[15] which weakened the

US policy of containment of Contadora while strengthening the perception of Costa Rica following an independent foreign policy. In addition, both the Foreign Affairs Secretary, Rodrigo Madrigal, and President Arias visited Europe in the first half of 1987 to meet European leaders in order to explain the new foreign policy of Costa Rica.

In Europe, Arias obtained support from European leaders. Even Prime Minister Margaret Thatcher, who was doubtful at the beginning, supported him.[16] Despite initial resistance because of a strong European support for the Nicaraguan revolution, most European leaders decided to follow the Spanish government in supporting the Arias initiative (Arias Sánchez 1997). After this the European Community, which had been supporting the Central American integration in opposition to the Reagan administration, expressed also its support for the Arias plan which marked the beginning of its success.[17]

Similar efforts were made before the US public and the Congress by Guido Fernández, Costa Rican ambassador in Washington. Fernández, a professional journalist, managed to align a large section of the US press and liberal congressmen, from both the Democratic and Republican parties, in support of the Arias plan (Fernández 1989). The inability to engage US public opinion both in Congress and in the press around the peace process is said to have accounted, among other things, for Contadora's failure to attain peace in the region (Gutman 1987). Contadora lacked a suitable interlocutor both in Central America and in the US. The Arias government, on the other hand, managed to overcome this shortcoming by displaying an active diplomacy which involved not only the leading decision makers at the Ministry of Foreign Affairs but also the President himself. Once external support had been ensured Arias presented his peace proposal 'Una Hora para la Paz' (an Hour for Peace) to the Central American presidents during a mini-summit convened in Costa Rica on February 15, 1987 which excluded Daniel Ortega.[18]

THE ARIAS PEACE PLAN AS AN INTER-STATE BARGAINING

The Arias Peace plan became a platform for bargaining between the states, especially between Costa Rica and Guatemala. Asymmetrical bargaining between Costa Rica and Guatemala essentially took the form of a strategic alliance between the two countries. The latter agreed to serve as the former's junior partner in the alliance but the agreement between them was pivotal in meeting the goals of peace and integration proposed by both governments. In short, the two governments' preferences converged, and both perceived peace in the isthmus as necessary to ensure the attainment of their political and economic goals both within and beyond the subregion. Hence they decided to cooperate on the basis of the lowest common denominator.

Unlike Cerezo's proposal, the Arias plan did not mention integration. Rather than taking integration as a precondition to peace, which seemed to be the logic of Cerezo's initiative, Arias concentrated on conflict resolution exclusively. Peace would be the result of democratisation and internal dialogue between the governments and their opposition. Integration in turn would be the result of peace and stability (Soto Acosta 1990). The emphasis, therefore, was placed on national reconciliation, democratisation, understood as free elections, avoidance of external aggression, and suspension of military aid with some sort of external supervision (Rojas Aravena 1990b; Moreno 1994).

The Arias plan was originally intended to function as a democratic alliance. To form a democratic alliance was another foreign policy objective of the Arias government (Arias Sánchez 1986). The peace plan, thus, could be applied to Nicaragua exclusively. It was this original reductionism which prevented the adoption of the plan in San José. Foreign Secretary Miguel D'Escoto and President Ortega had spoken to President Cerezo and asked him 'not to sign the document without Nicaragua, a request that Cerezo accepted' (D'Escoto Brockman 1997, 172). But Cerezo had his own reasons for not signing the plan in San José. First, he wanted to include Nicaragua in the new process of negotiations. President Ortega was invited to the first Esquipulas summit convened by Cerezo in 1986 and was a signatory of the Esquipulas I declaration.

Second, the Arias plan did not explicitly elaborate on integration, which was a major concern of the Cerezo government. Therefore, the inclusion of both Nicaragua and the issue of integration were preconditions for Guatemalan support of the Arias plan. But, following President Arias' logic, regional integration would be subordinated to the attainment of peace and subregional political stability, not the contrary as the Cerezo administration had wanted. For Arias, ignoring integration seemed to have been intentional. The Costa Rican government considered that, given the gravity of the political situation, with President Reagan asking Congress for $100 million in aid to the Contras, to talk of integration at that juncture would have been unrealistic. There was also the fact that Arias was fully engaged pursuing an export boom under Plan-2000. This plan embraced Arias' strategy for expanding Costa Rica's exports, especially non-traditional products, to third markets, which was crucial for attaining other national goals such as employment and economic growth. Thus Costa Rica was already engaged in a strategy of internationalisation that went beyond the subregion. The goal was to increase exports up to $2 billion by 1990. Funds for this purpose were provided under the structural adjustment programme, which the country had been implementing since 1985. This was happening while the CACM had become redundant. Most investment allocated in Costa Rica in the 1980s went to non-traditional sectors exporting mainly to the US market, whereas exports to the CACM at least until 1986 remained stagnated (Artavia et al 1987; Clark 1995). Cerezo was also implementing an export-led strategy similar to the Costa Rican one, based on non-traditional exports, but it was very unsuccessful because of the lack of external funding. As a result the country remained highly dependent on the CACM (Colindres 1993).

Although the Arias administration was not against integration, there was a clash of interests regarding the scope of integration between Guatemala and Costa Rica. Guatemala favoured 'positive integration' with a relatively high level of institutionalisation capable of attaining common policies.[19] This is a sort of de-emphasised intergovernmentalism, close to neo-functional regionalism with PARLACEN at the core of the system of integration, but without replacing the nation state. Costa Rica, on the other hand, perceived integration as 'process rather than as structure' (Soto Acosta 1990, 56). The government favoured intergovernmental negotiations where sovereignty would not be compromised by supranational structures. Its preferred policy option, in line with its successful programme of export promotion, was therefore strengthening the economic integration understood as *negative integration*, the CACM rather than PARLACEN, which should be opened to the global market.

Costa Rica therefore, co-operated in the efforts to bring peace and integration to the region, but at the same time accelerated its negotiations for a quick adhesion to the GATT (General Agreement on Trade and Tariffs). Costa Rica pressured the other governments to guarantee a 'concerted defection' (opt-out) regarding the Central American External Tariff (CET). This was required in order to secure its GATT membership. This led the Central American Tariffs Council to modify the CET to allow the governments to carry out unilateral modifications of their tariff structures in accordance with their own national programmes of economic reform. This move in effect left the region without a common external tariff by the end of the 1980s.

For the peace plan to be successful, therefore, the accommodation not only of this fundamental difference between Guatemala and Costa Rica was required, but also embracing the interests of the other governments. A negotiation looking for a large win-set, as Rojas Aravena points out (1990b), is the result of the incorporation of the fundamental interests of the parties. In other words, this involved placing the Esquipulas process within the context of asymmetric interdependence where the preferences, options, and interests of the states would be mutually constrained in accordance to their relative power. Asymmetric interdependence, as Moravcsik (1998: 60) points out, 'dictates the relative value each state places on an agreement, which in turn dictates its respective willingness to make concessions'. This implied embracing PARLACEN, which was at the core of Guatemala's interests, and recognising the security needs and political interests of the other governments, which led to a redefinition of the Arias Plan. The main bargaining took place between Costa Rica, Guatemala and Nicaragua, while Honduras and El Salvador largely adhered because of the pressure of what Northedge (1976, 150) calls 'enforced vicinity or involuntary propinquity', following a reassessment of their strategic standing in the face of a US foreign policy collapse.

Thus, the Esquipulas process became essentially a negotiated process between Costa Rica and Guatemala. It, therefore, reflected the preferences and interests of the governments of these states. The bargaining process focused on the following aspects:

1. It concentrated on the inclusion of PARLACEN in the Arias Plan and its location in Guatemala (Esquipulas). As said, integration was central for Guatemala's interest and PARLACEN embodied the materialisation of such an interest. But, although integration was important for Costa Rica as well, the establishment of a regional parliament was not favoured. A compromise was reached consisting of including PARLACEN in the Arias plan (Preamble of the Esquipulas Declaration, August 7, 1987), but its relevance in terms of both integration and pacification was largely de-emphasised.

   Rather than be the core of the process of integration and pacification as Guatemala wished, PARLACEN was limited as a forum for deliberation and analysis of regional matters but without a major significance for the region's politics. In this sense, PARLACEN lost the systemic character with which Guatemala intended to endow it within the integration system. Costa Rica even failed to sign up to it because the Parliament refused to ratify the treaty. The national Parliament was led by the fear that PARLACEN could evolve into a supranational institution which could curtail its powers (Soto Acosta 1990). Articles 5.c, 22 and 25 of the revised version effectively empowered PARLACEN as a quasi supranational body by allowing it to appoint the high-ranking personnel of regional institutions and by attempting to enforce Guatemala as the capital of the Presidents and Vice-Presidents' summits. Costa Rica was against these prerogatives which until then were entrusted to intergovernmental bodies. Thus, although the Arias government paid lip-service to PARLACEN, its peace plan concentrated exclusively on conflict resolution and the management of the external co-operation granted both for the peace plan and the rebuilding of the CACM, which was central to Costa Rica's interest. None of its eleven points refers explicitly to integration. By degrading the scope of PARLACEN, Costa Rica not only avoided compromising its sovereignty but also managed to bring economic integration in line with its own policies of export promotion, creating new opportunities for the country's exports. Costa Rican exports to the CACM grew accordingly during the Arias administration from $109.5 million in 1987 to $150 million in 1989. This growth, however, was viewed by the government more as a resonance of the success of its programme of export promotion than the recovery of the CACM itself (SIECA

1989). The CACM began to take the form of a regional bloc pursuing the integration of the region into the global economy (Soto Acosta 1991), but lacking internal cohesion.

2. Central to the bargaining between the two states was the signing of the Arias plan in Esquipulas, Guatemala, in honour of the first Esquipulas meeting, which was entirely due to Cerezo's diplomacy. Cerezo had worked hard to ensure that the launch of the revised Arias peace plan would be done in Esquipulas. He tried to move all diplomatic activity and international attention to Guatemala. This included an attempt to bring to Guatemala a preparatory meeting of ministers of foreign affairs originally planned to take place in Honduras, which produced a diplomatic fiasco. He also tried a last-minute change in the presidents' agenda, 'introducing proposals of his own apart from the Arias plan' which brought the summit to the brink of collapse.[20] As a result of these actions, the presidential summit originally planned to take place in Esquipulas on 25–26 June was postponed until August 6–7, 1987. Both Cerezo and Arias had to work hard to convince the other Presidents to accept the later date. The branding of the process as the 'Esquipulas process' ensured that Guatemala would get a share of the international credibility brought about by the Arias plan which as Soto Acosta asserts (1991, 16), 'would somehow clean the image of the country as a militarist state violator of human rights'.
3. Nicaragua should be admitted as a full player in the process of negotiation. Guatemala had opposed the attempts by the US government and its allies in the region to isolate Nicaragua. Therefore, Cerezo was interested in preventing the Arias plan from working as a democratic alliance against Nicaragua. Thus, the peace plan would be a regional agreement, not an alliance for democracy as the Arias administration proposed, and Nicaragua would take an active part in it. Cerezo's bargaining on this was strong because those who preceded him in the presidency had managed to coexist with the Sandinistas and because he had the support of Contadora and the EEC which Arias could not ignore if his plan was to have a chance of success
4. Costa Rica's sovereignty would not be compromised with the agreement; neither would the plan involve altering the political system of this country. As Costa Rica was already a democratic and pluralist society without any semblance of a domestic conflict since 1948, it did not have to internalise the peace plan; except in relation to curtailing the activities of the Contras and releasing some Salvadorian prisoners claiming to be political prisoners. The creation of a Reconciliation Commission was more a symbolic act than a real necessity, just to comply with the plan. The peace plan therefore, did not imply a limitation to Costa Rica's sovereignty or altering the existing constitutional order of the country. It was on this basis that the government presented the peace plan and accepted the jurisdiction of

the previously agreed presidential summits (Soto Acosta 1990). But Arias rejected Guatemala as the institutional capital of the presidents and vice-presidents' meetings as intended by president Cerezo under PARLACEN. Thus rather than structure, the presidential summit became a dynamic process-building mechanism destined to boost the intergovernmental bargaining and could be used by the presidents to enhance their own political credibility domestically.

Thus, rather than being the recipient of the peace plan, Arias viewed himself as the leader, as 'the mediator and in some occasions as spectator of the other governments' negotiations' (La Nación 1989, 18A). Most importantly, the Arias government would enlist Guatemala as its ally and regain the external credibility of the country by avoiding being seen as a puppet of the US. This credibility would increase Arias' domestic and regional leadership while simultaneously recovering the territorial integrity of the state, attract international recognition as the creator of the peace plan, propel the rebuilding of the CACM, and reassure foreign investors of the suitability of Costa Rica for the allocation of capital. It is not surprising, therefore, that FDI increased substantially during the Arias Government from $56 million in 1986 to $115 million in 1989 (Ramírez B and Sánchez S 1995).

5. It was also Oscar Arias' interest that the Esquipulas declaration should be taken by the governments as a peace plan, not as a simple declaration. As such, it would be the core of the region's peace process. The other governments had to drop their own proposals and commit themselves to the Arias plan. This would place the Arias government at the centre of the process. Guatemala's support would ensure Contadora's approval of the Arias plan. This was particularly important because Mexico was unhappy with Costa Rica taking the lead in Central America and was determined not to support the Arias plan if it became an arrangement for excluding Nicaragua. Arias perceived Mexico as an obstacle to the peace plan, which prompted his visit to the Mexican president Miguel De la Madrid in order to hammer out the differences.[21] Launching the peace plan as a Costa Rican-Guatemalan alliance was indispensable to secure the Contadora countries' support as well as that of the European Economic Community (EEC), which was strongly backing the Guatemalan integrationist agenda. This reinforced Esquipulas, a city of religious significance for Central Americans, as the best place for signing the peace accord.

For the Sandinistas, the modified Arias plan meant two things: survival in the face of an economy destroyed by the war and legal recognition by the presidents, something that, as Soto Acosta asserts (1991, 16) 'the 1984 presidential elections did not secure'. Arias did not question the legality of the Sandinista government, but its democratic legitimacy (Rojas Aravena 1990b). With the Contras militarily defeated, the peace plan could only mean their final political collapse, which would allow the government to concentrate on rebuilding the economy, to reintegrate the country into the CACM, and to pursue its talks with the unarmed opposition. This is why the Reagan administration rejected the revised version of the Arias plan, despite its support for the original initiative, viewing it as harmful to Contadora and the Sandinistas (Schulz and Sundloff Schulz 1994).

The main Nicaraguan bargain consisted, first of all of a compromise among the governments regarding the non- use of their national territories to support irregular forces (Contras) against another state (Nicaragua) and a call to foreign powers (the US) to cease aiding irregular forces fighting the governments. Second, a compromise regarding peace and democratisation in the region. According to D'Escoto (1997), the Arias plan was designed to be applied exclusively to Nicaragua. In line with Reagan's policy, the other governments were reluctant to assume responsibility for peace and democratisation. They did not recognise having a problem of democratic legitimacy despite the civil war in El Salvador and Guatemala and the military overshadowing of the democratic government in Honduras. For them their legality was based on their democratic legitimacy, something they did not extend to Nicaragua, but which provided some ground for bargaining.

It was Nicaragua that insisted that the issue of democratisation had to be extended to the other states as well, not just to Nicaragua. Under the Arias plan the Sandinistas committed themselves to allow free elections, to talk directly to the armed opposition, something they had refused to do before, to guarantee free speech and political pluralism. Nicaragua became the most responsible state in implementing the peace plan. 'The government indicated that it would meet its obligations even if the other signatories did not' (Schulz and Sundloff Schulz 1994, 182). When on January 14, 1988, the International Commission for Verification and Follow up (CIVS) created by the Arias plan presented its report to the presidents during a summit in Alajuela (Costa Rica), only Nicaragua was found to be in full compliance of the Esquipulas agreement. The other states, except Costa Rica, had put numerous obstacles up to it (LASA Report 1988; Moreno 1994). In the Presidential summit at Costa del Sol in El Salvador on February 14–15, 1988, Ortega proposed the holding of an election even earlier than stipulated in the Constitution. This was considered to be a strategic move aimed at capitalising on his high popularity. The Sandinistas thought that because of their popularity an earlier call of the elections would ensure their victory. But this was a miscalculation. Instead, it dragged the FSLN to an astonishing defeat by a pro-American liberal coalition led by Violeta Barrios on February 25, 1990.

As with El Salvador, President Duarte's participation in the Esquipulas process was for three reasons:

1. As his government had already been in conversations, although unsuccessfully with the FMLN-FDR, the Arias plan would not imply a

major policy change. The region's accord could be used instead to delegitimate the guerrillas' demands for negotiations because the Arias plan did not mean talking with the FMLN, but with the unarmed opposition and those who embraced the democratic process.

2. The government could also use the peace accord as a bastion against the army and the extreme right opposition to its policy of dialogue, therefore increasing its power and autonomy. Duarte won the elections in 1984 on a promise to pacify the country and to ensure social and economic reforms to bring about social justice to the impoverished population (Dijkstra 1993). However, he was prevented from doing so by the extreme opposition from the army, the extreme right and the Reagan administration, to negotiation with the guerrillas. The peace plan opened a theoretical possibility of carrying out his promise as it could be used to internationally isolate the guerrilla movement by taking up the democratic banner and cutting off some of its external support. As a result, it was hoped that the FMLN-FDR would be persuaded to negotiate on the terms set out by the government.

   The solution to the internal conflict under the Esquipulas accord would have also meant concentrating on the economic recovery of the country and rebuilding the CACM, which was vital for Salvadoran economic recovery and stability. This would have saved the Duarte government and the Christian Democratic Party (PDC) from the discredit of failing to pacify the country and rebuild the economy. The government was perceived as corrupt and incapable not only of pacifying the country but also of embracing the major economic reforms required to rebuild the economy. This explains why Duarte paid lip service to the Arias plan, even calling it a second act of independence for Central America, although he also boycotted it on several occasions by linking the dismantling of the Contras to the simultaneous dismantling of the FMLN which was a US demand.

3. The Duarte government viewed the peace accord as a real alternative for its own survival. The rationale was that Reagan's policy towards Central America, particularly to El Salvador and Nicaragua was collapsing as a result of the Iran-Contras scandal and the restrictions imposed by congress through the so-called Bolland Amendments.[22] The two Bolland Amendments approved by Congress in September 1982 and October 1984 heavily restricted the power of the president to intervene in Central America. They prohibited the CIA and the Pentagon from using American funds to finance, train or equip any irregular force or Army to conspire, destabilise or overthrow the government of Nicaragua or to provoke a military exchange between Nicaragua and Honduras (Rouquié 1994).

Duarte realised that once Reagan left the presidency it would be difficult to sustain American aid to his government and Honduras, to fight the FMLN and to continue harbouring the Contras, respectively. Duarte was quite informed about this because he had good contacts in Congress, especially with the democratic Speaker of the House, Jim Wright. He knew that Wright and his party were outnumbering the Republicans in Congress and they were casting their full support behind the Arias plan (Moreno 1994). Aware of this, Duarte resolved to support the Arias plan and convinced President Azcona of Honduras to follow suit. Duarte said to President Azcona, 'Remember that Ronald Reagan is only President for sixteen more months. Jim Wright is going to be Speaker of the House for the next ten years' (Moreno 1990, 131). As a result, Azcona who had promised the US he would not sign the Arias plan had no option but to sign it, which represented a major diplomatic defeat for the Reagan administration. Two main reasons account for Azcona's change of mind:

1. Security concerns. Azcona was worried that with the collapse of the US policy to the region, the Contras, which outnumbered Honduras' army in men and weaponry, would become a major threat to the state. This in turn would have signalled the failure of Azcona to deliver one of his main promises during the election campaign, which was to regain the territorial integrity of the state by 'dismantling the Contras and avoiding a war with Nicaragua' (Durán 1997, 138).
2. There was the fear of exclusion. As President Duarte was determined to go ahead with the peace plan, Azcona could not avoid following suit without being isolated again from the CACM, something Honduras wanted to avoid. The Hondurans learned that being outside the CACM proved to be costly in terms of their economic development. From 1970 onward, they strove to find a solution to their differences with El Salvador in order to get back to Central American integration, but they failed to do so because they tied themselves by following inflexible policies. Now that they were on the way back they were not prepared to withdraw just because of pressures from the already fading Reagan administration.

PEACE, REGIONAL INTERDEPENDENCE VERSUS FOREIGN INTERVENTION

The combination, of territorial proximity and the other governments' willingness to align with the Arias plan, became a major political pressure on the Honduras government to avoid exclusion from the new wave of integration. The logic of strategic interdependence prevailed, limiting the options available to the government. Belonging to a region largely determines the policies of a state in relation to its neighbours reinforcing 'vicinity or involuntary propinquity' (Northedge 1976, 150). Besides, the fact that international co-operation was largely granted to the region within the framework success for Central American diplomacy and regional integration. The fact that the Bush administration was willing to follow the diplomatic track instead of the bellicose policies of his predecessor allowed the governments of the region to carry on the pacification and integration of the area through the Arias plan.

The Bush administration not only gave conditional support to the Arias plan but also pressured the Salvadoran government to accept a proposal by the FMLN to end the war in exchange for democratic participation and fundamental constitutional reforms. This was something that the right-wing government of Alfredo Christiani and the army accepted only after the FMLN launched a major military operation in San Salvador in November 1989. The FMLN proved its assertiveness in taking the war to the capital and sustaining it for several weeks whereas the army proved unable to defeat the guerrillas. The bombing of working class neighbourhoods in the capital together with the killing of civilians (including Jesuit priests) brought a strong international condemnation of the army and the right-wing government, which further weakened their position, forcing them to negotiate with the FMLN.

THE IMPACT OF THE ESQUIPULAS NEGOTIATIONS ON INTEGRATION

The Peace accord had a great significance for Central America not only in terms of its pacification but also its integration. It meant a reassertion of the importance of the region as a political and economic unit. Although integration in the way of institutional reconstruction as advocated by Guatemala did not become the core issue under the Arias plan, the Esquipulas process was a return to integration in terms of policy-co-ordination, interdependence and the rebuilding of the CACM. It allowed the governments to reassess their geopolitical interests within a context of strategic interdependence. Thus, the peace accord became a clear example of negotiated policy-co-ordination under which peace and the return to integration could be attained, creating important degrees of interdependence among the governments. The domestic and foreign policies of the governments, despite their failure in fully implementing it, began to converge around the peace accord. In some respects the peace process lessened the distinction between the domestic and foreign policies of the states. The region was moving towards a common agenda grounded in the pursuit of peace, integration and economic rebuilding.

Although economic integration was not the central issue of Central American diplomacy under the Arias plan, the fact, that most international co-operation granted to the region was given for peace and integration purposes, largely favoured integration. The efforts at integration in the second half of the 1980s concentrated on three areas. The first area was rebuilding of peace and integration highly conditioned the preferences of H favour of co-operation with the Arias plan. There was also the fa lation would have meant dealing with the Contras and the US g on their own, without the support not only of the region but : rest of the international community, which in itself represented : alternative for Honduras' security. Therefore, signing the Arias Pareto-improving for Honduras in the long run.

The adoption of the principles of 'symmetry' and 'simultanei involved mutual recognition of the governments and the sim implementation of the agreement, made the decision-making sy interdependent and self-reinforcing, which the Reagan administra not easily break down (Rojas Aravena 1990b; Soto Acosta 1991). gan administration was left without veto power in this process an the possibility of establishing alternative coalitions, something t cessfully did during the Contadora process, which brought it to 1 the same token, it was difficult for the governments to run away agreement (defection) because the consequences of fully defecting agreement would have been a loss of international credibility, pre inability to resolve the conflicts by acting alone.

There could have been a welfare loss as well, as a result of exclu the main stream of economic co-operation. Under the peace acc government enjoyed veto power, which made it difficult for an ment to disengage from decisions in which they had already bee No government wanted to risk being seen as responsible for the the peace accord. Even Azcona and his negotiators, who threat to sign the Coronado declaration on December 12, 1989 and eve negotiating table, were forced to get back and sign by the pressure ity and the new region's high politics once some differences were se with Nicaragua.[23]

The Reagan administration tried hard to derail the process, attempting to prevent its adoption, secondly, by financially punis governments and, thirdly by discrediting the agreement, calling it Munich, 'the appeasement of a totalitarian regime by its democrat bours' (Moreno 1990, 130). Both the Arias and the Azcona gove were financially penalised by the Reagan administration for their of the Esquipulas accord. This involved cutting and withholding ec and military aid for 1988–1989 (by 42 per cent in the case of Cost strengthening the conditionality for loans from the financial insti and financing the opposition to defeat the governing parties (S: 1992; Grugel 1995a).

Although the US administration nearly succeeded in disrupting t cess via Honduras and El Salvador, it could not stop it. The Ari became a diplomatic success, a success that was reinforced by the g of the Nobel Prize to Oscar Arias in 1988. It represented, as Du asserts (1994, 40), 'a significant setback for realism', and an unqu the region's payments system in order to re-establish intra-regional commerce, which was highly disrupted. The integration of political decisions around the peace plan spilled over into economic co-operation. Efforts were made through the Central American Monetary Council (CMCA) and the Central American-EEC mixed commissions in order to co-ordinate external co-operation to rebuild the region's payments system. Second, resources were allotted to strengthen the export capacity of the states, particularly Honduras and Nicaragua. The EEC helped in this endeavour donating $205 million. $40 million out of it was given to Honduras and Nicaragua to help rebuild their export capacity (CMCA 1989; SIECA 1991).

Furthermore, additional resources were granted to the region as part of a reconstruction programme under the United Nations. Throughout 1987 the ministers of economy were working on a Guatemalan-devised plan of regional reconstruction (Plan de Acción Inmediata) which aimed at attracting international co-operation to deal with many of the consequences of the civil wars and the economic decline of the region. The Plan included help for refugees, food security, energy supply, foreign debt and reactivation of the CACM (INTAL 1988). The Action Plan was approved by the region's Vice-Presidents in January 1988 and was subsequently submitted and adopted with little modification by the UN as the Especial Plan for Central America.

Revitalising Central American economic integration became a central component of the UN plan and most multilateral agencies, including the WB, IMF, ECLAC, and the OAS were involved in the process of co-ordination (Fuentes K 1989). The US did not participate in this endeavour, whereas from 1984 the EEC consistently opposed any attempt by the Reagan administration to isolate Nicaragua from European funding (Latin American Weekly Report, 6 April 1984; Hazel 1993). Although the impact of these measures was not dramatic in the very short term, intra-regional trade began to recover from 1987, as can be seen in Table 5.1. Most integration efforts during the second half of the 1980s concentrated on peace and the rebuilding of integration in terms of policy co-ordination which involved tackling the payments system of the region and managing external co-operation.

However, the restructuring of the CACM and the process of integration as a whole was avoided because of the need to concentrate specifically on the security side of the conflict. The conflicts of the 1980s turned Central America into a 'security complex' creating interdependence on security matters which highly restricted the peace process to the areas of conflict resolution and confident building. Rebuilding the process of integration became the main concern in the 1990s when the salience of conflicts and the ideological and territorial divisions among the states had receded following the electoral defeat of the Sandinistas in Nicaragua. This reflects the dependence of integration on political convergence not just macroeconomic convergence among the states.

Table 5.1 Central America: Intra-Regional Trade Value of Imports (current US dollars)

Year	*Value*	*Year*	*Value*
1983	896.6		
1984	814.9	1991	861.7
1985	601.1	1992	1,123.1
1986	530.8	1993	1,204.7
1987	587.7	1994	1,411.4
1988	600.8	1995	1,712.8
1989	738.0	1998	2,200.*
1990	750.4	2002	3,088.0

Source: ECLAC (Economic Commission for Latin America and the Caribbean) (1995, 13); *SIECA 1999

The Esquipulas mechanism was not only the instrument under which peace would be attained, but also the bastion for the re-launch of the process of integration in the 1990s, in a new context of democratic governance and market liberalisation across the region. As such it helped both politics and economics. While the territorial integrity of the states was recovered allowing the governments to regain political control over their territory and their people, so was the market restored. This allowed the business interests of the region during the 1990s to work in alliance with the governments and international capital in the redefinition of the CACM in line with neoliberal principles. This, as Robison argues (2003, 69), 'included a shift in policy to "democracy promotion" as a means to neutralise through *incorporation* the threat posed by anti-systemic forces in the broader effort to construct a new historic bloc in the region'.

CONCLUDING REMARKS

In the 1980s Central American integration was severely disrupted as a result of civil wars, American intervention, protectionism, and failure of the governments to reform the CACM in line with distributional demands stemming from some states. Distributional and high politics conflicts, and protectionist measures adopted by the governments paralysed the CACM in the 1970s, a situation that got worse in the 1980s. The advent of the civil wars aggravated the problems, as the states had to prioritise security rather than economic development, which was detrimental to integration. The wars and the economic recession created ideological, economic, territorial and political divisions among the states, which affected the political and economic stability of the region, giving rise to negative rates of growth, external debts, trade and fiscal deficits, inflation and capital flight in all the states. This in turn prompted protectionist responses by the governments, dragging the region increasingly towards disintegration both in terms of intra-regional trade and policy co-ordination.

The American policy of isolating Nicaragua became a major obstacle to integration. Aid was given to the governments by the US in order to combat the left in the region, including the Sandinistas, and to redress the strategies of economic development of the states in line with market-oriented principles and integration into the global economy. This militated against regional integration and even prevented the governments for a long while from working on the rebuilding of the CACM. The US objection to a negotiated settlement, which involved the survival of the Sandinistas and a compromise with the FMLN in El Salvador, largely prevented the pacification and the resumption of the integration agenda during the first half of the 1980s.

It was not until 1986, following the arrival of a new generation of governments who were dissatisfied with the U.S policy and who also shared the desire of regaining the territorial integrity and independence of their states, that both pacification and integration began to be seriously re-considered. Under the Esquipulas process the governments created a distinct system of political interdependence which allowed the return to integration in terms of policy co-ordination. Under the Arias plan the governments began to reconstruct a common agenda which opposed US foreign policy, favouring regional rebuilding and co-operation. The governments reassessed their geopolitical interests within a context of regional strategic interdependence, which forced them to co-operate in the pursuit of peace and integration. The peace accord allowed each government to bargain in accordance with its relative power. The opportunity cost of not co-operating, given the cost of foreign intervention, was perceived as counterproductive by the governments, and forced them, especially the beleaguered governments of El Salvador, Honduras and Nicaragua, to make concessions in order to carry out the peace accord. The Arias plan, therefore, became an alternative for the governments or a compromise led by the logic of the lowest-common denominator under which the governments bargained for their survival and for the achievement of the national interests of the states.

Although integration in the form of institutional restructuring did not become the central issue of the negotiations under Oscar Arias leadership, integration was largely benefited through the rebuilding of the process of policy-co-ordination and the gradual recovery of the market out of the regional divisions. The regional market in the 1980s became a captive market, not just because of protectionist measures adopted by the governments, but also because of the loss of security owing to the civil wars and Reagan's foreign policy. The Arias plan not only gave rise to the gradual recovery of the territorial integrity of the states and the re-assertion of political control on the part of the governments. It also freed the market from economic and security constraints allowing its reconstruction and restructuring, giving rise to new alliance formations in accordance with the a new convergence of interests between the state and the market (Phillips and Buxton 1999). Intra-regional trade began to recover after 1987 and so did the role of the business groups of the region, which began to gain centrality in the process of negotiation leading to the restructuring of the CACM.

6 Rebuilding Integration in the 1990s[1]

In the 1990s, following the success of the Esquipulas process to end the civil wars, the governments of the region focused their attention on rebuilding and re-conceptualising Central American integration. This chapter looks at this process of rebuilding integration under SICA as a result of strategies pursued by the states in order to promote both regional co-operation and the insertion of the region into the world economy. In this chapter, three contentions are advanced:

1. That the rebuilding of regionalism in the 1990s and onwards reflects a compromise between the desire of the governments to pursue the historical project of integration and the need to respond to the pressure and stimulus brought about by globalisation.
2. Despite the restoration of integration within a context of open regionalism and given its importance for intra-regional trade, government preferences remain a central feature of the process, which determines the scope, geometry and pace of it. In some cases there has been an integration plateau.
3. There is a conceptual divide within the region concerning the meaning of intergration. The Northern states (El Salvador, Guatemala, Honduras and Nicaragua) have shown a preference for integration as "structure" (institutional building) whereas Costa Rica and to some extent Panama have emphasised integration as "process" and global integration which they have largely pursued unilaterally. The result has been variable geometry and fragmentation, which has led to sub-optimal outcomes both in terms of consolidating a regional bloc and in relation to the pursued goal of inserting the region into the global economy.

REGIONAL FACTORS EXPLAINING THE RE-LAUNCH OF REGIONALISM

It might seem paradoxical, but although the military conflicts of the 1980s exacerbated disintegration in Central America, they also created some political conditions for reinventing regionalism in the 1990s. Politically, the rise of the left and the conversion of Central America's crisis into an East-West conflict meant that previous 'high politics' such as the border dispute and political rivalry between El Salvador and Honduras lost political importance. The Cold War and the guerrillas were the only significant threat or enemies. Some of these threatened the survival of the military regimes. Therefore, co-operation on security matters became a high politics necessity for the governments.

The deepening of Cold War tensions and the rise of the left in some of the states of the region were not the only catalysts uniting the governments. Concerns with the implications of President Carter's human rights-driven foreign policy towards the region also worked as a catalyst, forcing the governments, especially the Honduran and Guatemalan ones, to co-operate with El Salvador. Although co-operation does not always succeed, the existence of common interests constitutes the psychological and material elements that move states into co-operation (Keohane 1984).

In the political context of the end of the 1970s and afterwards, these common interests consisted of preventing a military defeat of the Salvadorian army by the guerrillas and opposing Carter's human rights policy. Increasingly, the governments of those states tended to see themselves as part of a regional 'security complex' [2] which implies that they recognised their interdependence on security matters and the need to reinforce co-operation on security and economic matters. Co-operation based on some communality of interests allows governments to overcome or manage their differences. Security complexes, as Buzan points out (1991,190) 'emphasise the interdependence of rivalry as well as that of shared interests' allowing for co-operation.

The governments thought that the Nicaraguan revolution could have a domino effect in the region and that the military regimes could collapse under the rising power of the left. They also knew that the Carter administration had stated its unwillingness to rescue governments facing popular insurrection as a result of social injustices and human rights abuses. The fall of Somoza in Nicaragua and the Shah in Iran provided the examples of Carter's policy. That was the conclusion that the Honduran deputy Foreign Secretary Carlos López Contreras drew following a meeting in Tegucigalpa with Viron Vaky, the Assistant Secretary of State for Inter-American Affairs in late 1979 (López Contreras 1984). This understanding led the Honduran government to reshuffle the Foreign Office. Foreign Secretary Roberto Palma Gálvez was dismissed. Palma Gálvez had been problematic because he was not rightwing enough: he had dared to support the OAS-XVII Resolution of June 1979 asking for the removal of the Somoza's regime in Nicaragua, thereby, contradicting the government's policy of non-intervention in other states' affairs (López Contreras, 1984).

The new foreign policy team led by Eliseo Pérez Caldaso and Carlos López Contreras (Foreign Secretary and Deputy, respectively) was distinctively right wing and obedient to the military establishment. High priority was given to the settlement of the border conflict with El Salvador and the enhancement of military co-operation between the two states despite mutual distrust since 1969. Previous demands tenaciously maintained by Honduras, of requiring a simultaneous solution to all differences with El Salvador, were withdrawn in favour of a compromise, which favoured the rapprochement between the two states. Preventing the success of the Farabundo Marti guerrillas (FMLN) became a national security interest of both governments, which dictated the need for co-operation and the relaxation of their political differences (López Contreras 1984). The outcome was the Peace Treaty of October 30, 1980 where the states recognised part of their common border and agreed to submit to international adjudication for the remaining areas on which there was still disagreement.

The peace treaty converted El Salvador, Honduras and Guatemala into a sub-regional bloc, which not only involved military, but also economic and trade-related co-operation. The three states began to co-ordinate their security policy as early as May 1980 (Dunkerley 1982; Schulz and Sundloff Schulz 1994). By 1986 these states were moving into full economic co-operation, originally through joined developmental programmes at El Trifinio, a natural resource and communal area involving the three states, (SIECA 1990).

The Trifinio co-operation was followed by a trilateral trade agreement in 1987 where the governments sought to strengthen their economic relations grounded on neo-liberal principles. The agreement fell outside the CACM. Costa Rica and Nicaragua were not invited to join.[3] Bypassing the CACM appears to have been intentional in order both to bring in Honduras which remained outside the CACM and to avoid annoying the Reagan administration, which opposed reviving the common market because Nicaragua was part of it. This trade agreement created the conditions for Honduras's return to the region's economic arrangements. It formed the basis for the creation by these states of the North Triangle area in 1992 and the formal re-incorporation of Honduras to the CACM in that year.

However, it was the Esquipulas process that became the instrument through which the governments would gradually rebuild Central American regionalism, enhancing macroeconomic co-operation, particularly after 1990. Under the Arias peace plan, which became the keystone of the Esquipulas process, the governments began to move away from the political fragmentation brought about by the Cold War. The Arias Plan operated as a political pact among the governments allowing the reestablishment of political and economic co-operation region-wide. In the same way that the trade agreement of 1987 helped bringing Honduras back to the CACM, the Arias Plan brought Nicaragua back into the regional process of negotiation and policymaking (Rouquié 1994).

The willingness of the Sandinistas to introduce democratic reforms as established in the Peace Plan increased the level of trust among the governments. Esquipulas was efficient as a conflict resolution mechanism and as a system of policy co-ordination. Bilateral differences such as the suspension of diplomatic relations between Nicaragua and El Salvador in November 1989 and a dispute in the International Court of Justice between Nicaragua and Honduras were properly defused through collective bargaining among the presidents and their foreign ministers. The reestablishment of integration, understood as policy co-ordination, allowed the governments to establish a process of political co-operation,[4] which let them work together in the process of rebuilding and reforming CACM in the 1990s.

Thus, the new regionalism in Central America has not been a spontaneous process brought about by the end of the Cold War or by the US turn towards regionalism as stressed by some authors (Bhagwati 1994; Hettne 2000). These factors, however, have operated as catalysts creating pressures for integration in the region. The main explanation for the resumption of integration in the 1990s has to be found in the integrationist tradition of the region, the political co-operation under the Esquipulas process of negotiation, and in the increasing level of political and economic convergence among the states (Sanahuja 1998). International agreement, as Moravcsik argues (1993a, 487) 'requires that the interest of dominant domestic groups in different countries converge'.

In Central America there has been an increase in the level of convergence and regionness. This increased level of convergence, however, is limited to the realms of politics, economic policy and trade. Other areas such as social issues, sustainable development, tourism, etc remain fragmented despite attempts to bring them under integration.

As far as the former is concerned, the fact that all governments are elected by fairly democratic processes has given rise to the idea of presenting Central America as 'a region of peace, freedom, democracy and co-operation'.[5] As a result of the Esquipulas process, the Central American states have consolidated the transition from authoritarianism to democracy. Consequently, the level of common interest among the states increased favouring intergovernmental co-operation. In the words of Ayala Agrimaldi:

> 'These are five countries, which have overcome the internal armed conflicts. Five countries, which have overcome other political problems, related to democracy. The governments are democratically elected and the democratic machinery is working in the five countries, which strengthens the regional process of negotiation leading towards integration'.[6]

There still remain differences regarding the degree of consolidation of democracy in the region ranging from a well-consolidated democratic system in Costa Rica to really fragile democracies in the other states.[7] However, the democratic legitimacy of the governments is no longer questioned. As Luis Guillermo Solis puts it:

> The region has enjoyed for some time a democratic normality whereby many of the problems that it faces are the kind of problems facing every country of the world, namely, high levels of criminality, low levels of popular participation in the decision-making processes, and unemployment etc. There has been a profound change in the way political power is distributed and the political elite is much enlightened. Currently no one is thinking of maintaining or supporting Death Squads to kill opposition leaders or impede the legal participation of the left in the political processes, and this has a direct impact on the process of reforming Central American integration. [8]

Regarding economic and trade convergence, most efforts since 1990 have been oriented towards the co-ordination (not yet harmonisation) of economic and trade policies through programmes of economic adjustment (PEA) and tariff reductions. The convergence of macroeconomic policy preferences is considered to be a precondition for the revival of integration (Moravcsik 1993a). The end of the civil wars coincided with the arrival in power of conservative governments committed to implementing the economic reforms long delayed during the 1980s. Thus, since 1990, a profound policy change towards the implementation of such reforms was undertaken in El Salvador, Honduras, Nicaragua, and less successfully in Guatemala.

As a result of the economic reforms the level of convergence of the economies of the region increased during the 1990s. This convergence of policy preferences became the basis for co-ordinating the macroeconomic policies through the adoption of PAECA (Central American Economic Action Plan) in June 1990. PAECA, hence, became the equivalent of the Arias Peace Plan on economic matters. By the beginning of the 1990s, a considerable level of macroeconomic stability had been achieved, which included greater control of inflation, a considerable reduction of the fiscal deficit and some stability in terms of monetary policy and in the exchange rate. The exchange rate and the financial markets were thoroughly liberalised in the region (ECLAC 1995).

In the agricultural sector, despite the lack of integration as shown in the next chapter, the governments, with the exception of Costa Rica, eliminated price controls and subsidies, reducing the level of divergence between domestic and international prices. In addition, the governments were increasingly reaching a greater convergence in terms of the external tariff, as can be seen in chapter 7. The co-ordination of the adjustment policies under PAECA thus contributed to the consolidation of macroeconomic stability in each country which in turn helped in the efforts at integration by increasing the level of convergence of the economies.

Thus, it is possible to assert that in terms of economic policy there has been an increase in the level of regionness in Central America since the 1990s. But there is still a lot to be done to turn the region into an integrated unit beyond geographical definitions which inevitably would require a greater convergence in aspects such as inflation, taxation, external tariff and monetary integration in the way of a single currency. Owing to these changes in economic policy, all countries, including Nicaragua after 1993, experienced a robust economic growth in the first half of the 1990s (CMCA, 1995). This good economic performance together with the resumption of policy co-ordination spilled-over into intra-regional trade, which, increased from $750.4 million in 1990 to $4.329 billion in 2006. There was a consistent trend of growth throughout the decade of the 1990s as shown in Table 5.1 (previous chapter).

The increase in the level of macroeconomic convergence of the economies was, first of all, the result of the adjustment policies applied by the governments with the support of the IMF and the World Bank. But the co-ordination of macroeconomic policies under PAECA also played an important role in promoting economic stability and integration in the region, particularly through rebuilding the payments system and co-ordinating infrastructure and developmental programmes (IILA/BID 1991).

EXTERNAL DETERMINANTS OF INTEGRATION

External factors also account for the rebuilding of regionalism in Central America. As has been stated, the impact of the external environment on the processes of regional integration was a variable ignored by the traditional neo-functional analysis. It was thought that integration would move forward led by a technical and political spillover (George 1993), which was automatic and internal to the integration process.

The new regionalism in Central America followed the pattern, which characterises Latin American integration in the 1990s. Integration in the region took a fresh impetus following the end of the Cold War and the increased polarisation of the world economy. The new wave of integration took the form of open regionalism. In ECLAC's conception, open regionalism implies combining external openness with regional reciprocity, which means maintaining preferential treatment to regional partners. In other words, there is no longer incompatibility between regional integration and globalisation. The aim of new regionalism is to increase the competitiveness of the economies and to create the basis for a world economy that is more open and transparent (CEPAL 1995b; Rosenthal 1995).

Market determinants and conscious policies of export promotion, what Varas and Tulchin (1994, II) term the 'international relations of market', constitute the new parameter of integration. New regionalism takes the form of 'a complex patchwork of negotiations', embracing negotiations of trade agreements at different levels of regionness, ranging from the global, the hemispheric, regional, sub-regional and bilateral arrangements (Varas 1995, 285; Varas and Tulchin 1994). Intra and inter-regional arrangements based on the content (negative lists of goods) rather than form and institutionalisation tend to be a central feature of these arrangements (Varas and Tulchin 1994; Mace and Thérien cited in Sanahuja 1998, 14).

The end of the Cold War and the turn of the US towards regionalism are considered to be the main reasons for the revival of regionalism in international relations (Bhagwati 1994; Hettne 1997; 2000; Mansfield and Milner 1999). Although this appears to be the case in Latin America, it is not the whole explanation for the revival of regional co-operation. Certainly, the US made a U-turn towards regionalism in Latin America as a result partly of stalemate in the multilateral negotiations under the Uruguay Round of the GATT as well as owing to the increasing economic power and influence of the European Union (EU) and Japan. The CIA advised the Bush administration in 1990 to create NAFTA, with Canada and Mexico, as a strategy to face the challenge represented by European unification and the incipient East-Asian bloc led by Japan which the CIA identified as the main threat to US hegemony (Palacios L 1995). A rapprochement with Latin America in the form of the Enterprise for the Americas launched by President Bush in June 1990, and integrating Mexico to the US economy were viewed as positive moves to reinvent Inter-American relations in order to countervail the new challenges stemming from globalisation. This would also accelerate the deconstruction and fragmentation of Latin America, a condition for reasserting US hegemony in the region (Grugel 1996).

However, Latin American's new regionalism is not entirely determined by the end of the Cold War or by the US hegemony. The move towards a new regionalism is to a large extent explained as a result of an evolution of the old regionalism. There has been an evolutionary move in the perception of integration in the region. This move has to do with a shift in the rationale of integration, largely due to the triumph of neo-liberal economics and the advance of democracy, which has increased the political and economic convergence of the states. This in turn has reduced fears and geopolitical rivalries, enhancing, as a result, the prospects for co-operation among the governments (Hurrell 1995b).

In the 1960s and 1970s integration was seen as a defensive strategy designed to promote the economic development and cohesion of the region and reduce its external dependence. In the 1990s there was a pragmatic view of regional integration. It was seen as an offensive strategy purposively pursuing the integration of Latin American economies into the world market. As such it is endowed with a political dimension whose aim is to enhance the bargaining power of the region vis-à-vis other states, regional blocs and multinational businesses (Rosenthal 1991; Palacios L 1995). But as Lahera asserts, external integration is not only an end, but also a means of regional integration. It is expected that integration into the world economy will bring economic efficiency to the region. In other words, it will accelerate the transformation of the productive structure of the region and improve the competitiveness of the economies in the world market (Lahera

P 1992). As a result, there has been a proliferation of regional, sub-regional and trans-regional arrangements concerned with the expansion of trade and external openness in the region.

RESUMPTION OF INTEGRATION IN THE 1990s

In June 1990 at the presidential summit held in Antigua, Guatemala, the process of rebuilding and reforming the Central American integration within a new regionalist conception formally began. Although the aim was to rebuild the integration process and to form and consolidate a 'Central American Economic Community', the purpose of integration would not be regional cohesiveness or community building, but integration to the world economy.[9] In this sense, integration becomes an 'association' purposively organised by the governments to pursue the external integration where the possibilities of growth of the region are said to lie.[10]

It is, thus, 'a return to the old outward model of integration that prevailed from the nineteenth century to the 1950s' (Lizano 1994, 3). This creates an ambiguity, which largely accounts for the weakness of integration as it leaves it prey of the vagaries in the international economy. The ambiguity is found in the fact that while building integration requires political co-operation and increasing economic convergence, participation in the global economy brings back home the conditions of anarchy where competition and differentiation are the key to success. The competitive ethos of the global economy thus conspires against the need to strengthen regional convergence and solidarity. Central American integration in the 1990s, therefore, took the form of open regionalism. Its aim was to negotiate preferential access to external markets and to attract FDI, new technologies and aid for the economic reconstruction of the region. It is seen, as Francisco Sorto points out, 'as an arrangement to increase the comparative advantages of the region by means of creating scale economies and encouraging economic competition with states of similar size, multinational firms and other regional blocs'.[11]

GOVERNMENTS AS STRATEGIC ACTORS

The force behind the re-launch of regionalism in Central America in the 1990s was the governments themselves. The re-launch was grounded on the governments' concerns with the economic decline and marginalisation of the states from the world economy (trade and investment) and its implications in terms of political power and the consolidation of peace and democracy to which the governments are committed.[12]

Thus, the interest in shaping a new regionalism in Central America largely came from within the region. But this also reflected the pressures of the structural environment of the post- Cold War era in which the states interacted. Nonetheless, this new regionalism has not been as spontaneous as suggested by some theorists. Hettne (1997; 2000) assumes the existence of a strong participation of diverse social actors alongside the state which feel the need for co-operation to deal with the new challenges brought about by globalisation.

Central American new regionalism fits the pattern identified by Gamble and Payne (1996), in the sense that there has been little popular involvement or influence in the process. It is mostly a governmental response first of all to the need to rebuild and reform the domestic economies in order to overcome economic decline and to adapt to the international restructuring taking place in the world economy. Even if the state takes the form of a 'transnational state' where its leaders act as midviwes of capitalist globalization, as Robinson argues (2003, 44), political power and domestic considerations remain central concerns of governments which compel them to co-operate on integration to achieve their goals.

With the exception of business groups, there has been very little participation or even influence from civil society organisations in the process of rebuilding Central American integration. According to Luis Guillermo Solis 'there is no civil society participation in the process of integration because the presence of organised civil society forces is limited to SICA's Consultative Committee. The Committee is a mere deliberative mechanism used by the governments to interact with civil society's forces, but it is entirely controlled and led by the governments'.[13]

This, however, does not mean that there are not civil societal forces concerned with integration. If social participation is emerging within new regionalism, it tends to operate as a counteracting force to the intergovernmental paradigm, skewing its trade and neo-liberal orientation. Mittelman (1996, 208) calls this 'transformative regionalism'. Its aim is the building of an 'egalitarian way of unity, away from US hegemony and towards Latin American integration with a nationalist focus and a continental perspective that addresses North-South inequalities' (Mittelman and Falk 2000, 184–185). Venezuelan president Hugo Chávez's project of a Bolivarian integration seems to follow this pattern of transformative regionalism. The emphasis is placed on regional co-operation and collective action rather than exclusively external integration.

In Central America diverse societal forces, ranging from small businesses, communal organisations and trade unions, have been opposing the neo-liberal project of integration carried out by the governments and the main economic groups. These forces have also opposed the negotiation of the free trade agreement with the US known as CAFTA.[14] Grouped in the Civil Initiative for Central American Integration (ICIC, Spanish acronym) these social forces have opposed the model of social integration agreed by the Presidents in San Salvador in 1995. The reasons for rejecting it were because it did not represent their interests and because they were not properly consulted about it (Rivera 1995; De la Ossa1996). As early as 1991 these social forces were pressing the governments to include the social dimension in the process of integration, which in their view should include Social Security, a Social Charter, sustainable development and economic democracy (Rivera 1995).

So, despite pressure from social movements, new regionalism in Central America takes the form of what De la Ossa (1994) terms the 'official integration', which is a neo-liberal regionalism effected by the governments and heavily concentrated on trade and external integration. It is the governments guided by their own interests that have been leading the cause for this form of integration. The speed and reach of the process of integration is largely determined by the preferences of the governments and the power asymmetries among the states, as well as by the structural environment, especially the interest of multinational investors given their increasing power in the international political economy.

REGIONALISM AS A BARGAINING CHIP IN EXTERNAL NEGOTIATIONS

As has been acknowledged, the external environment has a strong impact on integration, constraining the power of the states. It impacts heavily in the region because of 'the extreme openness as well as the small size of the economies' (Bulmer-Thomas 1988, 212). This may not only constrain the capacity of the governments to carry out effective countervailing policies, but as in the case of CAFTA, also encourages them to pursue some level of co-ordination in order to increase their bargaining position. In a context of international interdependence and globalisation, week states can not only use their weakness to extract concessions from developed states. They can also form alliances and regional groups and use multilateral diplomacy to boost their influence (Hoffman 1978) not only vis-à-vis states but, also transnational actors such as multinational corporations.

Although the process of rebuilding Central American regionalism is in line with the established evolutionary trend in the Latin American integration process, it was also a clear attempt by the governments to use regionalism as bargaining to avoid exclusion from the world economy. The main external challenge that the region faced consisted of a shift in the strategic interests of both the US and the EU. With the end of the Cold War, US interests had been shifting away from security regionalism (Mittelman and Falk 2000). As a result, Central America had lost importance within the new US and EU geo-economics. The interests of these external actors concentrated increasingly on 'the larger countries of Latin America, but emphasising economic problems created by the debt crisis' (Varas 1995, 282). Other US interests such as the environment, democracy, labour and drug trafficking did not give Central America any political lever vis-à-vis the US or the Europeans.

Trade and drug trafficking became major concerns of both the US and the EU in the 1990s, placing the attention on the biggest states of the region and in the Andean Group. Reforming Central American integration was therefore an attempt to reengage both the US and the EU in Central American affairs. Particularly, the governments would use it to demand the extension of the benefits enjoyed by Mexico within NAFTA (North American Free Trade Agreement) and the Andean countries in the EU. These are the so-called NAFTA and Andean parity both in the US and the EU markets. The Central American governments view themselves as losers out of the concessions granted to Mexico and the Andean states by the US and the EU, respectively, and spent the decade of the 1990s demanding the extension of the benefits.

The reinvention of regionalism was reinforced following the crisis faced by EXA in 1989, and considerable losses in economic aid, especially from the US. The International Coffee Agreement collapsed in July of 1989, seriously affecting the Central American economies. In addition, the US announced a 60 per cent cut in the sugar quota and a 30 per cent reduction of economic aid.[15] The US Senate also approved on July 17, 1990, a bill freezing garment imports, which threatened the textile industry of the region, one of the most important ones in the 1990s.

The EU also granted preferential access, to its market, to the Andean states, which threatened the stability of Central America's exports to the EU market. The EU was also restricting imports of Latin American bananas in 1990, which affected investment and caused losses in revenues to some Central American states. There was, thus, the perception that reinventing regionalism was the answer to these new challenges and to gain or even maintain preferential access in both the US and the EU markets. This led the Presidents at their summit in Montelimar, Nicaragua, in April 1990 to shift their attention from conflict resolution towards the economic integration, a task designed to be the focus of the summit at Antigua. Conscious of the importance of rebuilding Central American integration and the need to enlarge the market, the presidents formally invited Panama to apply for membership and participate actively in the process.[16] A similar invitation was issued to Belize, and on some issues even the Dominican Republic has become close to Central America. The move towards integration was reinforced following the US rejection of pursuing negotiations with each state to participate in the Enterprise for the Americas Initiative (EAI) and NAFTA. As it is said in chapter 7, it was this rejection which forced Costa Rica to get back to the integration agenda.

DEEPENING THE INTEGRATION PROCESS

Rebuilding and reshaping Central American integration is the task that the governments of the region have undertaken since 1990. This move reflects both the realities of Central American politics and the impact of globalisation. The former includes the success of the peace process in bringing peace to the region, the need to address the economic failures of the 1980s, the conversion of significant sectors of the economic elite and itellectuals to marketisation. The latter refers to the shared interest of governments and private businesses in facing the challenges stemming from globalisation. The governments, therefore, have found both domestic and structural pressures to come up with a new regionalism which is at tune with the age.

FROM ODECA TO SICA

From 1990 to 1993 with the adoption of Antigua's Declaration, the Tegucigalpa Protocol (TP) and the Guatemalan Protocol (GP), the governments reinvented Central American integration. The integration, which the governments rebuilt through presidential summits and the adoption of regional instruments such as the TP and the GP has been the outcome of intergovernmental bargaining. As such, it responded to the interests and preferences of the main governments, leading to a political compromise. The TP, adopted in December 1991, created the Central American Integration System (SICA) as the new institutional framework of Central American integration, which was based on a reform of the Organisation of Central American States (ODECA).

Reforming ODECA instead of getting into a deeper integration, as originally intended by Guatemala with PARLACEN, underlined the concern of the governments with sovereignty. The intergovernmentalist hypothesis regarding institutional building argues that governments create institutions in order to ease the intergovernmental bargaining and co-operation as well as to increase their leverage and autonomy vis-à-vis domestic groups which might not be supporters of integration (Moravcsik 1993a).

The above hypothesis neatly fits the process of institutional building carried out in the Central American integration of the 1990s. The institutional rebuilding underway in the region aimed at facilitating the governmental process of decision making. The institutions and bodies created were reduced to the role of secretariats of the presidential summits and the meetings of ministers and other governmental bodies. This is clearly the case with the General Secretariat of SICA (CEPAL 1997). The reasons underlying this are, first, the unwillingness of the governments to transfer sovereignty to regional institutions, second, the preference for market arrangements as opposed to economic planning. As the minimalist or little state has become a national preference of both governments and business interests, the institutions of integration cannot escape this rationale.

There have been no moves towards supra-nationality. Although it can be argued that the reach of integration has been expanded with the inclusion of new issues, there has not been a transfer of sovereignty to regional institutions as predicted by neo-functionalism. This is a major difference, for instance, between the re-launch of regionalism in Central America and in the EU in the 1980s and 1990s. In the EU, the move towards deeper integration through the Single European Act and the Maastricht Treaty brought about greater pooling of soverignty and transfer of competence to regional institutions (delegation). For instance, qualified majority voting was expanded, new powers were given to the European Parliament and the European Court of Justice (Nugent 1993). In Central America, the move has been towards creating a sense of order within the system, simplifying the institutional milieu and pooling sovereignty on issues of common interest. But in contrast to the EU, the move in Central America has been towards centralising rather than decentralising the decision-making system which remains in the hands of government officials. One of the failures of the traditional institutional framework as Schmitter (1970b) argues was the ineffectiveness and lack of overlap in the decision-making process. There was no sense of interconnectedness among the different bodies and institutions as they refused to be subordinated under ODECA. Clearly the idea of interconnectedness was imbued in the structure of ODECA but it failed to develop because the institution became an arena for high politics conflicts.

The undertaking under SICA has been about creating interconnectedness and overlap, although in practice this has been difficult to sustain. SICA is in practice a synthesis between ODECA and the original Guatemalan project of PARLACEN, which was presented as a system of integration. Most of the bodies and institutions established under SICA existed in ODECA but they did not have a juridical personality of their own. They were councils, especial committees or simply gatherings of states' officials which normally met once a year in order to co-ordinate public policies such as education, justice, social security, and foreign policy (ODECA's Charter 1962: Arts, 1–21). Under SICA there is in principle institutional overlap and hierarchy. The SICA System comprises four principal bodies of decision-making:

1. The Presidents' Summit;
2. The Council of Ministers;
3. The Executive Committee; and
4. The General Secretariat.

Of these bodies, the Presidents' Summits and the Council of Ministers are the most important. The former has a wide range of responsibilities, including defining and leading Central America's regional politics, harmonising the foreign policy of the states, approving reforms, and admitting new members (TP, Art.15). Regarding the Council of Ministers, its main function is to follow up and ensure the implementation of the decisions adopted by the Presidents (TP, Art.16). The Foreign Secretaries are the most important within the Council. They are the real carriers of the process of integration, as they constitute the principal co-ordinating organ of SICA. They represent the region in external relations, execute the presidents' decisions, recommend the admission of new SICA's members, and are responsible for democracy and the security complex of the region. Jointly with the Economic Ministers, they define the strategy of the region for its external integration (TP, Art.20). Finally, they are the link with the presidents. Any proposal submitted to the presidents has to be channelled though them (TP, Art.17).

The Executive Committee and the General Secretariat of SICA (GS-SICA) are considered the permanent bodies of SICA. The former consists of states' representatives appointed by the Foreign Secretaries. It has the same kind of functions as its equivalent in the CACM. GS-SICA is the highest administrative authority of SICA and represents SICA externally. It is dependent on the political bodies and under authorisation by these it can negotiate international accords, especially, technical and financial agreements. Its main function, however, is to act as a Secretariat for the Presidents and Council meetings and implement their decisions (TP:Art.26). In practice, however, GS-SICA has been uneasy performing such a central function and has been de facto overtaken by the so-called "Protempore Secretariat" (the equivalent of the Presidency in the European Community) shared on a rota basis by the Foreign Secretaries (CEPAL 1997; Cerdas 1998).

The TP also includes the Meeting of Vice-presidents, PARLACEN, the Central American Court of Justice (CCJ) and SICA's Consultative Committee as part of SICA. Their inclusion, however, gave rise to a form of discontent, which obstructed the ratification process of the TP by Costa Rica and Guatemala. These two states constitute a conservative bloc, which opposes supranationality. Both states rejected signing the CCJ. In the case of Costa Rica this rejection included PARLACEN. As it is discussed in the next chapter, Costa Rica initially refused to sign the TP and the GP because of domestic opposition to deeper integration. It was only when Figueres Olsen took over the government (1994–1998) on a more committed agenda to integration that Costa Rica ratified such instruments. In the case of Guatemala, it is committed to deepening integration within the North Triangle or CA-4 Area [17] as it is shown below and in chapter 7, but it has refused supranationality and the surrender of national control, particularly on trade disputes and emigration policy. To a large extent, this reflects the government's preference for PARLACEN as core of the system of integration instead of SICA.

With regard to SICA's Consultative Committee (SICA-CC), it represents an attempt by the governments to reflect the new trend of global governance of the region where governments find in their own interest to interact with diverse societal forces. It is also used as an instrument to defuse domestic opposition to integration by co-opting leading social forces and business groups. Its aim is to allow the participation of societal forces in the process of integration, but such an aim has not been properly achieved. This is in part due to the weakness of the neo-liberal democratic process in the region which weakens rather than empowering forces in civil society such as trade unions and non-governmental actors.

SICA-CC has been strongly criticised for not being representative enough (Rivera 1995; De la Ossa 1996; 1997; Sanahuja 1997). Most analysts consider that the Committee is basically an instrument to promote the business interests to the detriment of other social forces. The popular movement grouped under ICIC has opposed the monopolistic presence of big businesses in both SICA and SIECA (Rivera 1995).

The prevalence of SICA over PARLACEN or SIECA, likewise, reflects the experience of negotiations under the Esquipulas process where the Presidents' summits and the Foreign Secretaries became the central bodies for decision making. Since Esquipulas, the Ministers of Economics and SIECA, the traditional bodies responsible for integration and regional development, have been placed in a position of subordination with respect to the Foreign Secretaries. This prevalence of SICA over PARLACEN also came out as a result of Costa Rica's disagreement with the latter owing to this state's preference for intergovernmental co-operation as opposed to supranationality.

Integration, therefore, has been moved from the realm of low politics to high politics. The reason for this is the difficulty in the international context of the 1990s to separate out domestic and regional economic issues from political and global ones. Because of this, regional economic co-operation has been increasingly taking place within the framework of foreign policy and foreign trade. Governments use integration to reap the benefits that it provides and 'to take advantage of the strategies of domestic interest groups' (Kahler 1997: 38). This has made the Foreign Secretaries, empowered by the Esquipulas process, the leading political force of Central American integration. This underlines the hierarchic ordering of SICA as core institution of integration to which all regional institutions and previous legal arrangements are subordinated, according to an advisory opinion by the Central American Court of Justice (Memoria 1994–1995). Thus the governments understood that integration was the way forward to respond to the challenges brought by globalisation, but they disagreed on the scope of integration. Some states are more prepared to support a quicker and more far-reaching integration than others.

THE NORTH TRIANGLE TAKES THE LEAD

In 1992 El Salvador, Honduras and Guatemala singed the Ocotepeque agreement instituting the North Triangle Area. Through agreement these governments seek to accelerate the establishment of a free trade area and a customs union allowing the free movement of goods and capital (Memoria 1992). The reach of the agreement was expanded in April of 1993 with the signing of CA-4 (a migratory agreement) with Nicaragua where the four governments agreed to allow the free movement of persons for tourist and commercial reasons.

CA-4 citizens can travel within the region without passport. Because of further advances during 2004 and 2005, travelers from outside the region (e.g. American or European citizens) are allowed to move freely across the region.[18] A single visa, designed to ease the burden on foreign travellers, was agreed by the interior ministers of the CA-4 countries who met in Tegucigalpa on March 4, 2005. As a result, from May 2005 foreign travellers no longer have to undergo check out procedures in each country. Thus a visa granted at entering the region and valid in the other member states will undoubtedly have a positive impact on the development of the tourist industry in the region, which has been growing since 2004. In the agreement the governments also committed to achieve 'the full integration (economic and political) of their countries'. [19]

In the area of customs union these states have made considerable progress with the setting up of the so-called Periphery Customs [20] (aduanas periféricas) which ease intra-regional trade. El Salvador has been leading this process by setting out customs union offices in the territory of the other CA-4 states. Their customs unions have been integrated since May 2004. This has created pressure on Costa Rica to join the endeavour of consolidating the customs union region-wide despite its previous reluctant attitude to it.[21]

Through this arrangement the CA-4 governments began the process of social integration and societal interdependence in the region, allowing the free movement of persons without the requirement of passports within their territories, thus lifting bureaucratic obstacles to intra-societal interactions (Memoria 1992; 1993). An agreement by the interior ministers in March 2005, creating a single passport within the CA-4 countries further consolidates this process of community building. This is an embryonic attempt at creating Central American citizenship. The governments have also adopted the principle of recognition of national standards of merchandise and granted national treatment to investment and capital originated in member countries.

Although conflict has not disappeared, the North Triangle-CA-4 area has become an area of intense economic and political co-operation, embracing joint actions at different levels. This includes co-operation in the Trifinio area, in the Honduras Gulf and Fonseca's Gulf, and other developmental programmes in fields such as electricity, transport and telecommunications (De la Ossa, 1999, 75). This effort has been largely led by El Salvador and Guatemala to which Honduras and Nicaragua have joined.

COSTA RICA'S AMBIVALENCE TOWARD DEEPENING INTEGRATION

Costa Rica has found it hard to engage at this level of regionness with the other states, first, because of the fear of losing sovereignty, but also because of divergence in the level of social development between Costa Rica and the other countries. Costa Rica has reiterated that it cannot agree on deepening integration as demanded by the other states until all the countries have the same social conditions. According to Patricia Solano, 'for political integration to go ahead, the social conditions in the other states must be improved, including labour conditions, welfare facilities and changes in the legislation. While convergence in the social conditions of the countries does not exist, Costa Rica cannot support or adhere to political union'.[22]

Costa Rica, therefore, during the 1990s did not support the deepening of integration, which was thought would lead to political or economic union. This is why it avoided participating in PARLACEN. Costa Rica has also avoided ratifying a regional treaty on Democratic Security agreed by the governments in Honduras in 1995. The argument is that, as Costa Rica has no army, the treaty would not be compatible with the constitution. Costa Rica dislikes the idea of giving regional attributions to the armies. Far from accepting the armies' influence in the process of integration, Costa Rica presses for their abolition. A deeper integration such as that agreed by the other states with the adoption of CA-4 would make Costa Rica the inevitable destination of economic migrants. Costa Rica, thus, fears being invaded by Central American economic refugees attracted by its higher standards of living and welfare provisions. As argued by Rodrigo Carreras:

> if with the border closed there are more than half a million of illegal Nicaraguans in Costa Rica, were the borders open as proposed by the CA-4 governments there would not be any person left in Nicaragua. The Nicaraguans would leave their country attracted by the better conditions offered by Costa Rica. Thus, these are the aspects that need to be overcome in order to proceed with the process of integration'.[23]

The social and economic differences between Costa Rica and the other states widened quite dramatically during the 1980s. All the states experienced a drop in per capita GDP with Honduras and El Salvador falling to the level of 1964, Nicaragua to that of 1955 and Guatemala and Costa Rica to the level of 1974 (Cáceres and Irvin 1989). By 1990, however, Costa Rica had fully recovered and had become socially and economically the most successful and stable state of the region. As there are already a large number of Central Americans, especially Nicaraguans, living in Costa Rica, Costa Rica fears becoming a safety net for the economic and social failures of the other states.

Finally, there is the high dependence of the state on customs duties and a sense of inferiority in terms of entrepreneurial capability, which deters Costa Rica from getting involved with far-reaching Central American integration. According to Luis Guillermo Solis, 'on economic matters Costa Rica is not the most advanced because it is the most protectionist state of the region. About 50 per cent of the state's revenues came from customs duties. Therefore, this is a country whose social development has been financed with taxes, especially customs duties'.[24]

Until recently, high dependence on import duties and disagreement over integration prevented Costa Rica from engaging with the other states in establishing a customs union because the loss in customs duties would severely affect the public finances and the social responsibilities of the state. As a result, Costa Rica has favoured a limited integration consisting of consolidating the CACM as a free trade area. As such it would be limited to trade integration. As pointed out by Amparo Pacheco.

> There are conceptual differences between Costa Rica and the other states. Costa Rica has two objections to a deeper integration. As far as political integration is concerned, it is viewed as a final stage following the advancement and consolidation of the economic integration. Regarding economic integration, trade integration is deemed a priority. There is no problem regarding capital markets and so on, but there is unwillingness regarding setting deadlines to achieve certain goals which are considered premature, as for instance, the adoption of a single currency or creating a single common authority. But there has been a great interest in proceeding with trade integration and economic integration in general which is regarded as a precondition for greater levels of integration, including political integration.[25]

Costa Rica's view of integration is, therefore, limited to the setting of clear rules of transparency based on the rule of law and a specific system to resolve trade disputes, which Costa Rica promotes. This, however, excludes getting into institutional building and political integration, which Costa Rica does not support. The reasons above mentioned underlie this preference for a limited integration. But there is another fundamental reason, namely, the fact that Costa Rica has developed a quite advanced system of export promotion and has been conducting its trade relations within a framework of foreign trade under the rules of the World Trade Organisation (WTO) rather than integration.

This policy change in Costa Rica has empowered the role of large firms, including big multinationals in the economic development of the country. These firms, therefore, press the government for further expansion of the export led model of growth. They are the real winners of the export boom, which also allows them to get the lion's share of the states' exports subsidises (Sánchez Sánchez 2004). As Busch and Milner (1994, 270) argue, an economic sector dominated by 'export-dependent and multinational firms is unlikely to demand import protectionism' or inward regionalism as intended by the other states of the region. For that reason the Rodríguez Echeverría administration (1998–2002) dissolved the Department dealing with integration at the Ministry of Economics, transferring its functions to the Ministry of Foreign Trade (COMEX). The initial step was actually undertaken by the Figueres Olsen government (1994–1998) in 1996 with the adoption of a law transferring the management of the economic and trade relations of the state to COMEX. However, the Figueres Olsen administration did not implement the law, perhaps because it decided to go ahead with the integration agenda of the other states.

For these reasons, Costa Rica in the 1990s, particularly under the Social Christian governments (1990–1994; 1998–2002; 2002–2006)[26] has actually favoured limited integration and unilateral action rather than regionalism as the way to carry out its external integration. This preference for unilateral action finds it roots in the structural differences in the level of development between Costa Rica and the other states and in the level of internationalisation achieved by Costa Rica since the 1980s. Thus, the government of Costa Rica has viewed the other states as unable to undertake their external integration at the pace required by Costa Rica. According to Amparo Pacheco:

> It was not voluntarism, but realism, in the sense of a lack of convergence of policies and interests of the states, which underpinned Costa Rica's preference for unilateral action. The governments favoured, in general, joint action but in practice they realised that their national priorities were not compatible. Some states wanted to advance faster in their external integration. Others wanted to advance slower, and others, even not to advance at all. The governments, therefore, faced the dilemma of whether to advance at the speed of the slowest state or to break down the integration. A compromise was reached to allow unilateral actions but the governments would avoid unnecessarily damaging the process of integration.[27]

Another reason is the self-image of Costa Rica as a weak economic state within the region. Costa Rica has never felt confident to influence the other states. The Costa Rican political elite feel that the other states, particularly El Salvador, possess more developed entrepreneurial power and better market conditions which give them leverage to influence economic policy within the region (Soto Acosta 1990).

Thus with a change in the Central American agenda in the 1990s towards economic integration and democratic security following improvement in the process of pacification, Costa Rica found it difficult to pursue a protagonist role in the fashion of the Arias Sánchez administration (1986–1990). Instead, the governments since 1990 have followed a quite passive but still positive engagement with the region (Muñoz G 1994), while unilaterally negotiating with third parties. Most initiatives towards a far-reaching integration, since 1991, have come from El Salvador. The reason for the Salvadorian leadership in the 1990s is explained not only by this country's coherent integrationist agenda, but also because integration strongly serves its interests. As Luis Guillermo Solis points out, 'El Salvador is the only country pulling the region towards a deeper integration mostly because it is the state which can reap the largest benefits of a full integration. The country possessing the most advanced, modern, and interesting concept of integration in this moment is El Salvador'.[28]

SALVADORIAN INNOVATION: A PRAGMATIC COMPROMISE

The Salvadorian president Alfredo Cristiani set out the cause for a pragmatic integration in his UN speech in October 1990. On that occasion, Cristiani invited the other governments to joint efforts in order to create what he termed 'the Central America of the nationalities'. This according to Cristiani would allow the states to 'keep their individuality (diversity) while at the same time assuming the dimension of a new international reality which does not accept isolation neither recognises self-sufficiency' (Cristiani 1990, 82–83).

Cristiani's speech reflects a major deviation by El Salvador, away from its traditional integrationist rhetoric focused on the reconstruction of the Central American Federation, to a more pragmatic approach more concerned with business and globalisation. Himself an active member of the New Right, as descibed by Robinson (2003) [29], a succesful businessman turned politician, he attempted to shape Central American integration taking into account pressures and demands by domestic as well as international business interests.

President Cristiani stressed that the world was already viewing Central America as a regional bloc and that the region could not avoid this external perception without the danger of being excluded from the New World order. Under this new logic of integration proposed by President Cristiani, the governments would find grounds for a compromise by sharing sovereignty on issues which demand joint action while opting out on issues which compromise their own national interest. This is a kind of integration that Costa Rica's political elite is more willing to embrace because it secures the country's sovereignty as well as its trade interests in and outide the region.

Thus the move under Cristiani's vision was to concentrate on negative integration and the building of the Central American bloc. El Salvador has been consistently providing leadership in the region, because of the success of its government in pacifying the country and in rebuilding the economy, but also owing to the political hegemony of the Republican-Nationalist

Alliance (ARENA), a right-wing party which has guaranteed the continuation in both economic and foreign policies.[30]

Progress in rebuilding Central American integration, thus, reflects the compromise between the North Triangle states and Costa Rica favoured by this pragmatic approach put forwards by Cristiani. As a result, the former could pursue their integrationist agenda while at the same time having a common cause with Costa Rica in the attempt to integrate the region in the world economy. External integration became a common interest for all the states in the 1990s, and therefore, a basis for co-operation. The governments have promoted it by different means (Lizano 1994). These range through unilateral initiatives, bilateral agreements, and pooling sovereignty in multilateral negotiations where they act as a bloc as in the Free Trade Agreement of the Americas (FTAA), the Central American-US Free Trade Agreement (CAFTA), and the Eropean Union.

In the Guatemalan Protocol (Art.1) the governments have agreed to promote the convergence of their economies and to co-ordinate their external trade relations. This commitment was reaffirmed in August 1994 during the Presidential Summit at Guácimo, Costa Rica, where the Presidents agreed to negotiate jointly on trade matters. In October 1997 during a meeting of Vice-Ministers held in Conchal, Costa Rica, as part of the negotiations for the FTAA, 'the governments pooled sovereignty for the first time. In the FTAA Central America acts as a bloc with a single voice'.[31] The region has acted as a bloc as well in the negotiation of trade agreements with the Dominican Republic, Chile, and more recently with the US.

Thus, there has been some progress in presenting the region as a bloc in external relations but, as Luis Guillermo Solis argues, 'the development of this vision of a bloc is fragmented and irregular. It is subject-dependent and sporadic rather than structured and coherent, and in the future it will depend on the conditions and on the national priorities of the governments'.[32] Thus, there is the danger that the Central American bloc would appear a hollow one because of the lack of internal cohesion. It is this hollowness, among other factors inhibiting the build up of regionalism, which has led some analysts to argue that Central America does not yet constitute a region as such other than in the geographical sense (Bulmer-Thomas and Douglas Kincaid 2001).

INSTITUTIONAL REFORM

The process of reforming Central American integration has been undertaken not with the view of decentralising, but to ensure integovernmental control of the regional process of decision-making. As a result, intergovernmental bargaining has tended to reinforce centralisation, thus constraining the competence of regional institutions. In the period 1994–1998, as a result of President Figueres' greater commitment to integration, regional institutional reform and political integration were given unqualified importance. Figueres' commitment strengthened the Liberal-Morazanic bloc led by El Salvador. Facing isolation, the conservative government of Alvaro Arzú in Guatemala also supported the cause of institutional reform whose aim was to transform San Salvador into the Brussels of Central America. Under a new institutional reform agreed by the presidents during the Panama summit in July 1997, all the integration institutions had to be located in El Salvador under the SICA system. The different sectors under integration such as the CACM, tourism, social and security had to be placed under SICA's framework as subsystems of it. Their Secretariats, including SIECA, had to be moved to San Salvador in order to establish an integrated system. The presidents also agreed to reduce the size, privileges and immunities of the bureaucracy in some regional institutions, especially PARLACEN and the Central American Court of Justice. The attack on regional institutions came from Costa Rica, despite the commitment of its government, under Figueres, to integration. The other governments accepted Costa Rican demands on regional reform in exchange for Costa Rican support for integration in other areas such as political integration and the consolidation of SICA as a regional system.

It is important to point out that despite this move towards further integration, the governments were in no way compromising their sovereignty. In Panama the Presidents were categorical when they stated that the institutional reform was in pursuit of the consolidation of the Central American Community. But this had to be done 'without diminishing the autonomy, specificity and the constitutional order of the states'.[33] Keeping sovereignty is a condition for integration and consensus or unanimity is the rule under the TP and GP (Arts, 14 and 52, respectively). The move was, therefore, to consolidate the Central American integration as a community of nations or more properly, as a confederation of sovereign states.

Institutional reform reflected this interpretation of Central American integration. But there were other reasons. First there was the need to ensure overlap within the system. The region's institutions had grown in number since integration began, but without a sense of interconnectedness. Despite efforts under SICA this was still the situation by the end of the 1990s (CEPAL 1997). By 2007 this situation was still prevailing because of setbacks in institutional reforms.[34] Lack of co-operation from regional institutions and governments' high politics and domestic constraints [35] got in the way, seriously delaying or undermining the process. Second, there were concerns about the economic cost of institutions and the lack of differentiation among them in terms of the allocation of resources. Some institutions consume resources out of proportion even though they contribute little to integration. The result has been that institutions which are relevant to integration such as SIECA and SICA, have been deprived of economic and technical resources (CEPAL 1997; Cerdas 1998:).

Following the Panama Summit, the governments attempted during 1997 and 1998 to correct the shortcomings of the institutional framework. Enlightened by studies carried out by ECLAC and based on proposals stemming from SG-SICA and other regional institutions, the governments were negotiating in February of 1998 the adoption of a 'single treaty'. This treaty sought to simplify the institutional framework of the region.[36] In 90 articles, the single treaty incorporates all the treaties and instruments that have been accumulated since the integration process began.[37] It has four grand areas:

1. Political, consisting of preserving the democratic system and the security of the region.
2. Social and Culture, comprising education, health, preserving the historical patrimony and protecting cultural communities.
3. Environment, consisting of promoting a sustainable economic development which takes care of nature.
4. Economic, which refers to economic integration and a commitment to accelerate it.[38]

The single treaty sought to create a unified General Secretariat under SICA. It was intended that all branches of Central American integration as well as technical and specialised institutions which had been dispersed throughout the region would be placed under a single administration within SICA, with San Salvador as the Headquarters. As a result, according to Agrimaldi, the system would show better levels of co-ordination both technically and politically. As explained by Eduardo Ayala Agrimaldi to the author, the most important effort is the creation of a unified secretariat as an administrative or technical institution which will support the whole system of integration. It will be a General Secretariat of integration (SICA-GSI) involving a re-composition of functional areas. SICA-GSI would be supported by sub-secretariats organised by issue-areas, e.g, environment, social, tourism or economic integration. This will allow better levels of co-ordination for the whole system of integration.[39] The treaty pursued the institutional reordering, but without altering the decision-making structure with the Presidents and the Foreign Affairs Ministers remaining as the core decisional body within the system. The treaty was a bold move in the fashion of Maastricht, but it was not adopted. Four reasons account for this political failure:

1. Change of government in Costa Rica in May 1998. While Figueres was supporting and even leading the institutional reform in 1997, and also signed the Managua Declaration on political integration of September 1997, the conservative administration of Miguel Angel Rodrígues did not support it. The Rogríguez government skewed the commitments cast by its predecessor on political integration and did

not support the Brussels' model and the relocation of all regional institutions in San Salvador. As pointed out by Carlos M. Echeverría:

We do not know why President Figueres went too far with something that is not going to work. By doing so, he created a problem for the current administration because the new government inherited a situation, which is not acceptable both to Costa Rica and other countries, e.g. Guatemala. Our position is more realistic and pragmatic. It is a position of carrying the integration forward through increasing levels of co-operation, but without bypassing phases and without talking, for instance, of political integration, knowing that it is impossible. It is not good to pay lip service to an idea that will not work. This is the thinking of the Rodríguez government. We do not believe that the Brussels model is suitable for Central America. It is not a good idea to take SG-SICA and turn it not only into a co-ordinator as stated in the TP, but also, following up, guiding and implementing the presidential accords. We believe that SG-SICA must be limited to the function of co-ordinating integration. Neither do we believe that centralising the institutions in a single country is the right thing to do. We think this will take away legitimacy from the system. It will bureaucratise it. It will turn it anti-democratic and it will make it less attractive for states which would lose institutions currently located in their territories.[40]

The triumph of Rodrígues in Costa Rica allowed for the temporary activation of the conservative bloc Rodrígues-Arzú. Both the Costa Rican and Guatemalan governments expressed discontent with the idea of removing regional institutions from their territories, despite the original commitments. It is quite likely that the retreat from supporting the Brussels model of institutional development was the fear of losing prestige and national pride, which is normally attached to the hosting of international institutions. The argument raised by both governments, however, had to do with their preoccupation with the loss of jobs as a result of the removal of regional institutions to El Salvador (Panorama Centroamericano 1998, 2). Guatemala has also been reticent because upgrading the role of SICA as the general secretariat of the whole integration system implies enhancing the systemic role of El Salvador in the region at its expense. Removing all the institutions to El Salvador implies for Guatemala losing SIECA, which has been located in this country since 1960. Guatemala, as Carreras argues, 'is still troubled by the nostalgia for Captaincy-General'.[41]

2. Hurricane Mitch. As a result of the damage caused by Mitch in October 1998, the governments changed the regional agenda from integration to reconstruction. Reconstruction became the priority and most efforts at regional co-operation focused on reconstruction. As a result, the single treaty and other integration matters were ignored.

For a long while the governments did not talk of integration together. As Patricia Solano states, 'Mitch was graphically what paralysed the process of integration at the end of 1998. Following Hurricane Mitch there were three months (October-January) in which integration was not discussed, because everything concentrated on the damage caused by the natural disaster. It was no longer a matter of urgency whether SIECA left or stayed in Guatemala'.[42] Mitch, thus, paralysed the process. Discussions on integration were resumed in February (1999) under Nicaragua's Presidency (Pro-tempore Presidency). But the focus during the first trimester of 1999 was on international assistance, e.g. Central America-EU co-operation, Japanese and Korean co-operation, etc. These were the issues on which the efforts concentrated in the first trimester bypassing the regional agenda on integration.

3. Bureaucratic resistance. Both regional bureaucrats and government officials underwent a crisis of loyalty to regional institutions. According to Carreras, 'the Ministers of Economics have been reticent in consolidating SICA at the expense of SIECA, which inevitably implied lowering their political position within the system. SIECA's bureaucrats also disliked the idea of being deposed from their historical role as the institutional core of the process of economic integration'.[43] Likewise PARLACEN and the CCJ refused to be reformed in the terms intended by the governments.
4. The rise of border conflicts. The major conflict occurred in November 1999 when the Honduran Parliament ratified a border treaty with Colombia in the Caribbean Sea. Nicaragua objected to the treaty because in it Honduras recognised sovereignty rights of Colombia in areas which Nicaragua had been disputing with both countries. As a reprisal, Nicaragua imposed a 35 per cent surcharge on Honduran goods and pursued a demand against the latter state in the Central American Court of Justice. Although both governments avoided exiting from integration, the process of integration was severely affected. A border difference also took place between Nicaragua and Costa Rica. Both conflicts affected intra-regional co-operation and strengthened the cause for unilateral action.

The surge of these conflicts and their negative impact on intra-regional trade and integration forced El Salvador to strengthen its economic ties with Guatemala and Nicaragua, retreating away from the rhetoric of political integration. This has proved a successful process creating externalities to the other states, which forced them to co-operate. Joined later by Honduras and Costa Rica the region is nearing completion of the establishment of a customs union, thus, creating an economic space for closer co-operation and integration. Through these actions El Salvador sought to avoid being cut off from the region, something that could happen in the eventuality of a rupture of relations between Honduras and Nicaragua. Because of this arrangement being orchestrated by El Salvador, if the situation between Honduras and Nicaragua deteriorates, Salvadorian trade South to the region would keep flowing through Nicaragua.

Central American integration, therefore, reached a plateau in 1998 and entered into a period of concern and instability in 1999, but it seems that it has managed to muddle through. By 2004, however, everything seemed to indicate that a new phase of co-operation was taking place in the region. This was shown by the commitment granted by all the states to the customs union and the joint efforts at negotiating CAFTA with the US. It was also shown through the regional support to the Salvadorian candidate, former President Francisco Flores, to take up the General Secretariat of the OAS [44] and progress on trade disputes. While conflicts still plague the region there has been a positive move towards integration, largely as a result of convergent national interests, but also due to pressures from the structural environment with the advance of globalisation and US demand for freer trade.

CONCLUDING REMARKS

In the 1990s, Central American integration was rebuilt as a new regionalism. The rationale for integration was no longer to protect infant industries or even to create a Central America Union, but to create economic competition among the states and to insert the region into the world economy. It is also a strategy through which the governments sought to negotiate or even maintain preferential access to external markets, particularly in the US and the EU. By increasing the level of regionness in areas such as trade, macroeconomic stability, and democracy, the governments aimed to increase their bargaining power in negotiations with other trading partners and multinational businesses in order to avoid being excluded from the new international restructuring.

The new regionalism is, among other things, an arrangement to promote the openness and competitiveness of the economies of the region. In the face of an increased globalising economy, enlarging the markets through integration has become a condition of survival, especially for small economies. This realisation brought the Central American governments to accelerate the process of reform of the CACM and the institutions of integration in the period 1990–1993. The end of the Cold War favoured the building of democratic governance and the peaceful resolution of conflicts in the region, but it also eroded the strategic importance of the region as the interests of the US and the EU have shifted towards economically important regions. In the face of exclusion from globalisation the governments upheld the banner of integration as a strategic imperative (Lizano cited in: Sanahuja 1998: 23).

The process of rebuilding integration, however, is not free of contradiction. The main problem is that integration taken as a trampoline for external competitiveness does seem to undermine regional cohesion. Integration is only one means to achieve the external objective. In the search for their external integration the governments have tried different ways ranging from unilateralism to joint action, in most cases at the expense of regional cohesion, which underlines the hollowness of the Central American bloc. Thus, although the governments have presented integration as a new regionalism in the sense that it goes beyond trade to include other issues, the centrality of trade and concerns with external integration have undermined regional cohesion and regionness. The imperative of survival in a globalising world economy gives primacy to competition which undermines the efforts at regional building.

In this respect, SICA and other regional arrangements do not guarantee that the region will move in bold steps towards an enduring process of regionalisation. The system reflects the preferences and interests of the governments and works as a compromise of competing preferences, where the states of the North press for cohesion and a deeper regional integration while Costa Rica looks outwards, favouring external integration and competitiveness. The result has been variable geometry, where groups of states move at different speeds and at different level of commitment. But the move is not always forward. It does not seem to be a way to escape this trend in the process of integration unless the governments willingly accept some level of supranationality. As Schneider and Cederman (1994, 657) argue in their analysis of European integration, 'the stop-and-go logic will be a typical feature of integration as long as both intergovernmentalism and unanimity characterise all major decisions'. The challenge for Central America is, therefore, how to reach a balance between the need for inward and outward integration or how to use integration in both senses for the promotion of sustainable development in the region.

7 Restructuring the CACM in the 1990s

The Move towards Open Regionalism

Since 1990 the Central American Common Market (CACM) has been the subject of major economic reforms through which the governments have sought to open the economies and bolster intra-regional trade. This chapter, therefore, analyses this process of reform and traces the interests and actions of leading governments. It also highlights some of the difficulties still hindering the process of economic integration.

Three contentions are presented here. First, that the process of economic and tariffs reform within the CACM has advanced as a result of a complex process of interstate bargaining where leading governments have sought to accelerate the process of openness in accordance with their own national interest. Second, the role of domestic and regional non-state actors remains relatively low key on the issue of economic liberalisation. One reason for this is that issues such as tariffs reform are divisive. Some groups demand protection, other pressure for greater openness. When domestic interest groups are divided over an issue, the level of autonomy of the government increases which allows it to pursue its preferred goals. Finally, the main constraints governments face stem from their own financial difficulties and from the strategic and structural environments. This largely refers to the inability of the North Triangle states to persuade Costa Rica to fully embrace integration, US views of the region and the impact this has in terms of shaping the regional bloc.

REFORMING THE CACM

Reforming the CACM has been a major concern of the governments since the second half of the 1970s. As far back as 1976, the Ministers in charge of integration set out guidelines and established technical groups to work on reforming the Central American External Tariff (CET) (INTAL/BID 1986). Nonetheless, this early attempt at tariffs reform and subsequent efforts made in the decade of 1980 were undermined by the acute political and economic crisis faced by the states since the end of the 1970s. As a result, the governments failed to implement a new external tariff adopted in

1984. By then the governments were embarked on implementing stabilisation and structural adjustment programmes under the International Monetary Fund (IMF) and the World Bank's supervision. These programmes were pursued on a national basis. It was not until October 1993, when the Guatemalan Protocol was negotiated that the reform of the CACM was undertaken again as part of the neo-liberal programme of economic reform and market integration.

RE-THINKING OF THE CACM UNDER THE GUATEMALAN PROTOCOL

The Guatemalan Protocol (GP), which was adopted in Guatemala in October 1993, is the instrument through which the governments reformed economic integration. Through it the CACM is refurbished and presented as a new regionalism, consolidating the free trade area within the region and opening the markets to external competition. Consequently, the GP abolished previous protectionist arrangements such as the Regime on Central American Industry, the Accord on Fiscal Incentives to the Industrial Development, and the Limón Protocol on basic grains, all part of the Import Substituting Model of growth of earlier decades.

In addition, with the GP, economic integration is converted into a subsystem of the System of Central American integration (SICA). Early on economic integration under the Secretariat for Economic Integration (SIECA) was viewed as a system of its own, untouched by the vagaries of Central American politics. The end of the subsystem of economic integration is 'to achieve development in the region by means of transforming its productive, social, and technological structures, and by integrating the region into the world economy' (GP, Art.3). Although the long-term goal of the governments is to achieve the economic union, the immediate objective is, according with Art.7 of the GP, to consolidate the CACM as a free trade area through the abolition of tariffs and non-tariff obstacles to intra-regional trade. This is consistent with economic theory of integration which places the emphasis for integration on the abolition of economic discrimination between states (Balassa 1961).

But the reform of the CACM in the 1990s went beyond economic theory of integration. It was grounded on neo-liberal principles as part of the so-called '*Washington Consensus*', which seeks the internationalisation of the Latin American economies based on open markets and international competition. Thus the CACM became a policy instrument in the same fashion as the national programmes of structural adjustment to strengthen the openness of the economies of the region in accordance with the demands of global capitalism. There is a convergence of interests between the neo-liberal governments that now rule the states of the region and those of multinational investors on the need to implement market-led reforms within regional structures and regimes. Thus, from the 1990s onwards the *structural environment* has shaped governments' preferences increasingly away from regional building, favouring external integration or globalisation. Tariffs reform within the CACM follows this logic.

Although some states remain committed to the idea of strengthening the regional bloc under SICA, there is a consensus in the elite that regional integration should also function as a launching pad into globalisation. There is the view that in the age of globalisation development can no longer be attained within the geographical confines of the states, or even the region, and that the nation states no longer have to perform market functions (Ohmae 1995; Robinson 2003). According to this view, national planning now undercuts rather than promotes development. The balance of power has shifted away from labour and the nation state to the hands of the transnational capitalist class. This capitalist class favours the shaping of what Ohmae (1995, 5) terms 'region states' or regionalisation which refers to economic and productive integration by market forces rather than regionalism which refers to strategies pursued by governments based on states' power and national interests (see Sideri 1997, 49).

Regionalisation reflects the interest of global capitalism to go wherever business opportunities exist regardless of national borders. In this sense, regionalisation and region states are synonymous with a borderless world and globalisation. This view of a borderless world, which is shared by the ruling elite in Central America, moved the governments to do away with the political and economic rigidity set out in the General Treaty of Economic Integration, which since 1962 regulated the CACM. The Guatemalan Protocol, instead, was presented as a flexible arrangement based on respect for the rule of law, transparency and solidarity embracing a holistic view of economic integration (Art.5). This flexibility highlights the move of the CACM towards new regionalism, although it relies heavily on consensus, reciprocity and constitutional restraints as the basis for moving the process ahead.

In the GP the governments institutionalise ECLAC's conception of open regionalism which combines regional preferences with external openness (ECLAC 1995). The Protocol was intended as a framework treaty defining the 'objectives, principles and means of actions to achieve the economic union of the region' (SIECA, 1993, 119). As such, it leaves grounds for further intergovernmental bargaining and negotiations. It is quite far-reaching in terms of the aims it pursues and it is full of general statements and does not specify clearly which aspects of it are binding for all the states and which are only binding for some of them (Pleites 1994, 29). This, however, may have been intended as muddling through in the negotiations facilitating its adoption. Quite often, in the diplomatic field, governments use ambiguous language in order to preserve some basic tenets as well as levels of agreement on substantive issues (Berridge 1992, 189).

Regional arrangements in Central America reflect this kind of ambiguity and generality in order to reconcile the interests of the governments and secure their co-operation, thus, enabling them to grant credible commitments to integration on issues where they generally agree.

THE GUATEMALAN PROTOCOL AND INTERSTATE BARGAINING

Under the Guatemalan Protocol strong intergovernmental bargaining developed through which the larger states [1] pursued the economic integration of the region. This bargaining was instigated by the domestic and external interests of the governments as well as the increasing level of convergence of the economies, leading towards the re-launch of economic integration. The evidence is that, as Moravcsik asserts (1999, 273), national officials, rather than supranational or multinational actors, act as entrepreneurs, 'initiating, mediating, and mobilising negotiations'. The gradualist way of proceeding with integration responds not to the neo-functional logic of sector integration or supranational planning, but to the need to accommodate national interests, in particular Costa Rican interests, given Costa Rica's reluctance to commit fully with the other states in building deeper integration. Although as a matter of principle the other states embrace gradualism in their economic arrangements, they are committed to a far-reaching and quicker inward integration.

THE NORTH TRIANGLE'S SEARCH FOR FULL INTEGRATION

Integration normally starts with states that want it, which later on extend it to reluctant states either by means of negotiation or as a consequence of the *'negative policy externalities'* [2] that it creates. Central American integration in the 1990s clearly illustrates this logic. The re-launch of economic integration under the Guatemalan Protocol responded, essentially, to the interests of the North Triangle states [3] and was intended as a bargaining chip against reluctant states, to obtain their acquiescence for the consolidation of the trade regime and economic union of the region.

These states, especially El Salvador and Honduras, joined later by Nicaragua, have been shaping a liberal-Morazanist bloc [4] whose aim is to accelerate the full economic and political integration of the region. Their concerted actions have created pressures on reluctant states (largely Costa Rica and Guatemala), [5] forcing them gradually to embrace aspects of the far-reaching integration agenda which the liberal Morazanic bloc pursue. The advance regarding the customs union is a clear example of this where even Costa Rica has declared that it wants to be part of it.

The Morazanist states tend to see integration as a substitute for national policies and, therefore, pursue the harmonisation of economic policies and greater closeness.[6] These states strongly proposed the building of the Central American bloc as leverage in the external negotiations. But this has not been an easy process because their ambition clashes with their domestic realities. As Patricia Solano argues:

> They want to be integrated. They want the single treaty. But they do not want to carry costs. Besides, in the cases of Honduras and Nicaragua, as they are the less developed of the region, they also want to be granted preferential treatment which generates conflict in the integration process.[7]

Moravcsik (1998) argues that in Europe leading governments pursue integration mostly for economic reasons. Geopolitics and ideology have not been as important as the search for economic gain for the re-launch of integration. At best geopolitics and ideology have played a complementary role. In the case of the CACM, especially within the North Triangle area, these elements seem to combine more markedly. Certainly, the pursuit of economic advantage gained centrality following the implementation of adjustment policies and the steady recovery of economic growth, especially in El Salvador, but so did the federalist ideology which has survived in the north of the region, stressing the cause for integration especially under SICA.

The revitalisation of the Salvadorian economy in the 1990s, following the end of the civil war, and its dependence on the CACM for sustaining economic growth became a major reason for re-launching integration. Rebuilding integration, in general, and the CACM, in particular, was strategic for the Salvadorian government in order to ensure a long-term recovery and the sustainability of economic growth. Government officials thought that 'if integration were strengthened El Salvador would become more attractive to foreign investors. Given the good conditions which in their view El Salvador possesses in the CACM, foreign investors would choose to invest in this country in order to export to the rest of the region and the world'.[8]

The end of the civil war placed El Salvador at the forefront of the integration process in the 1990s. The end of the civil war, the demobilisation of the opposition with the peace accords, together with a 97 per cent of public support for integration (see Seligson 1993), gave the government high levels of domestic autonomy to pursue the reactivation of the CACM. The fact that other governments also needed integration to bring about support for their policies of economic reform and revitalise their foreign trade gave rise to a political consensus around the issues of economic liberalisation and integration. This gave El Salvador leverage to pursue the re-organisation of the North Triangle area in accordance with Salvadorian interests, whose aim was to open the markets of the other states to Salvadorian exports of goods, capital and to the free movement of persons.

Honduras became the strongest supporter of the Salvadorian programme of integration in the 1990s. Under the presidency of Rafael Leonardo Callejas (1989–1994) and his successors Honduras became fully engaged and committed to a programme of economic liberalisation and integration. Bringing Honduras back to Central American integration became a political priority for the government and a condition for the success of its economic policy. As a result, previous objections, such as the principle of balanced development so tenaciously defended by this country in the 1970s, as precondition for participating in the CACM, was dropped.

President Callejas faced strong opposition from local industrialists and trade unions who did not support the integration of their country to the CACM because they viewed themselves as losers. But the government skilfully weakened these opposing forces by building up alternative supportive coalitions, i.e., trade unions and consultation mechanisms to co-opt labour unions and business organisations.[9] Attempts were also made by the government to reform the armed forces in order to reduce their influence in the political process. This was an important step because of the suspicion and hatred of the Salvadorian army held by Hondurans since the 1969 war between the two states. Through these actions the Callejas government sought to increase its autonomy from domestic forces in order to secure the implementation of the policies of economic reform and the re-incorporation of the country into CACM.

Consequently, in February 1992, despite strong opposition from labour unions and industrialists the Callejas government signed a Transitional Multilateral Trade Accord with El Salvador and Guatemala which prepared the ground for the return of his country to the CACM.[10] Callejas was also instrumental in the attempts at persuading Costa Rica to go along with the commitment of the North Triangle states to full integration, 'stressing that political co-operation was not a short-term goal'.[11]

As far as Guatemala is concerned, it co-operated in creating the North Triangle, attracted by the economic advantages that it could extract from integration, but also to apply pressure to weaken domestic opposition to economic liberalisation. Economic integration is very important for Guatemala. As with El Salvador, Guatemala is export-dependent within the CACM and this alone represents a strong reason for co-operating with integration. El Salvador and Guatemala's commercial exchanges account for about 50 per cent of intra-regional trade. Table 7.1 shows details of intra-regional trade in 2002 for all member states of the CACM.

The main reason for Guatemalan participation in the North Triangle was the level of economic interdependence with El Salvador, but there was also the political commitment that this country had professed to integration since 1986 with the creation of the Central American Parliament. Because of this economic interdependence, the success of the

North Triangle required Guatemala's participation. Its participation is also important in terms of bargaining with Costa Rica because the success of the North Triangle can be used to press the latter country to bring its support to a far-reaching integration region-wide. This has been a Guatemalan aspiration since 1986 and its failure to enlist Costa Rica's support for PARLACEN may be one reason for consolidating its links with its most immediate partners of the North Triangle.

Ideology is an important component of the move towards integration, especially in the North Triangle area, but is also a variable accounting for stagnation and plateau in the integration process, especially on the political side. The share of the federalist ideology as well as the prospect of economic gains explains the move of Nicaragua to join the North Triangle through the signing of the CA-4 migratory accord in April 1993. Side-payments were given to Nicaragua in order to secure its participation in North Triangle. This involved debt relief and preferential treatment in order to reduce the adjustment cost of this country to integration.

Although in terms of external openness Nicaragua has shown some preference for unilateral action, as in the case of the negotiation of a trade accord with Mexico, ideologically it has been as enthusiastic as Honduras and El Salvador in promoting political integration. This explains the logic of the Managua declaration of September 1997 on political integration. The declaration was a joint project by Honduras and El Salvador. These states, partly inspired by the integrationist ideal of the nineteenth century leader General Francisco Morazán, have led the cause for the re-establishment of federal government in the region.

Guatemala and Costa Rica, on the other hand, have traditionally opposed this move, owing to a preference in the former for a centralised Central American republic with Guatemala as its core, and self-determination and defence of the national sovereignty in the latter. However, in the 1990s both states sought to compromise with the integrationist rhetoric of

Table 7.1 Intra-Regional Trade in the CACM 2002. (millions of US dollars)

	Exports	%	*Imports*	%
Total	2,883,872	100	3,087,527	100
Guatemala	910,914	31.6	688,367	22.3
El Salvador	751,945	26.1	816,448	26.4
Honduras	285,750	9.9	792,767	25.7
Nicaragua	251,724	8.7	454,530	14.7
Costa Rica.	683,539	23.7	335,415	10.9

Source: Adapted From http:// www.sieca.org.gt/ Boletín 9.1/marzo 2003.

the Morazanist states. Some of the instances where they moved towards co-operation are the ratification (although delayed) of the Tegucigalpa and Guatemalan Protocols,[12] and the adoption of the Managua declaration on political integration which the presidents re-stated in their speeches at the LII UN General Assembly on September 22–23, 1997 (SICA 1997).

The North Triangle/CA-4 states, as explained in the previous chapter, are committed to full integration. Their commitment to integration is explained by the levels of convergence of their economies, the political and economic interests of governments, ideological convergence, and pressure stemming from economic interdependence and the structural environment.

COSTA RICA'S PREFERENCE FOR A LESSER INTEGRATION

Costa Rica, as mentioned in the previous chapter, has found it difficult to embrace the advanced programme of integration put forward by its regional partners. As a result, its governments in the 1990s onwards have favoured slow and limited integration. Costa Rica regards integration as 'necessary to consolidate the peace processes and the advance of democracy',[13] but does not follow the euphoria of the other states. Different administrations have emphasised disarmament and education as bases for integration.

For Costa Rica integration is important, but not as substitute for domestic policies. As seen in chapter 6, the government has not shown willingness to support the structuring of a regional process which may imply the full integration of the country into the region. Costa Rica sees and pursues the building of the Central American bloc as an outward strategy, as the pooling of efforts to bargain vis-à-vis other states and regional blocs, but it is reluctant to compromise sovereignty and its freedom of action. This is reflected in the unwillingness of the Oscar Arias government in 2007 of signing a regional programme with its regional partners to accelerate the customs union as required by the European Union as condition for the negotiation of an inter-regional trade and association agreement.

Accordingly, Costa Rica supports integration in areas which serve its national interest, particularly areas related with infrastructure and in sectors where it can both supply the region or attract capital which can be used to enhance the trade position of the country within the region. This involves projects such as 'creating a regional stock market for electricity, the building of a regional railway system or the interconnection of the financial markets'.[14] The government has avoided the pooling of efforts in issues which do not serve the national interest or limit its capacity of manoeuvre. These have included issues such as foreign debt, security, emigration, commercial policy and building regional institutions which may require compromising sovereignty.

Regional integration is not what Northedge (1976, 151) calls 'the hedonistic type of association' driven by the pleasure of being together or by a sense of belonging. It is fundamentally a pragmatic association through which governments pursue the realisation of their goals. Governments favour the integration of policies (pooling or delegation) when there is not an alternative option though which they can fulfil their expectations or when they wish to reinforce their policies with credibility. Delegation and pooling, as Moravcsik (1998, 75) asserts, 'are more likely to arise in issue-areas where joint gains are high and distributional conflicts are moderate, and where there is uncertainty about future decisions'.

Costa Rica is sceptical about integration and this scepticism is shared both by the public and by large sections of the elite (see Seligson 1993, 15). Scepticism is entrenched as a result of the strong loyalty of the elite and citizens to the nation-state. It is also the result of endless campaigning by right wing interests who are against integration and who use their economic power and the media to voice their views. It was the overwhelming influence of right wing interests which prevented presidents Oscar Arias Sánchez (1986–1990) and Rafael Angel Calderón Fournier (1990–1994) securing the ratification of integration arrangements such as PARLACEN, SICA and the Guatemalan Protocol.

Because integration does not evoke public enthusiasm, 'political leaders avoid playing politics with it. They do not have to get involved in this kind of rhetoric'.[15] But the importance of the CACM for industrialists and exporters compels the government to compromise with the region in the efforts at consolidating the trade regime and ultimately supporting, at least in statement, the customs union by the Abel Pacheco administration in 2002. About 50 per cent of the country's industrial exports go to the region, and the CACM is becoming Costa Rica's second largest market. By year 2004 exports to the CACM slightly overtook those going to the European Union.

This increase of trade with the region means that Costa Rica is becoming more trade dependent within the CACM. As a result, the country is likely to become more vulnerable to trade discrimination within the region. This may compel it to co-operate with the efforts at regional building carried out by the North Triangle states. Business groups supplying the CACM, fearing discrimination in the other states, have pressed the government since 1994 to go along with the North Triangle efforts at integration.[16] In contrast, right wingers who oppose integration have pressed the government 'to negotiate bilateral free trade agreements with states outside the region and even to withdraw from the region' (Fajardo Salas 1993, 46).

In the face of the North Triangle's far-reaching programme of integration, in 1993 Costa Rica was forced to compromise with the CA-4 states (El Salvador, Guatemala, Honduras and Nicaragua) offering a minimum commitment to integration under the Guatemalan Protocol. By signing (but not ratifying) the Guatemalan Protocol the government sought not only to avoid being excluded from the CACM, but also to calm down domestic pressures against and in favour of integration. The compromise was limited to rebuilding the free trade area, but with clear safeguard rules. Costa Rica rejected proposals aimed at establishing a customs union or a common market, as this would have undermined the economic sovereignty of the state such as the right to impose or maintain barriers to imports (Morales G 1994). In Costa Rica's view integration has to be 'gradual based on co-operation, without jumping phases, not least jumping to political integration'.[17]

Threatened with exclusion from integration by the other states, the Calderón Fournier administration signed the Guatemalan Protocol, but only after it negotiated modifications to the original version in order to guarantee opt-outs on all these issues which conflicted with Costa Rica's national interest. Guatemala acted as broker, bridging the differences between Costa Rica and the North Triangle (SIECA 1993; Morales G 1994). As a result of conflictive states' interests, the Guatemalan Protocol sets out an integration process, which allows the states to proceed at their own pace. Articles 6 and 52 legally sustain variable geometry. These Articles recognise the governments' right to opt-out from issues or policies which are against their national interests. The North Triangle governments can, therefore, deepen their integration process. But Costa Rica, and indeed, any state, is also permitted to negotiate trade accords with non-CACM states in accordance with its national interest.

The final document, thus, allows Costa Rica to reject the goals of free movement of labour (GP:Art.18), financial and monetary union (Art.19), policy harmonisation on taxes and state subsidisation (Art.17). It also guarantees to Costa Rica the capacity to negotiate trade agreements unilaterally with third parties (Art.12). This was a practice that the government had been following even before the adoption of the Guatemalan Protocol (e.g., the negotiations with Mexico and the US). The Guatemalan Protocol also secured to Costa Rica the requirement of consensus or unanimity in the decision-making process (Art.52), which prevents decisions from being imposed on the country by the other states.

In spite of its government's lesser willingness to embrace deeper integration, Costa Rica was a real winner in the negotiations to re-structure the CACM. This conclusion is derived from the opt-outs that the country managed to extract from the other governments, as described above. Costa Rica effectively used its internal divisions and the inability to fully embrace the grand project of integration put forward by the North Triangle governments as a bargain, which allowed it to strike a deal close to its domestic preferences.

Putnam (1988) argues that a government facing a small win-set domestically can turn it into bargaining advantage externally. The opposite may happen when the domestic win-set is large. A government enjoying a large domestic win-set may face a lower bargaining advantage in the external negotiation, although enjoying domestic autonomy may place it in a position of leadership. As a result of having a large win-set domestically, a government may be able to lead a process of negotiation because of its ability to compromise from the very beginning (Putnam 1988). This is what explains the Salvadorian leadership in building integration since the 1990s.

The threat of exclusion was a major reason for Costa Rica's acquiescence with the Guatemalan Protocol. The North Triangle governments let it be known that they were prepared to go ahead with the process of integration without Costa Rica. They adopted the first draft of the protocol without Costa Rica during a meeting of Economic Ministers in Managua (Morales G 1994). Deprived of the possibility of building an alternative bloc regionally owing to the unavailability of prospective allies,[18] Costa Rica was forced to compromise both to avoid exclusion and to constrain the ambitions of the other states.

Costa Rica's compromise with the region in building the Central American bloc was also reinforced by its failure to secure a trade agreement with the US. The Calderón Fournier government was eager to negotiate a trade agreement with the US government. A framework agreement was signed between the two states in November 1990 which was seen by Costa Rica as the gateway to the Enterprise for the Americas and NAFTA. But the illusion was short-lived. By April 1992 the Costa Rican trade minister was criticising the US for not complying with the agreement.[19] The US government had decided to treat Central America as a bloc rather than doing unilateral deals with each state. At that stage, however, no state of the region met the convergence criteria set out by the US government for a free trade treaty.[20] This forced Costa Rica to re-evaluate its interests in the CACM and compromise with the other states under the Guatemalan Protocol. In this way, the structural environment also instigates pressures which in the case of Central American integration may encourage interstate compromises.

Yet, the threat of exclusion from integration and US pressures are not the only variables explaining Costa Rica's compromise with the region. The move towards integration was also consistent with the priority given by the government to the attraction of foreign investment and the opening of the economy. The negotiation of trade accords with other states (bilateral, regional or multilateral) was central for the fulfilment of these goals, becoming, therefore, a central foreign policy issue (Abarca Amador 1995). Thus, the threat of exclusion, structural pressures and policy convergence in terms of opening the markets combined in producing interstate commitments and compromises in the region.

TARIFFS REFORM IN THE 1990s

Tariffs reform within the CACM became a central aspect of the process of re-launching of integration in the 1990s. The resumption of tariffs reform, after the failures of the 1980s, was the concern of those governments which had already made progress on economic reform and trade liberalisation as were the cases of Costa Rica and El Salvador. With the support of predominant economic interests (e.g. foreign investors, exporters, and international institutions) these governments pursued the consolidation of the free trade regime in the CACM in order to bolster economic growth and speed up the integration of the region into the world economy.

GOVERNMENTS: THE MAIN POWER BEHIND TARIFF REFORM

Although business interests have been actively promoting the transformation of the CACM through their activities in FEDEPRICAP,[21] their integrationist euphoria was spurred on by the commitment given by the governments to integration.

In his analysis of European integration Moravcsik (1995, 618) argues that 'only unanimous decisions by governments backed by institutional commitments triggered significant corporate reactions'. The increasing activism of business groups in Central America seems to conform to this hypothesis. What triggered their interest and enthusiasm for integration in the 1990s was, first of all, the commitment of the governments under the Arias Peace plan towards democracy, and the rebuilding of the CACM under the Special Action Plan for Central America (PAECA).

Although PAECA was formally adopted by the governments in Antigua (Guatemala) in June 1990, the initial discussion about it began during the Presidential summit at Montelimar (Nicaragua) in April of that year (Soto Acosta 1993). The renewed interest, by the governments, in regional integration since Montelimar, awoke the enthusiasm of business groups which not only co-operated with the governments but also drew up their own agenda of transnational interactions, getting deeply involved in discussions regarding integration. It is clear, then, that as Moravcsik argues (1998), demands by powerful governments and their readiness to bargain, not supranational proposals, impose the binding constraints on regional co-operation.

Thus, the move towards tariff reforms in the region does not respond necessarily to pressures from business groups. It is the way neo-liberal governments respond to the problem of underdevelopment and their interest in bolstering the free trade regime as the engine for economic growth and integration. Tariff reform also embodies the way states, through co-operation, tackle the negative policy externalities stemming from decisions and policies undertaken by national governments as part of their programmes of economic reform. Because of levels of economic interdependence these decisions and policies generate costs for individuals and governments in other states. Governments, then, feel compelled to co-operate in order to ameliorate the impact of these externalities on individuals, especially *'inflexible rent seeker'* (groups which favour protectionism), and on the states' revenues. They may also do so in order to compel compliance by other states or even the national government in the future (Moravcsik 1998).

By 1989–90 there was a clear trend of convergence in the region on tariff reform. The governments were considering reducing the external tariff, targeting a ceiling of 20 per cent for finished goods and a floor of 5 per cent for intermediate goods and raw materials, to be put in place no later than 1992. The governments were committed not only to reducing, but also tackling the level of dispersion and complexity of their external tariff structures. The expectation was that by 1994 there would be a unified structure in the region, ranging between 20 to 5 per cent.

After the Presidential summit at Antigua in June 1990 the governments began to co-ordinate the external tariff under integration. In PAECA, the Presidents charged the Economics Ministers with the responsibility of outlining a regional programme and a calendar on tariff reduction (PAECA, numeral 3, in Rodríguez et al 1991, 245). On that basis, a new CET was agreed in 1991, establishing a ceiling of 20 per cent for final and intermediate goods and a floor of 5 per cent, with an intermediate of 10 and 15 per cent for raw materials and capital goods. It was expected that the new CET would be implemented by January 1993. A limited list of goods with fiscal interest was left outside the CET, but it was hoped that it would be integrated into the CET no later than December 1994. Thus, by 1993 there was a consensus among the governments on the need for tariffs reduction, which provided the basis for bargaining and co-operation. Even Panama, which does not participate in the CACM, decided to reduce its tariff to 40 per cent (ceiling) with a floor even lower (2.5 per cent) than that adopted by the other states. Before this reduction Panama had a tariff higher than 100 per cent (ECLAC 1995).

According to the programme of tariff reduction adopted by the Presidents in July 1991 in San Salvador, it was expected that by the year 2000, there would be a CET binding for all states. The ceiling would be 5 and 15 per cent for intermediate and final goods and '0' for capital goods and raw materials. The evidence is that despite setbacks in the process of adjustment, the governments were achieving this objective (SIECA 1999). El Salvador, Guatemala and Costa Rica (in this order) were the countries which showed more progress in their programmes of tariff reduction in the 1990s. Nicaragua and Honduras, whose status as less developed states was recognised by the other governments under the Guatemalan Protocol,[22] enjoyed greater flexibility and longer periods for adjusting their tariffs. They were also allowed to impose Temporal Protection Tariffs (TPT) on imports, including those from the region.

On the basis of this prerogative, in 1996, Nicaragua imposed a TPT on more than 400 goods, but 'it was forced, especially by El Salvador, to back down because the government was too abusive in implementing it'.[23] The existence of such measures together with other irregular practices followed by the states [24] gave rise to the accusation that 'the CET agreed in 1991 was not really working as a common and co-ordinated policy' (Stevens 1997, 19). In other words, the region did not really have a CET. The argument was that economic convergence was not fully established in the region which undermined the prospect for co-operation.

SALVADORIAN LEADERSHIP ON TARIFFS REFORM

In the 1980s Costa Rica was the state which pushed ahead in the region with tariff reductions as part of its programme of structural adjustment. By 1990 its external tariff had a ceiling between 40 and 50 per cent for finished goods and a floor of 5 per cent for raw materials (Willmore and Máttar 1993). Surcharges on the importation of capital and finished goods were eliminated in the period 1986–1990 (COMEX 1991). Nonetheless, El Salvador was catching up with Costa Rica and quickly became more assertive in its process of economic reform. By 1989 El Salvador was placing itself at the forefront in the region on the issue of tariffs reform.

El Salvador, governed by the right-wing ARENA[25] since 1989, has implemented broad-ranging economic reforms. Under the Development Plan of June 1990, the government of President Alfredo Cristiani abolished price controls, dissolved the state's monopoly on coffee, sugar, banking, and foreign trade. It also extinguished non-tariff barriers to imports and carried out a drastic reduction in the external tariff. With the reform, the external tariff was placed at 5 and 20 per cent for intermediate and final goods and '0' for raw materials and capital goods.

The tariffs reform involved both reducing the level of protection and the level of dispersion ingrained in the tariffs structure. Contrary to the other states of the region, El Salvador was less dependent on customs duties and more on other kinds of internal taxation and revenues such as tax on profits. Moreover, it has the lowest interest rate in the region, and throughout the decade of the 1990s, El Salvador received more than $1.5 billion per year in remittances from Salvadorians living in the United States.[26] Therefore, 'the tariffs policy followed by the governments since the beginning of the decade did not represent an unbearable burden for the state in terms of loss of revenues. This gave El Salvador a larger stand on tariff reform over the other states'.[27]

Being the state with the largest stake in the CACM, with over 40 per cent of its exports going to the region, as well as the least dependent on import duties, El Salvador has pressed the other governments to accelerate the programme of trade liberalisation within the region. In 1995 the government of Armando Calderón Sol proposed the acceleration of the programme of reform of the Central American External Tariff mirrored in the country's own advanced tariffs programme. The proposal consisted of lowering the CET in 1995 to 1 and 5 per cent for raw materials and capital goods and to 15 and 20 per cent for final goods with annual reductions since 1996 by 3 per cent until it reached '0'. By 1999, according to the Salvadorian government, 'the programme of tariffs reduction should be completed with a ceiling of 5 and 15 per cent and a floor of '0' per cent'.[28]

Although reluctantly, the other states sought to accommodate their positions to the swift Salvadorian move on tariff reform. The Salvadorian programme demanded strong bargaining between the governments because of the distributional side of tariff reduction. Domestic as well as regional interest groups, which felt they would become losers out of tariff reduction, opposed the move. Indeed, the industrialists of the region grouped in FECAICA (Central American Federation of Industrialists) objected to the Salvadorian initiative. The reaction from some governments of the region, especially, Costa Rica, Honduras and Nicaragua, was also against further reducing the CET. But the credibility of the Salvadorian action, in other word, the ability of El Salvador to go it alone forced the other governments to back down in favour of asymmetrical bargaining and co-operation.

According to Moravcsik (1993a, 487), 'only where governments can collectively overcome such opposition is co-operation possible'. Unilateral reductions are undesirable because the benefits would accrue unevenly in favour of the country which instigates the process of reform. Furthermore, given the increasing integration of the economies in the 1990s, a unilateral reduction would seriously undermine economic integration. In addition, contraband would become a common problem sparked off by the lack of policy co-ordination, leaving most states at serious disadvantage. The intergovernmental bargaining, therefore, centred on the need to assume the Salvadorian programme of tariff reform, with slight modifications, within a context of policy co-ordination. The Salvadorian tariff policy, thus, was taken as a regional programme. In exchange for this regionalisation, which involved constraints for El Salvador, the other governments committed themselves to allow a greater liberalisation of the market, therefore dismantling barriers to intra-regional trade.

The Salvadorian proposal on tariffs reduction was, in effect, used by the governments as an opportunity for collusion in order to overcome the opposition from regional and domestic corporate interests. On March 30, 1995 a compromise was reached under which the Central American Tariff Council adopted the Salvadorian proposal. Earlier in February, at a meeting held in Guatemala, the Ministers of Economics had agreed that 'the Salvadoran proposal was valid and had to be adopted' (La República 1995). The distributional side of tariffs reduction was, therefore, largely settled in favour of the Salvadorian interests.

The reactions against the Salvadorian proposal on tariff reduction (from private interests and governments) showed that the pressures against liberalisation in the region were still strong, despite the doctrine of open regionalism shared by governments and most business groups. The pressure against full liberalisation has been strong and became stronger as the governments consolidated their trade negotiations with non-CACM states, such Mexico, Chile and the United States under CAFTA.

THE CACM AS A REGIME FOR INDUSTRIAL TRADE

Tariff reduction in the CACM has traditionally concentrated on the industrial sector. From the 1980s there was a consistent move towards reducing the CET as can be seen in Table 7.2. Attempts in the 1990s at free trade at all levels proved difficult to sustain because of the heterogeneity of the economic structures of the region as well as governments' preferences.

Intra-regional trade in industrial goods enjoys free trade within the region. But the same does not apply in other sectors. Although there has been a considerable degree of liberalisation in other sectors, they have not been fully integrated into the free-trade regime within the CACM. Agriculture, services and foreign investment are the cases. Despite liberalisation and its formal integration within the CACM, the agriculture sector remains highly protected (ECLAC 1995, 11). The Third Protocol to the Central American Agreement on Trade and Tariff allows the governments to impose a tariff higher than 100 per cent on agricultural products (SIECA 1999). This section analyses the difficulties faced by the states of the region to extend the regime of free trade to sectors other than the industrial one, particularly the service and agriculture sectors.

Table 7.2 Central America: Level of Tariff Protection in the Industrial Sector (percentage of nominal protection)

	1972		*1987*		*1994*	
	Ceiling	*floor*	*Ceiling*	*Floor*	*Ceiling*	*Floor*
Costa Rica	214	-	100	-	20	5
El Salvador	221	-	130	-	20	5
Guatemala	246	-	150	-	20	5
Honduras a/	226	-	90	-	20	5
Nicaragua a/	209	-	100	-	15	5
Panama	-	-	247	-	40	2.5

Source: ECLAC (Economic Commission for Latin America and the Caribbean) (1995, 19).
a/ In 1994, Honduras had surcharges between 5 and 10 per cent, and Nicaragua 18 per cent.

LIBERALISATION IN THE SERVICE SECTOR

In services there is no integration. Even if the CACM includes regulations on services these are not in operation (Canales-Kriljenko et al 2004). Traditionally developing countries have been reluctant to open their service sector because of national pride, groups' interests, or developmental and security concerns. Nonetheless, they have failed to coalesce in order to prevent the inclusion of services in international negotiations such as in the GATT or the World Trade Organisation (McDowell 1994).

Services though are very important for economic development and for the consolidation of well-functioning national and regional economies. It is said that 'the price and quality of services influence cost and productivity of all other sectors in an economy including manufacturing and agriculture' (USCSI 2002, 1). This calls for transparency and competitiveness in services. Services are important components of the economic activity in Central America. According to the World Bank, they contribute between 44 per cent and 64 per cent of the GNP (cited in USCSI 2002, 1).[29]

In Central America the countries have opened their service sectors as part of the efforts at integration within the GATT/WTO and CAFTA with the US, but not that much under the CACM. The external openness has been mushrooming on a national basis without proper regional or international agreement on market access and rules of national treatment and transparency (Canales-Kriljenko et al 2004). This has given rise to a complex universe of commitments and dispersion, which in turn has handicapped regional negotiations and economic efficiency. Because of the stringent rules on nationality, for instance, in the financial sector, 'not just international competitors, but even other Central American financial entities are barred access' (Mazzei, 1998, 5). El Salvador, for instance, which is the more opened economy of the region, has consolidated the openness of its service sector, particularly in such areas as banking and telecommunications. This consolidation has taken place at the level of the World Trade Organisation, but not at the regional level.

The service sector has been included in free trade negotiations with Mexico, the US and other extra-regional partners. This has increased divergence within the region because regionally, until very recently, there was no instrument regulating or integrating services into the regime of free trade. It was not until March 24, 2002; that the governments adopted a regional convention on investment and trade for services, the implementation of which will be undoubtedly difficult given the level of dispersion and lack of transparency in the service sectors across the region. This ranges from huge differences in national conditions about capital share, to protectionism on employment and wages in favour of nationals.

In Costa Rica there is a state monopoly on telecommunications, electricity and insurance, whereas in El Salvador and Guatemala these sectors have been largely privatised and open to foreign investors. Honduras and Nicaragua impose significant restrictions including a 60 per cent capital share by nationals in the former, whereas El Salvador extends national treatment to foreign bidders and investors.

Regarding employment and wages some countries impose strong conditions. In Guatemala and Honduras 90 per cent of jobs and 85 per cent of wages have to go to nationals, 75 per cent in Nicaragua. In Costa Rica foreign professionals face strong limitations and it is the only country in the region where foreign banks are not allowed to have branches, although they can open new commercial banks using the names of their home firms, e.g. Banco Cuscatlán which is a Salvadorian firm. But strong financial restrictions apply to them (USCSI 2002; Canales-Kriljenko et al 2004).

Thus, the idea of the regional convention alluded to above is not only to set out clear rules within the region, but also 'to produce a regional agreement in order to extend preferences first to the states of the region before concessions are made to non-CACM members'.[30] An embryonic integration of services exists in the financial sector, particularly within the North Triangle, which basically responds to the interest of Salvadorian and Guatemalan banks in expanding their activities region-wide.

El Salvador and Guatemala are the most advanced in the region in terms of openness of the financial sectors, and services in general, because it serves their interests. In these two states the interests of powerful financial groups and leaders of the parties in government are intertwined. In Costa Rica there has been a considerable degree of openness in the service sector, but the move is slow because some sectors such as banking, insurance and telecommunications remain under state control and there is no consensus to privatise them. As a result, the government has prioritised openness in the way of concessions to foreign bidders as an alternative to privatisation. The strong social opposition to CAFTA in Costa Rica is linked to this preference for national control of services.

The process of integration, therefore, rests unevenly, on the transaction of industrial goods for which a free-trade regime exists, and on infrastructure development, which is required for the expansion of intra-regional trade. Most instruments adopted during the 1990s have concentrated on the promotion of intra-regional trade in industrial goods. The process of trade liberalisation within the CACM (services excluded), as opposed to trade with the rest of the world, has, however, nearly been completed. According to SIECA by 1999 only four products faced trade restrictions within the region (coffee, sugar, wheat flour, petroleum and derivatives), while the rest which encompasses a range of about 8,000 products enjoyed free trade.

This comprehensive inward liberalisation largely accounts for the considerable increase in intra-regional exports during the 1990s and the first half of the decade of 2000, as seen in Table 5.1 (in chapter 5).

Foreign investment has also increased in line with the economic openness of the region, but there is no common legislation on this subject.

The governments have lifted most of the restriction to FDI, but they have done so on a very competitive national basis. FDI follows the traditional pattern, concentrating on the states which offer the best economic and political prospects. In 1998, according to ECLAC, Costa Rica and Panama took up more than 70 per cent of inward investment accruing to the region (La Nación 1998). This situation has shown a slight modification during the first decade of the twenty-first century, according to ECLAC. However, by 2004 Costa Rica was still far ahead with 29 per cent ($585 million) of inward investment, followed by El Salvador with 19 per cent ($389 million) [31] of the total of $2.022 billion received by the sub-region in that year (Leal C 2005).

THE CASE OF AGRICULTURE AND SENSITIVE PRODUCTS.

Substantial progress has been made in the region in removing obstacles to intra-regional trade, especially in industrial goods. Most non-tariff barriers such as import licences, quotas and other administrative obstacles have been either eliminated or transformed into tariffs, which is in line with the obligations assumed by the governments before the WTO (Lizano 1994, 4). Bottlenecks still exist, however, in trade of agriculture and animals products, including poultry, eggs, milk, cheese, bacon, onions, potatoes, etc.

Despite the integration of agriculture into the regime of free trade within the CACM since July 1991, intra-regional trade in agriculture remains subjected to mounting obstacles. These range from non-tariff obstacles (administrative procedures, quotas, inefficient customs facilities and inadequate road systems), to disagreement on rules of origin, giving rise to accusations of unfair trade practices among the states. The main reason for lack of integration of trade in agriculture is the lack of convergence of the economies in this sector as well as protectionist pressures from domestic producers.

Lack of convergence, particularly, has deepened as a result of the external negotiations to integrate the states into the world economy. According to Amparo Pacheco[32] by the end of the 1990s about 10 per cent of the tariffs applied by the states in their intra-regional trade had not been harmonised. By March 2005, according to the Costa Rican newspaper la Nación, 96 per cent of the tariff universe was harmonised which covered about 6000 goods which benefit from free trade, leaving 4 per cent still pending harmonisation (Leitón 2005). The remainder covers 'sensitive products', particularly agriculture and animal products where the governments are allowed to impose higher import restrictions. Because of their sensitivity the Ministers in charge of integration agreed in June 1997 to postpone the inclusion of these items into the harmonised tariff until the year 2005 (Mazzei 1998).

It has been difficult to eliminate this divergence completely because it is ingrained in the different levels of openness unilaterally negotiated by the governments under the programmes of structural adjustment and the accession of the states to the GATT/WT0. Just to mention one example, Honduras negotiated in the WTO a 35 per cent tariff for milk derivatives whereas Costa Rica negotiated a 65 per cent. Opposition to lower protectionism in Costa Rica is so intense that the government has encouraged the private sector to enter direct negotiations with its regional counterparts in order to avert discrimination in the Central American markets (Leitón 2005).

In the face of crisis, the governments are allowed, under the rules of the GATT/WTO, to apply safeguards to protect 'sensitive products and sectors'. This, however, has become a permanent rather than an occasional practice owing to the deep crisis which the agricultural sector has suffered since the 1980s, and because of pressures from interest groups, especially small industrialists and farmers. The main divergence is between Costa Rica and the other states. This is in part because Costa Rica does not receive the preferential treatment that the countries of the North Triangle extend to themselves. Therefore, Costa Rican goods have suffered discrimination in the other states. This moved Costa Rica to press the other governments to agree on the adoption of an efficient system of resolving trade disputes in order to protect its trade interests in the region. The lack of such a system represented a major weakness of Central American integration.

Striking a workable compromise on trade disputes is a necessity for the programme of integration to succeed, and for the programme of tariff reform within the region to be completed as programmed. This would allow the governments to isolate the discussion of technical matters such as trade regulations from the intensity of political ridden disputes which have a high potential to disrupt integration. A working compromise on external negotiations is also required. The fact that the governments only negotiate as a bloc the generalities of trade accords, but not the rules of access to the markets, represents a long-term problem for integration and for the building of the regional bloc. It may prove difficult in a single treaty, to harmonise the diversity that exists over the issue of access to the markets where the negotiations would involve not only the interests of the Central American states, but also those of third parties. Underlying this disjointed way of proceeding in the external negotiations is the recognition that there is divergence in the productive as well as tariff structures of the states, particularly in agriculture as well as the service sectors. But the fragmented way in which negotiations with external partners are conducted deepens national divergences in the region.

The impact of national preferences, economic heterogeneity, especially between Costa Rica and the other states, and the emergence of high politics differences between some states, particularly by the end of 1999, seriously affected integration and the programme of tariff reduction. As early as 1997, these differences diverted the region from the goals of both consolidating the free trade regime within the CACM, and having a CET by the year 2000. As a result, the latter goal was postponed to the year 2005. Nonetheless, overcoming many of these differences, progressing in establishing the customs union and the conclusion of CAFTA negotiations with the US in 2004 allowed for the presentation of a positive outlook for integration since 2005.

CONCLUDING REMARKS

It seems clear that in terms of consolidating the CACM as a free trade regime the region has made considerable progress. Rules designed to ease the free movement of goods within the region have been adopted. From 1990 the governments began to co-ordinate their programmes of tariff reform with the purpose not only of creating a freer CACM, but also of harmonising their tariff structures under a common external tariff, which was expected to be in place by the year 2000.

The progress in the processes of liberalisation and integration in the region has been the result of bargaining between the CA-4 states and Costa Rica. The Guatemalan Protocol came out as a compromise between the governments, allowing the CA-4 states to carry out their commitment to full integration, while at the same time permitting Costa Rica to accelerate its external integration through bilateral negotiations with non-CACM states. The GP, thus, rescued the process of integration by accommodating the interests of the states. The lowest-common-denominator, however, has prevented integration from becoming far-reaching. Although the free-trade regime within the CACM prevails for the transaction of industrial goods, other sectors and goods have faced difficulties. In some important sectors integration is still lacking. In many cases liberalisation has been negotiated first at the level of the WTO, but it is still lacking or progresses slowly at the level of the CACM.

The external liberalisation negotiated by the governments, mostly unilaterally under the national programmes of economic reforms and the WTO, has constrained the notion of Central American preference. This preference, perhaps more normative than real, is recognised in most regional arrangements such as the General Treaty of Economic Integration and Guatemalan Protocol. If the governments do not tackle the divergence that still exists between them in different areas (e.g. tariffs, rules of origin, safeguards, trade disputes, etc) there is the danger, as ECLAC warned in 1995, that the external liberalisation could work against integration within the CACM (ECLAC 1995, 18).

Likewise, the resurgence of high politics conflicts, especially border conflicts, suggests the need for working not only on a mechanism to resolve trade differences but also political conflicts and border disputes. Strengthening the Central American Court of Justice, for instance, with the support of all the states would be a step forward in the process of consolidating integration. These sorts of arrangements are required if the region is to evolve into a form of 'security community' based on the observance of the rule of law as the basis to resolve peacefully regional conflicts and sustain integration.

8 Concluding Chapter

As has been argued throughout this book, it seems quite clear that traditional integration theories do not provide an adequate account of current integration in Central America, and of regionalism, in general. They over emphasise the plurality of interests, attitudinal aspects, modernisation imperatives, and structural conditions as variables explaining integration. The overriding influence of pluralism and modernisation in industrialised societies led scholars, working within the framework of functional theories, to ignore or neglect the central role of politics and the resilience of the state in international relations.

These theories assumed that the state as a centre of authority and political allegiance had become obsolete. They view regional integration as the new international governance of the future through which societal and political actors could be persuaded to transfer their allegiance to a supranational authority which would provide for their welfare and security. Central to this view of integration was the idea that by transferring political allegiance to a supranational authority, individuals would be free from the vagaries of the social and economic life which is largely circumscribed by the territorial state. Thus, with integration societies would be transformed into security communities, free from the anarchical nature of the international system and therefore, free from war. Gains in welfare would be the outcome of economic progress, integration and democracy. Modern governments could not avoid the logic of incrementalism for to do so would conspire against their national interests.

Theories from the power politics and structural perspectives, on the other hand, ignore the domestic political economy of the states, the importance of agency and the intensity of preferences, focusing instead on interstates rivalries, hegemony, international anarchy and systemic forces as variables accounting for integration and disintegration.

Intergovernmentalism is a reaction to these perspectives on integration. For intergovernmentalism (far from being mechanistic, power- and structure- laden or incremental) integration largely relies on the rational choice and preferences of national governments and on the level of convergence of their policies. Integration is based on the intensity of preferences and on asymmetrical interstate bargaining, through which leading governments seek to resolve domestic and regional distributional conflicts. To a certain extent, these conflicts arise as a result of negative policy externalities brought about both by national measures or policies adopted by the states and by virtue of their economic and strategic interdependence. States, especially the larger ones, pursue integration in search of political and economic gains. Their support for integration is conditional on the level of utility they can derive from it. As part of this interstate bargaining, side-payments are granted to smaller states, in order to gain their acquiescence, while a reluctant state may face the threat of exclusion as a way of inducing its co-operation with the strategy of integration preferred by the larger states.

Although a level of plurality in the domestic politics of the states is assumed to exist, especially in Europe, the competing interests and pressures from domestic groups do not necessarily trap the governments. Intergovernmentalism asserts that the governments can create substantial levels of autonomy through negotiation and manipulation of decisional processes.

This book has pursued two objectives: to introduce the intergovernmentalist analysis into the study of Central American integration, and to look at the process of reform of the Central American Common Market in the 1990s and onwards. Evidence shows that, to a great degree, integration in Central America follows the pattern of negotiation and rationality set out in the intergovernmentalist framework. Intergovernmentalism asserts the centrality of the state and governments' preferences as the indispensable process shaping integration in Central America. The states are assumed to act under constraints, both domestic and external, but they largely define the scope and character of integration in accordance with their national interests.

In the liberal intergovernmentalist view developed by Moravcsik, domestic constraints spring from the demands of interest groups which want to influence the governments' policies, either in favour or against the opening of the markets. The governments then aggregate these demands in their economic foreign policies through which they seek to take advantage of the 'incentives generated by patterns of international economic interdependence' (Moravcsik 1998, 6). The external constraints, on the other hand, stem from the strategic environment which refers to the strategic interactions of the states in which patterns of interdependence constrain their unilateral choices, setting the context for co-operation.

Interdependence leads governments to co-operate not only because of the negative externalities caused by their unilateral actions, but also because the achievement of their domestic goals is dependent on the willingness of other states to co-operate. This mutual dependence of the states for the achievement of their goals is termed strategic interdependence (Schelling 1960; Milner 1993). In regions, such as Central America, where economic interdependence is not as strong as in the EU, strategic interdependence provides a strong rationale for states' co-operation and for shaping regional integration.

Moravcsik (1998) has argued that a theory of integration should be actor-oriented, highlighting the constraints faced by rational actors rather than the unintended dynamics of broader structural processes. Structural factors constrain states' behaviour, but do not determine it (Ikenberry 1991, 157). The central weakness of neo-functionalist analyses of integration was that they ignored what Moravcsik (1998, 15) terms 'exogenous constraints (state economic interests, political constraints, and delegation)'.

As was mentioned at the beginning of this book, with some modifications intergovernmentalism applies to Central American integration. The two main limitations of the theory when applied to Central America are, first, the lower importance of domestic politics and regional interdependence in the process of preference formation, and second, the greater importance of the structural environment and structural constraints.

Firstly, in Central America, domestic politics and regional interdependence do not seem to play a role as central as in Europe in the process of preferences formation. Because of underdevelopment and external dependence, the role of economic and social actors is weak. This reinforces the overriding role of the state in social and economic development. States' preferences reflect basically the interests of the political elite (the one in power) and the constraints this elite faces as a result of interactions with the strategic environment, which is not limited to states' interactions within the region.

As far as the second is concerned, because of the dependent and underdeveloped condition of the Central American economies, the structural environment and defensive motivations played a greater role than in Europe in the process of preference formation. Together with their mutual relations the strategic interactions of the states also involve the constraints stemming from the structural environment whereby rules, interests and pressures from the global political economy restrict the options of the governments, and therefore, have an impact in the process of preference formation. Hence, when the governments began the process of integration in the 1950s, they did so not only as a result of a rational decision to promote the industrial development and strengthening intra-regional trade and co-operation. They did so as well because they wanted to use integration as a cushion against external shocks, particularly the negative effect of the fall of the prices of their traditional exports. Thus, even though the governments began the process of integration to fulfil some domestically defined objectives and interests, they also worried about pressures stemming from the international political economy. Particularly, they took into account, as they still do, the willingness or unwillingness of the US government and other external actors to co-operate with their efforts at economic development and regional integration.

Thus, while in Europe integration may be grounded on the rational choice of governments influenced essentially by domestic constraints and regional interdependence as Moravcsik argues, in Central America, the structural environment conditions the process of states' preferences. For this reason, intergovernmentalism cannot automatically be transposed to Central America. An adaptation of the theory, in line with the ideas presented in chapter one, is required in order to account for the impact of the structural environment in shaping states' preferences. In other words, the understanding of the strategic environment in which bargaining and intergovernmental relations occur needs to take into account the structural environment in which the Central American states find themselves. The strategic interactions of the region need to include the impact of the structural change, especially the shift in terms of power relations following the end of the Cold War and technological developments, which limit states' behaviour. For instance, since the 1990s the governments could not ignore their obligations under the World Trade Organisation. Neither could they ignore US policy on hemispherical integration, pressures stemming from the rise of China in world trade which challenges Central American exports in the US and other international markets, nor even the greater bargaining power of multinational investors and their demand for macroeconomic and financial stability.

The unequal distribution of power in the international economy implies that small states cannot ignore the interests of dominant actors and come to terms with the consequences of their actions (Wallerstein, 1979; Gilpin 1981). In the current globalised world the notion of dominant actors is no longer restricted to larger states. It also includes large multinational businesses, trading blocs such as the EU or NAFTA, giving rise to new sources of asymmetries in the relationship between actors, both governmental and non governmental ones (Stopford and Strange 1991).

These kinds of factors limited the ability of the governments to act purposively both in terms of shaping integration and in their response to external changes. States' preferences, particularly in developing areas, would therefore reflect not only what the governments want to achieve domestically or regionally, but also the barriers that the structural environment imposes on them which could either encourage or discourage cooperation. These facts, to some extent, modify intergovernmentalism as a theory of integration based on states' power and preferences. Although the state remains the central force determining policy action, as Gilpin (2001, 23) argues, 'economic and technological forces also shape the policies and interests of individual states and the political relations among states, and the market is indeed a potent force in the determination of economic and political affairs'.

Therefore, the state-centric or agency-oriented view of integration portrayed by intergovernmentalism does not fully explain Central American and other Latin American processes of integration. This calls for a rethinking of the theory. Although the core tenets of intergovernmentalism can be identified in Central America, integration also reveals the impact of external and structural factors. States' preferences are formed within an environment in which the broader contours of their political economy are determined elsewhere. Therefore, the rational choice of the states incorporates their reactions and adaptation to broader processes taking place in the global political economy.

Thus, the experience in Central America tells us that for intergovernmentalism to account for integration in developing countries, the reach of the strategic environment needs to be expanded with the incorporation of the notion of the structural environment. This would allow for a more adequate account of the role and impact of external and structural factors in the process of preference formation. But the fact that structural factors influence state's preferences formation in Central America does not invalidate Moravcsik's contention that integration needs to be actor-oriented. Intergovernmentalism still offers a useful way of analysing the processes of political interactions in the region and allows making predictions about the extent and limits of integration.

Consequently, integration still takes the form of negotiated policy co-ordination or co-operation as Moravcsik proposes where sovereignty would be preserved or compromised depending on the interests of the states. The level of credible commitment granted to integration, which could involve pooling or delegating sovereignty, is determined by the intensity of governments' preferences, the desire to ensure compliance with regional arrangements and perceptions of the importance of the future. Integration does not progress incrementally. It does so through hard interstate bargains where states can veto proposals, withhold financial support to states and institutions and form coalitions to elicit pressure on a recalcitrant state. Integration is, therefore, guided by the logic of diversity and the lowest common denominator. The hard interstate bargaining around the Guatemalan Protocol clearly reflects this logic of proceeding with integration in Central America.

Thus, the process of preference formation largely reflects the economic and political interests of the governments constrained by the structural environment. Therefore, as well as focusing on domestic determinants, intergovernmentalism needs to take into account defensive motivations in order to account for the process of preference formation in Central America or in Latin America in general. Consequently, the liberal strand of intergovernmentalism developed by Moravcsik, which emphasises political economy determinants for integration does not fully apply to the region. Even when the governments face pressure from domestic interest groups such as industrialists, in most cases they do not seem to be constrained by these pressures. In the face of a weak state-society relationship, the state's elite in Central America enjoys a greater level of autonomy from domestic politics than its counterparts in the European Union.

In addition, because of the strong external dependence, the Central American states face strong pressures to embrace concerted actions, particularly in relation to other strategic regional partners and trading blocs. Because of these constraints, the need to secure agreement seems to deter governments from vetoing decisions that they do not like or which affect their interests. Instead the compromise of the region tends to favour deflecting differences by allowing the states to deviate from regional policies through '*concerted defection*' [1] as a way of re-balancing distributional conflicts.

Concerted defection differs from other kinds, such as voluntary and involuntary defection, in that there is a previous agreement, which allows discrimination and deviation from agreed policies. In other words, concerted defection takes place within policy-co-ordination. The other forms respond more to behaviours stemming from the anarchical nature of the international system, dictated by the primacy of competition and survival such as cheating or the incapacity of a government to comply with an agreement because of domestic limitations (see Putnam 1988). The aim of concerted defection is to soften the effect of the asymmetrical distribution of benefits caused by integration. In practice this works as side-payments granted by the most advanced states to secure the participation and co-operation of the less developed in the CACM. An example of this was permitting Nicaraguan in 1996 to impose temporal protection tariffs to imports from the region.

Thus, although interdependence may be a force pressing for integration, regional integration has less to do with managing interdependence, more to do with creating conditions for convergence and co-operation which is central for the consolidation of the free trade regime. Intergovernmentalism, therefore, provides a comprehensive explanation of peace and integration in Central America. Both governments' interests and structural factors combine to explain the process of preference formation in the region.

With the understanding that certain aspects (e.g., low domestic and regional demands and strong pressures from the structural environment) may, to a certain degree, limit the intergovernmentalist framework, the theory still offers a comprehensive way of viewing integration in Central America. The intergovernmentalist's argument regarding the centrality of governments in the process of European integration is also relevant in Central America. The centrality of the state is paramount in the region. The interstate bargaining backed with the threat of exclusion and concerns about transferring sovereignty to institutions and transnational forces have placed considerable barriers to integration in the region. So have changes of government. When a coalition of interests which does not favour integration takes power in some countries of the region, integration tends to stagnate or decrease. In these four aspects there is not a mayor difference between Central America, Europe or Mercosur in South America (Kaltenthaler and Mora 2000; Bouzas and Soltz 2000; Malamud 2001).

Integration in Central America has largely reflected governments' preferences and coalitions' power politics through which likeminded states have sought to advance their interests, encouraging and forcing the adaptation of other states' policies. The main interest of the governments has been to legitimate their tenure of power and the preservation of the status quo. Integration has served these causes by providing markets and additional resources, which the governments have used to promote the industrial development, economic modernisation and the internationalisation of the economies. Intergovernmentalist assertions can be verified at least in three concrete episodes of the Central American integration. These are: the process leading to the formation of the CACM in the 1950s, the Esquipulas peace process of 1986–1990; and the process of reform and re-launch of integration in the 1990s, including the process of tariffs reform. These processes clearly reveal the kind of interactions between governments highlighted by intergovernmentalism.

As in Europe, it is the intensity of preferences, policy convergence, and asymmetrical bargaining that have determined outcomes in the interstate negotiations. A central reason why Guatemala joined El Salvador and Honduras under the Tripartite treaty of February 1960 was the fact that the Salvadorian-Honduras alliance threatened Guatemalan geopolitical and economic interests. This forced Guatemala to abandon its bid for leadership in the region, striking instead a compromise with El Salvador.

A secondary reason underlying the Guatemalan search for a compromise with El Salvador and Honduras was the fact that Guatemala shared the integration ideology. This made its policy and preferences convergent with the interests of the Salvadorian and Honduran governments. The integration of Guatemala with El Salvador and Honduras forced Nicaragua to follow suit. But neither Guatemala nor Nicaragua surrendered to the Salvadorian strategy of integration. Instead, their support for integration was based on the convergence of their preferences and asymmetric bargaining involving the threat of exclusion and their strategic need for co-operation. These allowed the governments to turn the Tripartite agreement into the framework for a general agreement of integration which led to the formation of the Central American Common Market.

The threat of exclusion from the funds of the Central American Bank of Economic Integration (CABEI) was used against Costa Rica in order to get its acquiescence with integration. So was US pressure to exclude Costa Rica from the US aid granted to the region in support for integration. But Costa Rica only joined to the General Treaty of integration following a change of government. The conservative government of Mario Echandi refused to join to the CACM. But, his successor from the National Liberation Party, President Francisco Orlich, did not hesitate in integrating the country to the region in 1962. In doing so he was following the ideology of its party which fully supported regional integration. But he was also responding to the need to avoid the isolation of Costa Rica from the region.

The above arguments give credibility to Moravcsik's contentions. First is his idea that if the threat of exclusion substantially undermines the vital interests of reluctant states, integration could become far-reaching. In other words, it could go beyond the logic of the lowest common denominator.

Second is the idea that governments' preferences are not necessarily connected to relative power. Therefore, regardless of relative power, a change of government can have an impact on integration (Moravcsik 1991). In the case of Costa Rica in 1962, the fact that the new government shared the integration ideology (convergence) served the cause of integration. As a result of a change in preferences, Costa Rica was brought into conformity with the growing policy convergence of the region, which largely reflected the interests of the large states.

The role of institutions in this process has been limited and very well in line with intergovernmentalist's predictions. Institutions such as ECLAC, SIECA, and the GS-SICA played an important role as catalysts for integration, but they did not determine integration, nor have they proved to be able to deal with distributional conflicts. The logic of the lowest-common denominator, policy convergence and the threat of exclusion have done so. For institutions to succeed in promoting integration, unambiguous political support from leading governments is required. Their success depends on whether they follow the 'path of least resistance', providing bargaining and co-operative solutions to the governments (Moravcsik 1993a; 1998). This was what underlined the helpful mediating role played by ECLAC and SIECA in the launching and development of Central American integration in the 1960s and GS-SICA in the 1990s onwards as mechanisms for intergovernmental co-ordination or international regimes around which states' expectations converge.

ECLAC was able to act as a catalyst for integration in the 1950s and 1960s because it possessed both technical and professional expertise which was helpful to the interests of the states. Its success as catalyst for integration was due to its conformity with the path of least resistance. Its conception of balanced development very much represented the view of predominant states. The same applies to GS-SICA and PARLACEN since the 1990s. The fact that these institutions promote the agenda of integration of the North Triangle states and provide space for interstates bargaining allows them to have some credibility and support from the governments. To the extent that regional institutions operate within the reach of government policies, it is likely that they can influence the decision-making process by reinforcing the interstate bargaining and providing to the governments information, which could ease the attainment and implementation of agreements.

The experience of the 1960s and the 1990s onwards revealed that the sustainability of integration depends highly on the capacity and willingness of governments to nurture it with political commitment. This, in turn, depends, as Moravcsik (1998) argues on patterns of asymmetrical interdependence. This implies that those states and social actors that gain more from integration will be willing to give credible commitment to the process and favour compromises, whereas those who gain the least, or for whom the costs of adaptation are higher, impose conditions and might be less willing to co-operate. This brings in the issue of distributional conflicts and their impact on integration. The traditional view of integration discarded the influence of both distributional conflicts and high politics on the process of integration because it was assumed that the process was self-sustained and incremental as predicted by the logic of the spillover. In addition, regional technocrats were supposed to deal with conflict prevention and conflict management in a scientific manner (Schmitter 1969; Fuentes Morh 1973; Lizano 1979). Great faith was placed on the virtues of planning and on economic rationality. Conflict would be averted through the planning of activities. Furthermore, liberal economics advocates that if decisions were left to rational economic agents, these would find their own solution by seeking their own self-interest.

For intergovernmentalism, distributional conflicts and high politics are central in the analysis of regional integration, and, therefore, need to be dealt with. Conflict and high politics differences can only be resolved politically through a hard interstate bargaining in which predominant governments resort to credible threats to veto proposals, grant or withhold financial side-payments, and form alternative alliances aimed at threatening a reluctant government with exclusion from integration (Moravcsik 1998, 3, 369).

In addition, because of asymmetrical interdependence, distributional conflicts are likely to be resolved in favoured of the larger states. Moravcsik argues that in Europe distributional conflicts between, for instance, strong- and weak-currency countries were resolved in favour of Germany, the strongest state (Moravcsik 1998). The way distributional conflicts are dealt with in Central America is consistent with intergovernmentalism. Examples of this are Honduras' demands to redress the balance of gains from integration in 1970s, tariffs reform, institutional reform and the building of the customs union in the 1990s. The solution to these issues reflected the relative power and the intensity of preferences of the larger states. The preferences of El Salvador have taken precedence in most of these issues. Even the negotiation of CAFTA seems to follow this logic where the Salvadorian and US interests have prevailed over the interests of the other states. This, among other things, explains why El Salvador was the first state to ratify and implement the agreement with the US.

But the rise and solution to distributional conflicts in Central America are not exclusively the result of governments' power, preferences or regional interdependence. External shocks also impact the region, reducing the gains from integration, and therefore, fleshing out conflicts. As Robson (1998, 7) argues, 'the purely static gains from integration, although they may be significant, can be -and often are- dwarfed by the operation of factors of domestic or international origin that have nothing to do with integration'. If crises or an increase in the level of divergence of the economies of the states become obstacles for adopting sound regional economic policies, rational governments will choose self-reliance as a way to tackle the problems.

Intergovernmentalism rightly argues that integration relies on policy convergence and willingness of the governments to co-operate. When convergence does not exist or is broken either by the pressure of external factors or by high politics differences between governments, then, integration subsides. Governments may feel that they are better off following their own course of action. This rationale largely explains the disruption of integration in the 1970s, throughout the 1980s, and at the end of the 1990s.

Policy convergence and the intensity of preferences were also major reasons for enhancing co-operation and integration. This is illustrated by the cases of the Esquipulas Peace process of 1986–1990, SICA, the Guatemalan Protocol in the 1990s, and the progress in establishing the customs union in 2002–2005. These processes were based on the interests of governments which sought to enhance their power and autonomy from domestic and external pressures and to accelerate the internationalisation of the economies of the region. Thus, the inability to prevent Costa Rica from going it alone with a comprehensive peace plan forced Guatemala to strike a bargain in order to present the peace plan as a Costa Rican-Guatemalan initiative. The external support obtained by the peace plan together with a crisis in the US foreign policy towards the region restructured the status quo for the other states of the region, which had no option, but to support the initiative.

The credibility of the Peace Plan forced the governments to rethink their strategic interests in a context of failing US foreign policy. Fearing isolation from the region the governments of El Salvador and Honduras decided to support the peace plan. The Costa Rican plan triggered a negotiating environment where the governments bargained in order to achieve a collective outcome which reflected their interests. The peace plan gave rise to strategic interactions whereby the achievement of the governments' objectives depended on the co-operation of the states. The peace plan allowed the governments to retake the initiative and become the central actors in the process leading to the implementation of an agreement that took the preservation of the sovereignty of the states as the precondition for co-operation. The governments enjoyed veto power, which allowed them to block decisions that endangered their national interests. The Foreign Affairs Secretaries acted as gatekeepers, ensuring that the process would be kept under governmental control. The peace plan, therefore, clearly reflected the logic of the lowest common denominator and the agreement took the form of a compromise where the interests of the states were represented. In other words, it was asymmetrical bargaining rather than a non-reciprocal submission to the Costa Rican-Guatemalan initiative, which explained the success of the peace plan.

Moreover, the process of re-launching integration in early the 1990s was based on intergovernmental bargaining backed by the threat of exclusion. It was the concerted interests and preferences of the states of the North Triangle (El Salvador, Guatemala, Honduras and Nicaragua) for integration and their willingness to go ahead without Costa Rica which forced the latter to bargain in order to avoid being excluded from integration. However, its inability to support the far-reaching integration of its partners did not disable Costa Rica's capacity to negotiate. Rather, it allowed it to strike a deal that reflected its preferences and national interest. This explains why Costa Rica obtained opt-outs, which substantially modified the far-reaching programme of integration favoured by the other states under the Guatemalan Protocol and the Central American Parliament. The logic of the lowest common denominator and diversity prevailed. The result was a compromise, which allows the states of the North Triangle to consolidate their integration while at the same time allowing Costa Rica to deviate from integration and pursue its preferred policy of global integration. Thus, the bargaining process and the lowest common denominator set a limit on the scope of integration. The process either moves at the pace of the slower states (the reluctant ones) or takes the form of *variable geometry* whereby some states (the enthusiastic ones) can move faster than others.

Regional institutions in the 1990s onwards played a limited role in shaping integration because of the unwillingness of some governments to compromise sovereignty. Regional institutions by the end of the 1990s were increasingly facing isolation and marginalisation. Moravcsik's contention (1998, 347) that governments act as political entrepreneurs 'initiating negotiations, mediating compromises, and mobilising domestic support' is strongly corroborated in Central America. The Guatemalan government, for instance, acted as broker to bridge the differences between Costa Rica and the states of the North Triangle in order to compromise under the terms of the Guatemalan Protocol which was adopted in 1993 (SIECA 1993; Morales G 1994). Likewise, in 1991, President Callejas of Honduras acted as broker in the attempt at bringing Costa Rica's support to integration under SICA.

The role of institutions is weak, in part, because the governments of Costa Rica and Guatemala refuse to transfer sovereignty, and because the governments, in general, facing domestic and high politics constraints have refused to discuss integration within regional institutions. Rather than empowering institutions the trend has been to reform them and reduce their competence and privileges. The instruments through which integration is discussed and carried out are the Presidential Summits and the Council of Ministers meetings in which the Presidents and the Ministers of Foreign Affairs have been the central players.

By-passing regional institutions allows the governments to avoid the demands they make for a far-reaching integration and to concentrate on shaping integration in line with their shared interest in inserting the region into the world economy. The problem, though, with emphasising the external integration at the expense of regional building is that it accentuates the weaknesses and divergence of the economies of the states, which in turn undermine the efforts at integration. The emphasis on external integration reflects the impact of the structural environment on Central American states. The increasing international competition for markets, technology and foreign investment and the reliance of the states on this for economic development, presses the governments to conform with the macroeconomic discipline of the neo-liberal consensus which has been shaping economic policy in Latin America since the 1980s (Phillips 2000; Robinson 2003).

Thus, as well as reflecting governments' preferences, integration in Central America and other Latin America regions shows 'defensive motivations'. In this sense, integration is also a government's response to events taking place in the global economy (Grugel, 1995b; Bouzas and Soltz 2000; Gruber 2000). As Gilpin (2001, 11) argues 'as the international economy has become more closely integrated, regional groupings of states have increased their co-operation in order to strengthen their autonomy, improve their bargaining position, and promote other political/economic objectives'. Thus, events, such as the formation of regional trading blocs (NAFTA, FTAA, the European Union) or the end of the Cold War provide limits on, and possibilities for, state action. These events may weaken the centrality of the state in some areas of economic policy, while at the same time strengthening it in others (Evans 1997).

The threat of exclusion from the process of global economic restructuring operates as a structural constraint for the Central American governments, forcing them to emphasise their global integration which in some cases has ran against regional building. In this sense the nation state also operates, as Robinson (2003, 44) argues, as a transnational state whereby the governing elite accepts the constraints set up by the so-called 'Washington consensus' in the sense of neoliberal economic discipline and the overriding influence of global interests.

Thus, intergovernmental co-operation in the 1990s onwards concentrated not only on enhancing regional building under SICA and the Guatemalan Protocol, but also at integrating the economies of the region into the global economy. The governments have done this through the implementation of Programmes of Structural Adjustment and the negotiation of trade accords with states from outside the region. As external openness increases the vulnerability of small economies (see Krasner 1991), the opportunity cost of emphasising internationalisation may consist of endangering the internal stability of the states and neglecting the process of regional building which requires convergence and regional cohesion. To the extent that internationalising the economies has become a central interest of the states and governments to bargain about, it does not seem to be a major conflict with intergovernmentalism. In the intergovernmentalist perspective of co-operation, states' interests and intergovernmental bargaining are central for the building of regional or international structures. The governments have sought compromises in relation to the external openness, as shown with the refurbishing of the CACM and the negotiation of the CET, turning integration into open regionalism. But regional building has been the casualty of this course of action.

The need to accommodate their interests to the changes taking place in the global political economy shapes the governments' options and interests regarding the building of regionalism. Two consequences arise from the pressures for global integration. First, it seems to heighten regional divergences and weakens intergovernmental bargaining on regional building. The pay off of global integration seems to be inversely correlated with levels of political instability and socio-economic polarisation. The result is that while economically the states have made progress, despite growing inequalities, politically they show increasing levels of polarisation and problems of legitimisation of the democratic processes, giving rise to high levels of abstention in national elections.

Thus, while globalisation presses the states to harmonise their economic policies, the pressure for global competition appears to accentuate regional disparities, undermining regional integration. Hence, states that are successful at the global level do not feel strong pressure to support deepening regional integration. According to Mattli, 'economically successful leaders are unlikely to pursue deeper (regional) integration because their expected marginal benefit from integration in terms of improved re-election chances (or simply in terms of retaining political power) is minimal and thus not worth the cost of integration' (Mattli 1999, 52).

This is clearly one reason why Costa Rica has rejected the call from the North Triangle states for a deepening of Central America integration. As Costa Rica is very successful in promoting exports and attracting FDI, its government, is not so sensitive or vulnerable to the pressures and policy preferences of its neighbours. This gives Costa Rica strong bargaining power over its neighbours which allows the government not only to influence the direction that integration should take, but also to deviate considerably from regional agreements.

A second consequence of emphasising the external integration at the expense of regional building relates to the inability of the region to increase its bargaining power vis-à-vis other states and regional blocs. Thus, although the governments have tried to co-ordinate their policies when undertaking international negotiations, they have failed to articulate proper regional responses. The North Triangle negotiates as a sub-regional bloc whereas Costa Rica favours to go it alone in most cases. Even when the governments agree to go together, as in the case of the negotiations with Chile, or CAFTA with the US, they only negotiate as a bloc the generalities of the agreements. On the issue of access to the markets, which involves commitments on tariff reduction, periods of adaptation and the inclusion of sectors likely to cause social disapproval, governments tend to follow their own independent way. Costa Rica, for example, has preferred a unilateral response while the North Triangle has consistently favoured negotiation as a sub-regional bloc.

Regarding CAFTA, this way of proceeding has increased regional divergence because the governments have failed to implement the agreement simultaneously which has brought costs and losses to the countries left behind. Because of these divergences the Central American states do not act purposively in the external negotiations as a regional bloc and are easily marginalised by larger actors. Two examples are worth mentioning to demonstrate this. First, at the beginning of 1999 the summit of the Rio Group [2] took place in Panama. In the Rio Group Central America participates as a regional bloc. In such a summit, the Salvadorian Ambassador to Panama, Mauricio Castro Aragón, represented the region. According to Ambassador Castro Aragón [3] he was completely ignored by the other Rio Group members. He was allowed to attend the summit, but not to speak. The other members of the Rio Group prevented him from effective participation in the summit.

The other example is the EU. A Proposal made by the Central American governments to the EU to negotiate a trade accord was initially rejected by the latter on the grounds that the Central American states have not yet sufficiently liberalised trade relations among themselves. The EU demands the full liberalisation of intra-regional trade in Central America as a precondition for negotiation of a biregional trade accord (SICA 2000). In other words, the EU does not see Central America acting as a regional bloc. Although the UE has finally agreed to embark on negotiations with the region in October 2007, its demand of regional unity on issues such as customs union and market access unveils the fragility of the Central American regional arrangements. Thus, although the governments began pooling sovereignty in some international negotiations, they have not been able to harmonise regional policies and present themselves assertively as a bloc. As a result, the Central American bloc is weak, lacking cohesion. This fact gives credibility to the accusation by Bulmer-Thomas and Douglas Kincaid (2001) that Central America does not constitute a region as such, except in a geographical sense.

Thus, because of the difficulty in getting agreements on some important issues such as institutional building, trade liberalisation and external integration, the restructuring of integration as a flexible arrangement has been a pragmatic necessity. It has been so in order to protect the process of integration from itself by releasing some stringent constraints, which if unabated could force governments to withdraw from integration. As a result, unanimity remains the basis for agreeing regional policies. The governments use it in a flexible manner in order to accommodate internal and external barriers. That is, they tend to use it to keep the decisional process as consensual as possible rather than jeopardising it with the threat of vetoing decisions. This way of proceeding reinforces co-operation to the extent that it forces the governments to adjust their interests more often. They all agree that whatever they do they should favour regional integration. In other words, it is in the interest of all to avoid unnecessarily hurting integration and by all means they should work under the integration agenda and favour the convergence of their policies.

This is the workable compromise that the region has sorted out under SICA and the Guatemalan Protocol. To go beyond that will depend on some of the following conditions. First, on whether the governments manage to increase the level of convergence, trade dependence and competitiveness of their economies within the CACM. Second, if governments facing weak support for integration domestically manage to assert their leadership and change the balance of forces in favour of integration. Third, if the governments manage to avert the impact of high politics conflicts on integration by means of co-operation. Fourth, if negative externalities are created by a group of governments over a recalcitrant one supplemented with a credible threat of exclusion, hence, forcing the latter to co-operate. Fifth, whenever uncertainties and external pressures force the governments to make credible commitments to integration in order to achieve a desirable outcome. One example of this is the unwillingness of external actors such as the US and the EU to negotiate with the states of the region bilaterally, pressing them to harmonise their policies and act as a regional bloc. These conditions predict intense intergovernmental negotiations which are likely to remain the bedrop of Central American integration in the years ahead.

Notes

NOTE TO THE INTRODUCTION

1. I have taken the notion of Regional Security Complex from Buzan (1991) which refers to patterns of amity and enmity in regional security arrangements. (see note 2 in chapter 6). I sometimes use the concept interchangeable with high politics. The concept stresses the interdependence that links states of a subregion in terms of power and security and brings some of the characteristics of international anarchy to the subregional level.

NOTES TO CHAPTER 1

1. The win-set refers to the level of domestic approval enjoyed by intergovernmental agreements (see Putnam 1988, 437). Thus, the larger the level of domestic support for governments' agreements the greater the likelihood that they will be approved or ratified domestically.
2. Negative policy externalities 'occur where the policies of one nation imposes costs on the domestic nationals of another, thereby undermining the goals of the second government's policies' (Moravcsik 1993a, 485).
3. I wish to express my gratitude to Professor Nicola Phillips for suggesting to me to rethink the *strategic environment* in terms of the *structural environment* in order to make intergovernmentalism more applicable to the analysis of Central American integration.
4. These include the creation of NAFTA with Mexico and Canada, and more recently CAFTA with Central America.

NOTES TO CHAPTER 2

1. Author's interview with Rodrigo Carreras, Deputy Foreign Secretary of Costa Rica 1994–1998, San José, Costa Rica, April 1998.
2. Author's interview with Rodrigo Carreras, San José, Costa Rica, April 1998.
3. Author's interview with Luis Guillermo Solis, Chief of Staff at the Costa Rican Foreign Office, San José, Costa Rica, April 1998.
4. Author's interview with Francisco Sorto, Director of Department of Integration at the Salvadorian Ministry of Foreign Affairs, San Salvador, March 1998.
5. Maquila refers to the assembly of parts, particularly in the garment sector (e.g. t-shirts, shirts and trousers, etc), sent from the US for completion and

re-exported duty-free to the US market. In the 1980s and 1990s this kind of industry became the main non-traditional product exported by the Central American states.

6. El Salvador had overtaken Costa Rica by 1999 in terms of the size of its GDP, but the earthquakes that hit the country in 2001 severely affected its economic growth, forcing it to fall back behind Costa Rica, thus remaining as the third largest economy of Central America.
7. This is according to Francisco Peña, Deputy Director of Department of Commercial Policy at the Salvadorian Ministry of Economics, interviewed by the author in March 1998.
8. Author's interview with Francisco Peña, Deputy Director of Commercial Policy, Ministry of Economics, San Salvador, March 1998.
9. Author's interview with José Francisco González, Deputy Director of Department of Integration at the Salvadorian Ministry of Foreign Affairs, San Salvador, March 1998.
10. Author's interview with Francisco Peña, San Salvador, March 1998.
11. A good comparative analysis of the Central American constitutions on the issue of regional integration is presented by Gallard, (1999).
12. Author's interview with Rodrigo Carreras, San José, Costa Rica, April 1998.
13. Author's interview with Patricia Solano, Director of Department of Integration at the Costa Rican Ministry of Foreign Affairs, San José, Costa Rica, April 1998.
14. Author's interview with Luis Guillermo Solís, San José, Costa Rica, April 1998.
15. Author's interview with Amparo Pacheco, Director of Department of Commercial Treaties at the Costa Rican Ministry of Foreign Trade, San José, Costa Rica, December 1999.
16. Author's interview with Amparo Pacheco, San José, Costa Rica, December 1999.
17. Author's interview with Carlos Manuel Echeverría, Chief of Staff at the Costa Rican Ministry of Foreign Affairs 1998–2002 San José, Costa Rica, December 1999.
18. Author's interview with Amparo Pacheco, San José, Costa Rica, December 1999.
19. These are El Salvador, Honduras and Nicaragua which share the ideal of Central American political union.
20. Author's interview with Amparo Pacheco, San José, Costa Rica, December 1999.

NOTES TO CHAPTER 3

1. Rosenau (1967, 22) defines issue-area as 'all the controversies within a society over the way it attempts to maintain or alter its external environment'. Keohane and Nye (1989, 65), define it as 'set of issues, which the governments see as closely interdependent and deal with them collectively'. They emphasise that decision-makers must perceive the issue (problem) as relevant to policy.
2. The Tegucigalpa treaties included the Multilateral Treaty on Free Trade and Central American Economic Integration, the Integration Industries Convention, and the Tariff Equalisation Convention, the last one signed in 1959. These treaties were of limited reach, granting free trade to nearly 300 products, and opened the way for further negotiations in order to include another 200 products (Bulmer-Thomas 1987).

3. The Eisenhower administration had first hand accounts of the contempt in the region for US policy and anti-Americanism in general. Vice-President Nixon experienced it during his trip to South America in the spring of 1958 where he and his wife were maltreated by angry protesters (Nixon 1978).
4. A good description of the US government position on integration is found in Cohen Orantes (1972, 29–31).
5. Author's interview with Francisco Sorto, San Salvador, March 1998.
6. For the concept see note no.1 in the introduction of the book, and note 2 in chapter 6.
7. By high politics risk I intend to mean the likelihood of conflict among the states even if conflict does not necessarily take the form of war. Following a classification presented by Little (1987, 592), this kind of conflict could take the form of 'salient' disputes and 'potential salient' disputes. The first one refers to 'those involving high levels of tension and actual or potential hostilities, while the latter to those where the grievance level is high but where there is little immediate prospect of an outbreak of hostilities.
8. According to ECLAC (1995) a natural partner (socio natural) is that country which concentrates a sizeable proportion of trade of a given country.
9. During the British hegemony, the negotiation of bilateral trade treaties, especially that between Britain and France in 1860, provided the standard for the expansion of trade across Europe which included the reciprocal extension of the most-favoured-nation-clause (see Lipson 1982).
10. In June 1951, the Central American delegations to the four sessions of ECLAC held in Mexico asked for ECLAC technical support in their efforts at economic development and integration. As a result, ECLAC created a regional office in Mexico to deal with the process of integration in Central America. In addition, ECLAC created a Technical Committee for Economic Co-operation of the Central American Isthmus (CEC) made up of the five economics Ministers of the region and some ECLAC Assistants.
11. See note 2 in this chapter.
12. CEC: Central American Committee for Economic Co-operation set up in 1952 with the support of ECLAC in order to foster regional co-operation.
13. President Ydígoras made membership of CABEI conditional to the signing of the General Treaty of Economic Integration. This may have compelled Costa Rica to sign the treaty in order to benefit from the resources from the Bank. Ydígoras had also embargoed some Costa Rican exports and offered the Echandi government to lift the embargo in exchange for Costa Rica's signing of the General Treaty of Economic Integration. This was confirmed to the author by Alfredo Vargas, Mario Echandi's Foreign Affairs Secretary. There was also the fact that the US government was backing the Managua negotiations which was a pressure enough for Costa Rica to go along with the treaty. Finally, there is the fact that the PLN was committed to the programme of integration. Its leaders had strongly criticised Echandi's administration for remaining uncommitted with the Central American negotiations.

NOTES TO CHAPTER 4

1. These figures presented by SIECA (1973) and Rosenthal (1975), based on the book value recorded by the US Department of Commerce may not be accurate. Barry and Preusch (1986), argue that such figures are not accurate because: 1) they report only the book value or historical costs of investment; not the resale value of the business; 2) they excludes figures, which fall below the $500,000 minimum investment standard, ignoring

hundreds of small- business operations or ventures like hotels and ranches owned by US citizens; 3) they include only direct investment, not the assets of foreign affiliates. According to them the assets of US affiliates in Central America (Belize and Panama excluded) in 1977 amounted to $1.8 billion while FDI was only $698 million.

2. In the 1990s, with a sense of shamefulness, sociologists such as Torres Rivas, accepted the importance of FDI and free market integration. This is something, as Torres-Rivas confesses, that in the 1970s would not have been acceptable because they were obsessed with dependency, imperialism and the loss of the national profile (Torres-Rivas 1999).
3. I am following Paul Taylor's notion of entrenched intergovernmentalism. By this he means the intricate nature of the decision making process within the European Community where member states 'imposed limits upon the extent to which the European Parliament and other institutions could acquire new powers' (Taylor 1983, 83).
4. The Modus Operandi in 1970 was intended as a provisional agreement to bring the CACM to a certain level of normality after the disruption caused by the war between Honduras and El Salvador. Honduras suggested it as alternative to a full reinstallation of the CACM, which it fully opposed. The Modus Operandi would temporally regulate the CACM while the whole programme of integration was submitted to a process of restructuring.
5. See note 2 in chapter 3.
6. At the beginning of 1969 Honduras was lagging far behind the other states in the ratification of integration accords. It had seven treaties pending ratification. The reason for delaying ratification was the dissatisfaction of the government because such treaties did not take into account the Honduran concern with balanced development and, therefore, the treaties were regarded as detrimental to Honduran interests (SIECA 1975).
7. For a full account of the crisis of the RII see Ramsett (1969) and Guerra Borges (1979).
8. For a fervent critique of the concept of the size of the market as a condition for economic development and competitiveness see Farley (1992).
9. Castillo asserts that external security, the need to protect the countries from external aggression and foreign domination, has also been a recurrent factor pushing for integration in Central America. 'They saw that union was a key factor to secure the sovereignty of their countries and that only by joining efforts could they hope to build a respected place in the concert of nations' (Castillo 1966, 68).
10. Voice Option basically means the capacity to complain or demand satisfaction which could involve using some power politics manoeuvre such as threatening to veto decisions or establishing linkages in the decision process.
11. These concessions were granted to Honduras through a special protocol signed in September 1966 where it was allowed a list of preferences which included: 1) Tax and raw material import exemptions to new industrial investors for a period ranging from two to ten years. 2) Preferential treatment in CABEI, IDB, and IBRD loans for improving its infrastructure. 3) Special consideration in selecting integration industries. 4) Longer time for adopting the CET. 5) Advantages on fiscal incentives.
12. The co-operation between Honduras and El Salvador was so high during the Villeda Morales government that both states were considering the possibility of union under a single common government (De la Ossa 1999).
13. El Salvador avoided being dragged to a negotiation on Honduras' terms by denouncing the Bogotá Pact of Peaceful Solution of Controversies and

sticking to Art.80 of the Constitution which declares that the Salvadoran territory is irreducible. Honduras, on the other hand, tied itself by clinging to the Carías Castillo doctrine, which inhibited negotiation of the peace with El Salvador without a global and simultaneous solution to the problems (López Contreras 1984).

14. The Modus Operandi was intended in 1970 to be a provisional agreement to bring the CACM to a certain level of normality after the disruption caused by the war between El Salvador and Honduras. Honduras suggested it as an alternative to a full reinstallation of the CACM, which this country fully opposed. The Modus Operandi would temporally regulate the CACM while the whole programme of integration was submitted to a process of restructuring.

NOTES TO CHAPTER 5

1. By security dilemma is understood a systemic pattern where the actions of a state to increase its defense capabilities in order to guarantee its national security automatically make other states feel insecure, forcing them to increase their defense capabilities as well. The result is an arms race, which makes all the states insecure.
2. Jeane Kirkpatrick was a right-wing professor of political sciences who provided intellectual content to the Republican Party foreign policy. During the Reagan administration she became the US Ambassador to the United Nations.
3. The National Bipartisan Commission was appointed by President Reagan in 1983 to carry out a study of the region's developmental crisis and to provide some recommendations on which the US policy towards the region could be guided. Henry Kissinger who in January 1984 published his report on Central America also known as the 'Kissinger Report' chaired the Commission.
4. In January 1983, Colombia, Mexico, Panama, and Venezuela created the Contadora Group. Contadora was presented as a mediating group searching for a Latin American solution to the Central American crisis, taking as basic the domestic roots of the conflicts and the need to protect the independence of the states (Durán 1988). As such, Contadora acted as a countervailing diplomatic force to US policy in the region.
5. Latin America Weekly Report, 30 May 1986.
6. Declaración de Esquipulas, May 25, 1986.
7. According to Miguel D' Escoto (1997, 172), Sandinistas' foreign affairs minister, before the Nicaraguan Revolution there had not been a presidential summit for eight years. A meeting took place after the revolution convened by President Rodrigo Carazo of Costa Rica. Since then there had not been another presidential gathering until 1986.
8. In the first draft elaborated by the Guatemalan vice-President Roberto Carpio Nicolle, PARLACEN was presented as the Central American Parliamentary System, where the Parliament was just one component of a more sophisticated structure with far-reaching responsibilities on integration. All the integration institutions of the region were placed on a subordinated dependence on PARLACEN.
9. Declaración de Esquipulas, May 25, 1986.
10. On November 17, 1983, the Costa Rican government declared Costa Rica a neutral country. Costa Rican neutrality was said to be "perpetual, active, and unarmed". The government committed itself to pursue a foreign policy according to the international obligations of a neutral state. But in 1985 there was evidence that Costa Rican territory was used by the Contras to attack Nicaragua. The Tower report in the US Congress had revealed that infrastructure had

been build by American military engineers to facilitate supply to the Contra by air and land from Costa Rica. In addition, US ambassador to Costa Rica, Lewis Tambs told the Tower Commission investigating the Iran-Contras affair that 'his main mission as ambassador was to open the Southern Front-in Costa Rica- against Nicaragua' (Moreno 1994, P.81).

11. Latin American Monitor, August 1988.
12. This refers to the experience of Honduras as a virtual occupied state. Honduras had been virtually occupied by the US army and the Contras in their attempt to overthrow the Sandinistas.
13. Latin American Weekly Report, 18 April 1986, 6.
14. According to Moreno (1994, 86), Arias refused to meet CIA director William Casey and Lt. Col. Oliver North from the National Security Council in San José who threatened him with cutting US aid to Costa Rica.
15. The Tegucigalpa Group was an alliance formed by Costa Rica, El Salvador and Honduras during a meeting of Foreign Affairs Ministers in Tegucigalpa in October 1984. It was orchestrated by the Reagan administration to undermine Contadora. These states suggested substantial reforms to the Contadora's Act on Peace and Co-operation, which brought the Contadora's process of negotiation into a standstill and finally killed it.
16. Oscar Arias confirmed this to the author during an informal talk in October 1998 on the occasion of a visit he made to London. In 1986 he made an appointment three months in advance to see Mrs. Thatcher. However, Mrs. Thatcher was refusing to see him. It was thanks to the Queen who was sympathetic to his peace initiative that Arias finally managed to see Mrs. Thatcher. Thatcher's original refusal to see Arias had to do with her support of the American policy in Central America.
17. Latin America Weekly Report, 9 July 1987.
18. The reason for not inviting Ortega, according to Arias, was that the conditions in Costa Rica were not favourable for the Sandinistas' leader. The media was lined up with the US policy against Nicaragua and, therefore, Daniel Ortega would have been maltreated by the media and by the Costa Rican rightists (Arias Sánchez 1997).
19. This distinction between negative and positive integration is taken from Pinder (1968, 90). By negative integration Pinder means the removal of discrimination or freer trade, whereas positive integration refers to 'the formation and application of co-ordinated and common policies in order to fulfil economic and welfare objectives'.
20. Latin American Weekly Report, 25 June 1987.
21. Latin American Weekly Report, 12 May 1987.
22. The Bolland amendments were introduced by Congressman Edward P. Bolland with the purpose of preventing the American intervention in Nicaragua (Moreno 1990; Rouquie 1994).
23. Azcona's withdrawal was due to a disagreement with Nicaragua regarding a threat by this state to re-issue a demand pending in the International Court of Justice against Honduras because of its lack of compliance with the demobilisation of the contra. Azcona only got back after mediation by the other Presidents who brokered a deal with Ortega to resolve the difference outside the Court by bilateral negotiations. (La República 1989, 2A).

NOTES TO CHAPTER 6

1. An earlier version of this chapter was published 2003. It has been updated for its inclusion in this book. Reprinted by permission of the Publishers from

'Rebuilding the Central American Bloc in the 1990s: An Intergovernmentalist Approach to Integration', in *Comparative Regional Integration* ed. Finn Laursen (Aldershot.: Ashgate 2003), pp. 31–52.

2. Buzan (1991, 190) defines security complex as 'a group of states whose primary security concerns link together sufficiently closely that their national securities cannot realistically be considered apart from one another '.
3. Latin American Monitor, June 1987.
4. Political co-operation in a regional context, as Laffan (1992, 151) applies it to Europe, 'deals with the ways and means by which the member states harmonise their views on world politics and speak with one voice in the external arena and on major world issues'.
5. Declaración de Puntarenas, December 1990: Preamble; Protocolo de Tegucigalpa, 1992, art.3.
6. Author's interview with Eduardo Ayala Agrimaldi, Deputy Economics Minister of El Salvador, San Salvador, March 1998.
7. For a good discussion of diversity in Central America, see GOMA, R and FONT, J. 1996. Political Change and Socioeconomic Policies in Central America: Patterns of Interactions. *Third World Quarterly* 17 (4), 737–751.
8. Author's interview with Luis Guillermo Solis, San José, Costa Rica, April 1998.
9. Declaración de Antigua, June de 1990, Numerals 24, 26.
10. I am drawing this qualification of integration as association based on a distinction made by DD Raphael (1970). For Raphael an association has two characteristics. First, the members of the group must have a specified common purpose or set of common purposes. Second, they must be organised for the pursuit of that purpose.
11. Author's interview with Francisco Sorto, San Salvador, March 1998.
12. Declaración de Montelimar, April 1990.
13. Author's interview with Luis Guillermo Solis, San José, Costa Rica, April 1998.
14. CAFTA was negotiated in 2003 and 2004 between the Central American governments and the US. As of June 2008 Costa Rica was the only state which remained outside the agreement. Despite getting CAFTA approved in a referendum in October 2007, the government has not implemented it because of failure to obtain parliamentary approval of complementary legislations.
15. Latin American Monitor, March 1990; November, 1990.
16. Declaración de Montelimar, April 1990.
17. This area is made up of Guatemala, El Salvador, Honduras and Nicaragua.
18. Costa Rica does not participate in this scheme.
19. Acuerdo de Managua, April 1993.
20. Currently there are three kinds of customs in operation (1) Integrated ones, with common rules for members states, (2) Juxtaposed ones with uniform procedures for two states at their common border, (3) Peripherical ones. These are customs offices placed by one state in the territory of another one aimed at accelerating the flow of merchandises into its own territory.
21. Costa Rica announced in March 02, 2004 that it supports the customs union and that it would join the other states as soon as some domestic legal aspects were sorted out (Barquero, 2004).
22. Author's interview with Patricia Solano, San José, Costa Rica, April 1998.
23. Author's interview with Rodrigo Carreras, San José, Costa Rica, April 1998.
24. Author's interview with Luis Guillermo Solis, San José, Costa Rica, April 1998.

25. Author's interview with Amparo Pacheco, San José, Costa Rica, December 1999.
26. For strategic reasons related not only to the determination of the other states to go ahead with integration, but also due to US policy of negotiating a free trade agreement with Central America as a bloc, the government of President Abel Pacheco felt forced to support integration. An additional factor was that because disagreement with his own party the President relied heavily on support from leaders from the National Liberation Party (PLN), especially from the charismatic former president Oscar Arias Sánchez. The PLN is an integrationist party.
27. Author's interview with Amparo Pacheco, San José, Costa Rica, December 1999.
28. Author's interview with Luis Guillermo Solis, San José, Costa Rica, April 1998.
29. According to Robinson (2003), the New Right groups waged battles in every country against the old economic groups. They turned to political mobilisation and went on in the 1990s to struggle for, and win, state power and to implement the programme of global capitalism in the region.
30. ARENA has remained in power since 1989, repeatedly winning presidential elections.
31. Author's interview with Eduardo Ayala Agrimaldi, San Salvador, March 1998
32. Author's interview with Luis Guillermo Solis, San José, Costa Rica, April 1998
33. Declaración de Panama, July 12, 1997.
34. The latest attempt at reforming institutions took place on December 11, 2004, where during the XXV Presidential summit held in San Salvador the Presidents agreed on reducing the number, budget and immunities of both PARLACEN and the CCJ. Each country is free to send between three to twenty deputies to PARLACEN and they will contribute to the budget accordingly while the number of judges in the CCJ is reduced from two to one per country. For the latter the serving period was also cut off from 10 to 6 years.
35. This latter applies specifically to Costa Rica where the Oscar Arias government in July 2007 conditioned its support to further consolidating the Customs Union, as demanded by the EU in the negotiation of an association treaty with the region, to the approval of CAFTA in the October referendum.
36. The basic proposals for reform was put forward by SICA in the document entitled 'Lineamientos para el Fortalecimiento y Racionalizacion de la Institucionalidad Regional', presented to the presidents in Panama on July 12, 1997. The document was based on an earlier version adopted by a High Level Group of Government Representatives in February and March 1997, under the title 'Propuesta para el Fortalecimiento y la Racionalización de la Institucionalidad Regional Centroamericana'.
37. Author's interview with Elber Durán, Deputy Director at the Department of Information of SICA, San Salvador, March 1998. The information regarding the content of the single treaty was provided in interviews to the author by both Elber Durán and Eduardo Ayala Agrimaldi. The single treaty was in an early stage of negotiation at the time when the interviews were carried out. It had not yet been released to the public. For this reason it was not possible to obtain a copy.
38. Author's interview with Eduardo Ayala Agrimaldi, San Salvador, March 1998.

39. As explained by Deputy Economics Minister of El Salvador Eduardo Ayala Agrimaldi in interview with the author, San Salvador, March 1998.
40. Author's interview with Carlos Manuel. Echeverría, Chief of staff at the Ministry of Foreign Affairs, San José, Costa Rica, December 1999.
41. Author's interview with Rodrigo Carreras, San José, Costa Rica, April 1998.
42. Author's second interview with Patricia Solano, San José, Costa Rica, December 1999.
43. Author's interview with Rodrigo Carreras, San José, Costa Rica, April 1998.
44. At the end former president Francisco Flores withdrew its candidacy, clearing the way for Costa Rican leader Miguel Angel Rodriguez who won the OAS General Secretariat, but was forced to resign a month later of taking up duties as a result of corruption accusations against him in his own country.

NOTES TO CHAPTER 7

1. The notion of larger states here refers not to the size of the territory but to the economic and political power of the state. In terms of the size of the territory the leading states in Central American integration are not the biggest of the region, but they are the largest economies and the most influential in terms of economic and political power.
2. Negative policy externalities, as mentioned earlier, refers to the costs imposed by some states upon others as a result of their unilateral or join actions. If the costs are great enough as to undermine the domestic policies or interests of the affected states these may feel compelled to co-operate in order to reduce the costs or attain an optimal outcome where either costs or gains are shared.
3. El Salvador, Guatemala , Honduras and Nicaragua.
4. I am grateful to Luis Guillermo Solis who talked to me about the survival of the traditional divide in the region between 'the liberal-Morazanist bloc' made up of El Salvador, Honduras and Nicaragua, and 'the conservative one' by Guatemala and Costa Rica. These political forces currently compete in the remaking of Central American integration. The liberal-Morazanist bloc consolidated its influence in the period 1994–98 following the election of Armando Calderón Sol in El Salvador, Carlos Reina in Honduras and Arnoldo Alemán in Nicaragua and the willingness of the Figueres administration in Costa Rica to follow the integrationist agenda.
5. Guatemala co-operates fully on economic integration, but is reluctant on political integration.
6. I am using here Martin's (1999, 86–87) typology of institutional effects. As the CACM can be regarded as an institution, the typology should be applicable. According to Lisa Martin international institutions 'might serve as 'substitutes' for domestic mechanisms and institutions; or they might 'complement' the effect of domestic-level process and structures'. In this interpretation states which view integration as a substitute for domestic policies will pursue the convergence of their economic policies or at least try to bring their practices more closely in line with one another. Conversely, states which view integration as a complement to domestic policies might avoid the convergence of policies or even exaggerate domestically generated practices.
7. Author's second interview with Patricia Solano, San José, Costa Rica, December 1999.
8. Author's interview with Francisco Peña, San Salvador, March 1998.

9. Latin American Monitor, May 1990, 789; March 1993, 1128.
10. Latin American Monitor, June 1992, 1032.
11. Latin American Monitor, January-February 1992, 976.
12. El Salvador, Honduras and Nicaragua were the states which first ratified the Guatemalan Protocol, bringing it into force on August 16, 1995. Costa Rica and Guatemala ratified it in May 19, 1997.
13. President Rafael Angel Calderón's speech to the Legislative Assembly (La República 1991, 4B).
14. Author's interview with Carlos Manuel Echeverría, San José, Costa Rica, December 1999.
15. Author's interview with Carlos M. Echeverría, San José, Costa Rica, December 1999.
16. Latin American Monitor, August 1994, 2.
17. Author's interview with Amparo Pacheco, San José, Costa Rica, December 1999.
18. Panama also signed SIECA's first draft of the Guatemalan Protocol (GP). Its signing of the GP, however, was worrying enough for Costa Rica, forcing it to compromise with the region.
19. Latin American Monitor, April 1992.
20. In 1991 Carla Hills, US Trade Representative, during a visit to Costa Rica presented the convergence criteria that the states have to meet before getting a trade agreement with the US. Among these were the abolition of tariff and non-tariff barriers to trade, the elimination of requirements of local content to exports, broad access to services, protecting intellectual property, and legislating on labour and the environment. For fuller details see (Lizano 1994).
21. Central America and Panama Federation of Private Businesses.
22. Preferential treatment to Nicaragua is acknowledged under the Guatemalan Protocol (Art.5, Transitory). In the case of Honduras preferential treatment was granted in June 1994 by the Executive Council of the General Treaty of Economic Integration through Resolution 4–94 (CE-II).
23. Author's interview with Francisco Peña, San Salvador, March 1998.
24. In 1995 Cost Rica, Guatemala, and Honduras temporarily reintroduced surcharges to imports, whereas El Salvador carried out further reductions in its external tariffs.
25. Alianza Republicana Nacionalista, a republican and Nationalist party.
26. Since 2006 remittances from the US have surpassed the $3 billions per year and are getting higher.
27. Author's interview with Eduardo Ayala Agrimaldi, Deputy Economics Minister of El Salvador, San Salvador, March 1998.
28. Author's interview with in 1996 Eduardo Ayala Agrimaldi, San Salvador, March 1998.
29. The contribution is Costa Rica 64 per cent, El Salvador 59 per cent, Guatemala 60 per cent, Honduras 47 per cent and, Nicaragua 44 per cent.
30. Author's interview with Eduardo Ayala Agrimaldi, San Salvador, March 1998.
31. The Salvadorian Central Bank informed in April 6, 2005 that the amount of inward foreign investment for 2004 was $496.6 million.
32. Author's interview with Amparo Pacheco, San José, Costa Rica, December 1999.

NOTES TO CHAPTER 8

1. I decided to coin the term *'concerted defection'* largely because I did not find another suitable term to describe the type of deviations from regional agreements that the most developed states of Central America allow to Honduras and Nicaragua.
2. Formed in December 1986. Most Latin American states are members of it. Central American states participate individually, however, the state holding the Protempore Secretary of SICA represents the region.
3. Author's interview with Mauricio Castro Aragón, Embassador of El Salvador to the United Kingdom, London, April 1999. At the time the summit took place, Mauricio Castro Aragón was the Salvadorian Ambassador to Panama. El Salvador was the holder of the region's Protempore Secretariat and the Ambassador was delegated by President Armando Calderón Sol to represent the region.

Bibliography

Abarca Amador, E. 1995. La Política Exterior de la Administración Calderón Fournier: Reducción de los Márgenes de Maniobra o Incorporación al Nuevo Contexto Internacional. *Revista de Ciencias Sociales* 70: 57–67.

Allison, G. 1982. Essence of Decisions. In *Decision making: Approaches and Analysis,* edited by A.G Mcgrew and M.J. Wilson, 36–40. Manchester: Manchester University Press.

ANEP.1996. El Manifiesto Salvadoreno: Una Propuesta de los Empresarios a la Nación. *Revista Unidad Empresarial* 40 (7): 57–66.

Araya Pochet, C. 1982. *Historia Económica de Costa Rica 1821–1971.* San José: Editorial Fernández Arce.

Arias Sánchez, O. 1986. Discurso de Toma de Posesión, Mayo 8th. *Relaciones Internacionales* 15–16 Segundo y Tercer Trimestre: 40–45

Arias Sánchez, O. 1993. El Proceso de Paz como Premisa para el Proceso de Integración. In *Una Contribución al Debate: Integración Regional*, edited by O.M. Sánchez and J. Delgado, 77–101. San José: Flacso-UNA.

Arias Sánchez, O. 1997. Ganamos la Batalla contra las Dictaduras, pero Estamos Perdiendo la Guerra contra la Pobreza (Interview). In *Esquipulas, Diez Años Después? Hacia Dónde va Centroamérica?, edited by* J. Ordóñez and N. Gamboa, 207–211. San José: Educa/Csuca/Hombre de Maíz.

Aron, R. 1954. *The Century of Total War.* London: Derek Verschoyle.

Artavia, R, Colburn, F. D. Saballos Patiño, I. 1987. La Experiencia con Exportaciones en Costa Rica. In *Centroamérica: Estrategias de Desarrollo*, edited by F. D. Colburn, 107–141. San José, Costa Rica: EDUCA.

Balassa, B. 1961. *The Theory of Economic Integratio.* Illinois: Richard D. Irwin INC.

Ball, A.R. 1977. *Modern Politics and Government.* London: Macmillan Press.

Baloyra-Herp, E. 1983. Reactionary Despotism in Central America. *Journal of Latin American Studies* 15 (2): 295–319.

Barry, T. and Preusch, D.1986. *The Central America Fact Book.* USA: Grove Press.

Barquero S, M. "Cadexco pide plan exportador."La Nación, December 5, 2000, http://www.nacion.com/.

Barquero S, M. "País apoya la unión aduanera". La Nación, March 3, 2004, http://www.nacion.com/

BCR. 1999. *Boletín Económico* 127 (12) El Salvador, Marzo-Abril.

Bell, J.P. 1971. *Crisis in Costa Rica: The Revolution of 1948.* Austin and London: The University of Texas Press.

Bell, P. 1984. Central America and the United States: Myth and Reality. In *Central America in the Midst of the Whirlwind: Essays on the Crisis and its Alternatives,* edited by Presidency of the Republic of Colombia. Bogotá, November 28–30: 59–65.

Benitez Manaut, R. 1992. Esquipulas: Perspectivas de una Década. In *Centroamérica ante las Nuevas Relaciones Internacionales*, edited by G. Aguilera Peralta et al. Guatemala: FLACSO: 45–62.

Bergsman, J. and X. Shen. 1995. La Inversión Extranjera Directa en los Países en Desarrollo. *Finanzas & Desarrollo* 32 (4): 6–8.

Berridge, G.R. 1992. *International Politics: States, Power & Conflict since 1945.* New York: Harvester Wheatsheaf.

Bhagwati, J. 1994. Regionalism and Multilateralism: an overview. In *Asia Pacific Regionalism: Readings in International Economic Relations,* edited by R. Garnaut and P. Drysdale. Sydney: Harper Education Publishers:145–166.

Block, F. 1991. Marxist Theories of the State in world System Analysis. In *Perspectives on World Politics,* edited by R. Little and M. Smith. London: Routledge: 395–403.

Bodenheimer, S.J. 1981. El Mercado Común y la Ayuda Norteamericana. In *La Inversión Extranjera en Centroamérica,* edited by S.J. Bodenheimer. San José: Educa: 24–147.

Bodenheimer, S.J. 1974. La Ayuda Externa no ayuda a la Integración Centroamericana. In *La Inversión Extranjera en Centroamérica*, edited by S.J. Bodenheimer. San José: Educa: 34–70.

Bouzas, R. and Soltz, H. 2000. The Institutional Performance of Mercosur: A Preliminary Assessment. Paper presented at the Workshop on *"Regional Integration in Latin America and the Caribbean: An Evaluation of the Political Economy of Open Regionalism",* Institute of Latin American Studies, London, July 7–8, 2000.

Bravo, A. "A la apertura de la integración de los mercados bursátiles. Próximo año arranca bolsa regional". La Prensa Gráfica, November 14, 2000, http://www.prensagrafica.com.sv/.

Bromley, S. 2004. International Politics: states, anarchy and governance. In *A World of Whose Making? Making the International: Economic Interdependence and Political Order,* edited by S. Bromley et al. London: Pluto Press: 95–129.

Bulmer-Thomas, V. 1987. *The Political Economy of Central America since 1920.* Cambridge: Cambridge University Press.

Bulmer-Thomas, V. 1988. *Studies in the Economics of Central America.* London: Macmillan Press.

Bulmer-Thomas, V. 1997. *Open Regionalism in Central America: Theory and Practic.* Paper presented at Annual Conference of Latin American Studies Association (LASA)-Guadalajara, Mexico, 17–19 April.

Bulmer-Thomas, V and Douglas Kincaid, A. 2001. *CENTROAMERICA 2020: hacia un nuevo modelo de desarrollo regional.* Cuaderno de Ciencias Sociales No.121. San José: Flacso.

Bushch, M.L and Milner, H. 1994. The Future of the International Trading System: International Firms, Regionalism, and Domestic Politics. In *Political Economy and the Changing Global Order,* edited by R. Stubbs and G. R.D. Underhill. London: Macmillan: 259–276.

Buttari, J.J. 1992. Economic Policy Reform in Four Central American Countries: Patterns and Lessons Learned. *Journal of Interamerican Studies* 34 (1):179–216.

Buzan, B. 1991. *People, States & Fear: An Agenda for International Security Studies in the Post-Cold War Era.* New York: Harvester Wheatsheaf.

Cable, V. 1969. The 'Football War' and the Central American Common Market. *International Affairs* 45 (4): 658–671.

Cáceres, L.R. 1980. *Integración Económica y Subdesarrollo en Centroamérica*. México: Fondo de Cultura Económica.

Cáceres, L.R and Irvin, G. 1989. The Reconstruction of the CACM and European Co-operation. In *Central America: the Future of Economic Integration*, edited by G. Irvin and S. Holland. Boulder: Westview Press: 163–185.

Caldera, T. H. (undated). *La Democracia Cristiana en Centroamérica*. Guatemala: Incep.

Cameron, M.A. and Tomlin, B.W. 2000. *The Making of NAFTA: How the Deal was Done*. Ithaca: Cornell University Press.

Canales-Kriljenko, J.I. et al. 2004. La integración financiera en América Central: Perspectivas y necesidades de ajuste. *Integración &Comercio* 20: 231–256.

Caputo, O. and Pizarro, R. 1982. *Dependencia y Relaciones Internacionales*. San José: Educa.

Carr, E.H. 2001. *The Tewnty Years' Crisis*. Houndmill: Palgrave.

Castillo, C.M. 1966. *Growth and Integration in Central America*.Westport: Praeger.

Castrillo Zeledón, M. 1970. *El Régimen de Libre Comercio en Centroamérica*. San José: Educa.

Cepal. 1975. Alcance y Requisitos de una Política de Integración y Reciprocidad Económica. In *La Integración Centroamericana*, edited by E. Lizano, 29–39. México: Fondo de Cultura Económica.

Cepal. 1995a. Las Relaciones Comerciales de Centroamérica frente a los Nuevos Esquemas de Cooperación, Integración y Comercio (LC/MEX/L.261/ Capítulo II). México DF, sede subregional de la CEPAL en México.

Cepal. 1995b. Informe de la Reunión Extraordinaria de Consulta del Comité de Cooperación Económica del Istmo Centroamericano (CCE) (LC/MEX/ CCE/L.421). Mexico DF, sede subregional de la CEPAL en México.

Cepal. 1997. Diagnóstico de la Institucionalidad Regional Centroamericana. In *Centroamérica: La Integración que no Cesa*, edited by C. Sojo, 15–54. Cuaderno de Ciencias Sociales No.103. San José: FLACSO.

Cerdas, R. 1998. Las Instituciones de Integración en Centroamérica. In *Centroamérica en Reestructuración*, edited by V. Bulmer-Thomas, 245–276. San José: Flacso.

Checchini, V et al. 1959. *Honduras: A Problem in Economic Development*. USA: The Twentieth Century Fund.

Clark, M.A. 1995. Nontraditional Export Promotion in Costa Rica: Sustaining Export-Led Growth. *Journal of InterAmerican Studies and World Affairs* 37 (2): 181–219.

Clark, M.A. 1997. Transnational Alliances and Development Policy in Latin America: Nontraditional Export Promotion in Costa Rica. *Latin American Research Review* 32 (2): 71–97.

Cline, W.R. 1978. Benefits and Costs of Economic Integration in Central America. In *Economic Integration in Central America*, edited by W.R. Cline and E. Delgado, 59–121. USA: The Brookings Institution.

Cline, W.R. 1986. El Papel de la Integracion Economica en el Desarrollo Centroamericano. *Revista de la Integracion y el Desarrollo de Centroamerica* 39: 75–94.

Cochrane, J.D. 1965. Costa Rica, Panama and Central American Economic Integration. *Journal of Inter-American Studies* 7 (3): 331–344.

Cohen Orantes, I. 1972. *Regional Integration in Central America*. USA: Lexington Book.

Cohen orantes, I. 1998. *Ensayos sobre la Integración Centroamericana*. Tegucigalpa: BCIE.

Colindres, A.M. 1993. Non-Traditional Exports in Guatemala. In *Economic Maladjustment in Central America,* edited by W. Pelupessy and J. Weeks, 111–127. New York: St. Martin's Press.

COMEX. 1991. *Adhesión de Costa Rica al Acuerdo General sobre Aranceles Aduaneros y Comercio GATT.* San José, Costa Rica: Comex.

COMEX. 2008. Costa Rica: Exportaciones totales por destino 2000–2007, http://www.comex.go.cr/estadisticas/exportaciones, visited on July 3.

CMCA. 1989. *Situación Económica de los países Centroamericanos en 1988.* San José: CMCA.

CMCA. 1995. *Situación Económica de los Países Centroamericanos en 1994.* San José: CMCA.

Cooper, R.N. 1972. Economic Interdependence and Foreign Policy in the Seventies. *World Politics* 24 (2):159–181.

Corrales Quesada, J. 1992. El Proceso de Ajuste Estructural en Centroamérica. In *Ajuste Estructural y Progreso Social: La Experiencia Centroamericana,* edited by M.A.Rodríguez, 251–275. San José: Asociación Libro Libre.

Corte Centroamericana de Justicia. 1995. Memoria. Managua.

Crick, B. 1962. *In Defence of Politics.* Middlesex: Penguin Books.

Cristiani, A. 1990. Discurso ante la Asamblea General de las Naciones Unidas. *Pensamiento Centroamericano* 45 (208): 81–87.

Cueva, A. 1985. *El Desarrollo del Capitalismo en América Latin.a* México: Siglo XX1.

Dada Hirezi, H. 1980. La Crisis de la Integración Centroamericana. *Revista Mexicana de Sociología* 42 (2): 731–747.

Dada Hirezi, H. 1983. *La Economía de El Salvador y la Integración Centroamericana 1954–1960.* San José: Educa.

Dahrendorf, R. 1972. A New Goal for Europe. In *European Integration: Selected Readings,* edited by M. Hodges, 74–87. London: Penguin Books.

Daly Hayes, M. 1982. United States Security Interests in Central America in Global Perspective. In *Central America: International Dimensions of the Crisis,* edited by R.E. Feinberg, 85–102. USA: Holmes & Meier Publishers.

Davis, C.L., Gabel, M.J. and Coleman, K.M. 1998. Citizen Response to Regional Integration in the Americas: The Cases of Costa Rica and El Salvador. *Studies in Comparative International Development* 33 (2) Summer: 88–109.

Delgado, E. 1981. *Evolución del Mercado Común Centroamericano y Desarrollo Equilibrado.* San José: Educa.

Delgado Rosa, J. 1984. *El Estado Centroamericano: Un Balance Político de su proyecto de modernización e integración 1951–1969,* Tesis. Mexico: FLACSO.

D'Escoto Brockman, M. 1997. La Pacificación no ha traído Mayor Bienestar a los Nicaraguenses (Interview). In *Esquipulas, Diez Años Después: ¿Hacia dónde va Centroamérica?,* edited by J. ordóñez and N. Gamboa, 171–178. San José: Csuca-Asdi.

De la Ossa, A, ed. 1994. *El Sistema de la Integración Centroamericana: Crítica de la Visión Oficial.* San José, Costa Rica: Fudación Friedrich Ebert.

De la Ossa, A. 1996. La Integracion Social: Nuevas Rutas Hacia la Discordia. In *La Integración Social: Nuevas Rutas Hacia la Discordia,* edited by A De la Ossa, 25–142. San José: Fundación Friedrich Ebert.

De la Ossa, A. 1997. La Revisión Oficial de la Institucionalidad de la Integración: ¿Otro Paso más en el Ajuste Neo-Liberal?. In *Centroamérica: La Integración que no Cesa,* edited by C. Sojo, 91–98. San José: FLACSO.

De la Ossa, A. 1999. *La Unión Centroamericana: Condiciones y Perspectivas.* (Managua: Cries.

Department of State. 1997. El Salvador: Economic Policy and Trade Practices Report, http://www.state.gov/Reports 1997.

Deutsch, K. W et al. 1957. *Political Community and the North Atlantic Area: International Organization in the Light of Historical Experience.* New Jersey: Princeton University press.

Dijkstra, G. 1993. The Limits of Economic Policy in El Salvador. In *Economic Maladjustment in Central America*, edited by W. Pelupessy and J. Weeks, 53–66. New York: St. Martin's Press.

Dunkerley, J. 1982. *The Long War: Dictatorship & Revolution in El Salvador.* London: Junction Books.

Dunkerley, J. 1988. *Power in the Isthmus: A Political History of Modern Central America.* London: Verso.

Durkerley, J. 1998. *The Pacification of Central America: Political Change in the Isthmus, 1987–1993.* London: Verso.

Durán, E. 1988. Pacification, Security and Democracy: Contadora's role in Central America. In *The Central American Security system: North-South or East-West?*, edited by P. Calvert. Cambridge: Cambridge University Press.

Durán, J.R. 1997. Honduras: El País durante la Guerra y en el Proceso de Paz de Esquipulas. In *Esquipulas, Diez Años Después: ¿Hacia dónde va Centroamérica?*, edited by Jo. Ordóñez and N. Gamboa, 137–148. San José: Hombres de Maiz-Csuca-Asdi.

Easton, D. 1971. The Analysis of Political Systems. In *Political Sociology: Selected Readings*, edited by A. Pizzarro, 39–56. London: Penguin Books.

ECLAC (Economic Commissión for Latin America and the Caribbean) 1974. "Planteamientos y posibles medidas en torno al problema del desarrollo equilibrado en Centroamérica" (LC/MEX/74/22), Mexico City, ECLAC subregional headquarters in Mexico.

ECLAC (Economic Commission for Latin America and the Caribbean). 1986. Central America: Bases for a reactivation and development policy. *CEPAL REVIEW* 28: 11–48.

ECLAC (Economic Commissión for Latin America and the Caribbean) (1995), "El regionalismo abierto en América Central: el desafío de profundizar y ampliar la integración" (LC/MEX/L.261), Mexico City, ECLAC subregional headquarters in Mexico.

El-Agraa, A. 1996. International Economic Integration. In *Current Issues in International Trade*, edited by D. Greenaway, 174–221. London: Macmillan Press.

El Diario de Hoy. 2000. Presidentes deberán solventar impasse/ C.A. sin acuerdo en solución de diferencias, Agosto 30.

Evans, P. 1979. *Dependent Development: The Alliance of Multinational, State, and Local Capital in Brazil.* New Jersey: Princeton University Press.

Evans, P. 1997. The Eclipse of the State? Reflections on Stateness in an Era of Globalization. *World Politics* 50 (1): 62–87.

Facusse, M. 1976. La Empresa Privada Hondureña en el Proceso de Integración. *Revista de la Integración Centroamericana* 18: 27–39.

Fagen, R. 1987. *Forging. The Challenge of Central America.* USA: Pacca.

Fajardo Salas, G. 1992. *La Desgravación Arancelaria en el Contexto Centroamericano.* San José: Mieco.

Fajardo Salas, G. 1993. El Papel de Costa Rica en el Proceso de Integración de Centroamérica. In *Una Contribución al Debate: Integración Regional* Sánchez, edited by O. .M. Sánchez and J. Delgado, 33–54. San José, Costa Rica: Flacso-UNA.

Faletto, E. 1989. The specificity of the Latin American State. *CEPAL REVIEW* 38: 69–87.

Farer, T.J. 1980. Searching for Defeat. *Foreign Policy* 40, Fall: 155–174.

Farley, R. 1992. Entrepreneurship and Economic Power: The Non-Relevance of Market Size. *Caribbean Affairs*, 5 (2): 30–46.

Fernández, G. 1986. *El Primer Domingo de Febrero: Crónica Interior de la elección de Oscar Arias*. San José: Editorial Costa Rica.
Fernández, G. 1989. *El Desafío de la Paz en Centroamérica*. San José: Editorial Costa Rica.
Fmln. 1990. *Proclama del FMLN a la Nación: Revolución Democrática*. San Salvador.
Fonseca, G. and Ramírez, D. 1970. Los Organos del Tratado General de Integracion Economica Centroamericana. *Derecho de la Integración* 6: 66–97.
Forster, A. 1998. Britain and the Negotiation of the Maastricht Treaty: A Critique of Liberal Intergovernmentalism. *Journal of Common Market Studies* 36 (3): 347–368.
Fuentes K.J.A. 1989. *Desafíos de la Integración Centroamericana*. San José: FLACSO.
Fuestes Mohr, A. 1973. *La Creación de un Mercado Común: Apuntes Históricos sobre la Experiencia de Centroamérica*. (Buenos Aires: BID/INTAL.
Furtado, C. 1970. *Economic Development of Latin America: A Survey from Colonial Times to the Cuban Revolution*. London: Cambridge University Press.
Gallard, J.I. 1999. La Unión Centroamericana: Bases y Requisitos constitucionales. *Cuadernos CRIES* 3: 7–29.
Galtung, J. 1991. A Structural theory of Imperialism. In *Perspective on World Politics,* edited by R. Little and M. Smith, 292–304. London: Routledge.
Gamble, A. and Payne, A. 1996. Conclusion: The New Regionalism. In *Regionalism & World Order,*edited by A. Gamble and A. Payne, 247–264. London: Macmillan Press.
García, R. 1988. Integration or Disintegration: The Central American Common Market. In *Central America: Crisis and Possibilities,* edited by R. García, 83–99. Stockholm: Institute of Latin American Studies.
Garrett, G. 1992. International Cooperation and Institutional Choice: The European Community's Internal Market. *International Organization* 46 (2), Spring: 533–560.
George, S. 1993. Intergovernmentalism and Supra-nationalism in the Development of the European Community. In *International Relations and Pan- Europe: Theoretical Approaches and Empirical Findings*, edited by F.R. Pfetsch, 159–171. Germany: Lit Verlag.
George, S. 1996a. The European Union: Approaches from International Relations. In *The European Union and National Industrial Policy*, edited by H. Kassim and A. Menon, 11–25. London: Routledge.
George, S. 1996b. The European Union, 1992 and the Fear of 'Fortress Europe. In *Regionalism & World Order*, edited by A. Gamble and A. Payne, 21–54. London: Macmillan Press.
Gerardi, R.E. 1986. La Repercusión de la Crisis en los Esquemas de Integración. In *Integración Latinoamericana* 116 (11): 43–60.
Gill, S. and D. Law. 1988. *The Global Political Economy: Perspectives, Problems and Policies*. Hertfordshire: Harvester. Wheatsheaf.
Gilpin, R. 1971. The Politics of Transnational Economics Relations. *International Organization* 25: 398–419.
Gilpin, R. 1981. *War & Change in World Politics*. Cambridge: Cambridge University Press.
Gilpin, R. 1987. *The Political Economy of International Relations*. New Jersey: Princeton University Press.
Gilpin, R. 2001. *Global Political Economy: Understanding the International Economic Order*. New Jersey: Princeton University Press.
Gobierno de El Salvador. 1972. General Treaty of Economic Integration. In Tratados, Convenios y Acuerdos Internacionales vigentes en El Salvador 1960–1963, Tomo vii, 162–177. San Salvador.

Goma, R and Font, J. 1996. Political Change and Socioeconomic Policies in Central America: Patterns of Interaction. *Third World Quarterly* 17 (4): 737–751.

Greiner, P. 1991. Causas y Desarrollo de los Agudos conflictos Comerciales en el Mercado Común Centroamericano. *Revista de la Integración y el Desarrollo de Centroamérica* 48: 11–52.

Grieco, J.M. 1993. Anarchy and the Limits of Co-operation: A Realist Critique of the Newest Liberal Institutionalism. In *Realism and Neo-Liberalism: The Contemporary Debate*, edited by D.A. Baldwin, 116–140. New York: Columbia University Press.

Gruber, L. 2000. *Ruling the World: Power Politics and the rise of Supranational Institutions*. New Jersey: Princeton University Press.

Grugel, J. 1995a. *Politics and Development in the Caribbean Basin: Central America and the Caribbean in the New World Order*. London: Macmillan.

Grugel, J. 1995b. El Nuevo Regionalismo en las Americas: Las Opciones de Centroamerica despues de NAFTA. *Sintesis: Revista de Ciencias Sociales Iberoamericana* 25: 205–221.

Grugel, J. 1996. Latin America and the Remaking of the Americas. In *Regionalism & World Order*, edited by A. Gamble and A. Payne, 131–167. London: Macmillan Press.

Grugel, J. 1998. State and Business in Neo-Liberal Democracies in Latin America. *Global Society* 12 (2): 221–235.

Guerra Borges, A. 1979. Algunos Aspectos de la Experiencia del Mercado Común Centroamericano en materia de Inversiones Extranjeras. *Integración Latinoamericana* 39 (4): 3–14.

Guerra Borges, A. 1990. Mercado Comun y Desarrollo Industrial en Centroamérica. In *Centroamerica: el Futuro de la Integracion Económica,* edited by J. Weeks et al, 71–90. San José: Dei.

Guerra Borges, A. 1991. Problemas y Perspectivas del Desarrollo Industrial dentro de un Nuevo Esfuerzo de Integración Centroamericana. *Revista de la Integración y el Desarrollo de Centroamérica* 48: 85–117.

Guidos Bejar, R. 1988. El Estado en el Proceso de Industrialización Salvadoreño. In *El Salvador: Una Historia sin Lecciones,* edited by J. Cáceres et al, 130–224. San José: Flacso.

Gunder Frank, A. 1969. *Capitalism and Underdevelopment in Latin America*. London: Penguin Books.

Gutman, R. 1987. The United States, Nicaragua, and Consensus Decision Making. In *Contadora and the Diplomacy of Peace in Central America,* Vol. 1, edited by B.M. Bagley, 142–155. Boulder: Westview Press.

Haas, E.B. 1964. *Beyond the Nation-State: Functionalism and International Organization*. San Francisco: Standford University Press.

Haas, E.B and Schmitter, P.C. 1964. Economics and Differencial Patterns of Political Integration: Projections About Unity in Latin America. *International Organization* 18 (4) Autumn: 705–737.

Haas, E.B. 1968. *The Uniting of Europe: Political, Social, and Economic Forces 1950–1957*. Standford: Standford University Press.

Hanrieder, W.F. 1991. Dissolving international politics: Reflections on the Nation-State. In *Perspectives on World Politics*, R. Little and M. Smith, 143–156. London: Routledge.

Hansen, R.D.1967. *Central America: Regional Integration and Economic Development*. USA: National Planning Association.

Hastedt, G.P and K.M, Knickehm. 1991. *Dimensions of World Politics*. New York: Harper Collins Pubishers.

Hazel, A.S. 1993. *European Community Policy Towards Central America in the 1980*. PhD. Diss. London: London School of Economics and Political Sciences.

Hernández, A. 1994. *La Integración de Centroamerica desde la Federación hasta Nuestros Días*. San José: Dei.
Hernández Alcerro, J.R. 1976. Los Conflictos en el Proceso de Integración Centroamericana: Teoría y Práctica de un Arreglo. *Revista de la Integración Centroamericana* 19: 53–62.
Hettne, B. 1997. El Nuevo Regionalism. *Relaciones Internacionales,* México, 73: 155–162.
Hettne, B. 2000. The New Regionalism: A Prologue. In *National Perspectives on the New Regionalism in the North*, Volume 2, edited by B. Hettne et al, xv-xxix. London: Macmillan Press.
Hirschman, A.O. 1969. *National Power and the Structure of Foreign Trade*. Berkeley: University of California Press.
Hirschman, A.O. 1970. *Exit, Voice, and Loyalty: Responses to Decline in Firms, Organisations, and States*. Massachusetts: Harvard University Press.
Hirschman, A.O. 1978. Exit, Voice, and the State. *World Politics* 31(1): 90–107.
Hobbes, T. 1914. *Leviathan*. London and New York: Dent & Dutton.
Hoffmann, S. 1965. The European Process at Atlantic Crosspurposes. *Journal of Common Market Studies* 3 (2): 85–101.
Hoffmann, S. 1966. Obstinate or Obsolete? The Fate of the Nation-State and the case of Western Europe. *Daedelus* 95 (2): 862–915.
Hoffmann, S. 1978. *Primacy or World Order: American Foreign Policy since the Cold War*. New York: McGraw-Hill Book Company.
Hoffmann, S. 1992. The Search for Power not the Sole End of States. In *Basic Texts in International Relations*, edited by E. Luard, 299–305. London: Macmillan.
Holsti, K.J. 1972. *International Politics: A Framework for Analysis*. London: Prentice-Hall.
Holsti, K.J. 2004. *Taming the Sovereign: Institutional Change in International Politics*. Cambridge: Cambridge University Press.
Huntington, S.P. 1968. *Political Order in Changing Societies*. New Haven: Yale University Press.
Huntington, S.P. 1996. *The Clash of Civilisations and the Remaking of World Order*. London: Touchstone Books.
Hurrell, A. 1995a. Explaining the Resurgence of Regionalism in World Politics. *Review of International Studies* 21 (4): 331–358.
Hurrell, A. 1995b. Regionalism in the Americas. In *Regionalism in World Politics,* edited by L. Fawcett and A. Hurrell, 250–282. Oxford: Oxford University Press.
IILA/BID. 1991. *El Proceso de Integración en América Latina,* Argentina: IILA/BID.
Ikenberry, G.J. 1991. The State and Strategies of International Adjustment. In *Perspectives on World Politics,* edited by R. Little and M. Smith, 157–168. London: Routledge.
Inotai, A. 1971. *The Central American Common Market: An Example of Integration Between Developing Countrie*. Budapest: Center for Afro-Asian Research of the Hungarian Academy of Science.
Intal. 1982. Centroamérica: Las Recientes Medidas Económicas y su Repercusión en el Comercio Intra-regional. *Integración Latinoamericana* 66 (7): 60–62.
Intal-BID. 1986. *El Proceso de Integración en América Latina en 1985*. Buenos Aires: Intal-BID.
Intal. 1988. Mercado Común Centroamericano. *Integración Latinoamericana* 133: 41–42.
Jiménez, E. 1974. *La Guerra no fue de Futbol*. La Habana: Casa de las Américas.

Jonas, S. 1988a. Reagan Administration and Central America. In *Central America: Crisis and Possibilities,* edited by R. García, 19–31. Stockholm, Institute of Latin American Studies.

Jonas, S. 1988b. The Reagan Doctrine and Nicaragua. In *Central America: Crisis and Possibilities,* edited by R. García, 219–241. Stockholm: Institute of Latin American Studies.

Jones, W.T. 1942. *Masters of Political Thought: Machiavelli to Bentham* Vol.2. London: George G. HARRAP & CO.

Kahler, M. 1997. El Nuevo Regionalism y sus Instituciones. In *Regionalización e Integración Económica: Instituciones y Procesos Comparados,* edited by R. Bouzas, 27–55. Buenos Aires: Gel.

Kaltenthaler, K and Mora, F.O. 2002. Explaining Latin American Economic Integration: The Case of Mercosur. *Review of International Political Economy* 9 (1): 72–97.

Karliner, J. 1989. Central America's other war. *World Policy Journal* VI (4), Fall: 787–810.

Keohane, R.O. 1984. *After Hegemony: Cooperation and Discord in the World Political Economy.* New Jersey: Princeton University Press.

Keohane, R.O. 1993. Institutional Theory and the Realist Challenge after the Cold War. In *Neo-Realism and Neo-Liberalism: The Contemporary Debate*, edited by D.A, Baldwin, 269–300. New York: Columbia University Press.

Keohane, R.O and Nye, J. 1989. *Power and Interdependence.* New York: Harper Collins Publisher.

Keohane, R.O and Hoffmann, S. 1991. Institutional Change in Europe in the 1980s. In *The New European Community: Decisionmaking and Institutional Change,* edited by R O. Keohane and S. Hoffmann, 1–39. Boulder: Westview Press.

Kindleberger, C.P. 1986. *The World in Depression 1929–1939.* California: University of California Press.

Kirkpatrick, J. 1979. Dictatorships and Double Standards. *Commentary* 68: 34–45.

Knorr, K. 1991. The Nature of International Economic Power. In *Perspectives on World Politics,* edited by R. Little and M. Smith, 84–90. London and New York: Routledge.

Krasner, S.D. 1978. *Defending the National Interest: Raw Materials Investments and U.S. Foreign Policy.* Boulder: Princeton University Press.

Krasner, S.D. 1985. *Structural Conflict: The Third World Against Global Liberalism.* Berkeley: University of California Press.

Krasner, S.D. 1991. State Power and the Structure of International Trade. In *Perspectives on World Politics,* edited by R. Little and M. Smith, 125–137. London: Routledge.

Krasner, S. 1996. The Accomplishments of International Political Economy. In *International Theory: Positivism & Beyond,* edited by S. Smith at al, 108–127. Cambridge: Cambridge University Press.

Kuhn, T.S. 1962. *The Structure of Scientific Revolutions.* Chicago: The University of Chicago Press.

Laffan, B. 1992. *Integration and Cooperation in Europe.* London: Routledge.

Lahera, P.E. 1992. La Nueva Actualidad de la Integración. *Comercio Exterior* 42 (8): 707–710.

La Prensa Gráfica. 2000a. Flores: He aguantado ocho meses de presiones, November 25.

La Prensa Gráfica. 2000b. Flores en defensa de aperture económica, September 16.

La República. 1960. Honduras repudia invasion a Nicaragua, January 5.

La República. 1961. Concentración industrial analiza el Ministro de Economía y Hacienda, January 17.
La República. 1961. Ministro de Economía concluye su exposición, January 21.
La República. 1989. December 12.
La República. 1991. May 12.
La República. 1995. February 6.
La Nación. 1989. Regreso anoche al país. Arias demanda alejar violencia del istmo, Augost 8.
La Nación. 1994. Discurso Inagural del Presidente Figueres Olsen, Mayo 9.
La Nación. 1998. Estudio de la Cepal. Más capital en el istmo, May 5.
La Nación. 1999. Auge económico arrastra flaquezas, December 22.
La Nación. 1960. Carta de Echandi a Ydígoras, January 9.
Latin American Studies Association. 1998. LASA Report. *Extraordinary Opportunities and New Risks: Final Report of the LASA commission on compliance with the Central American Peace Accord*. University of Pittsburg.
Latin American Monitor: Central America, June 1987.
Latin American Monitor: Central America, August 1988
Latin American Monitor: Central America, March 1990; November, 1990.
Latin American Monitor: Central America, May 1990; March 1993.
Latin American Monitor: Central America, June 1992.
Latin American Monitor: Central America, January-February 1992.
Latin American Monitor: Central America, April 1992.
Latin American Monitor: Central America, August 1994.
Latin American Weekly Report: Central America, 6 April 1984.
Latin American Weekly Report: Central America, 18 April 1986
Latin American Weekly Report: Central America, 30 May 1986
Latin American Weekly Report: Central America, 12 May 1987
Latin American Weekly Report: Central America, 25 June 1987
Latin American Weekly Report: Central America, 9 July 1987
Laursen, F, ed. 2003. *Comparative Regional Integration: Theoretical Perspectives*. Hampshire: Ashgate.
Leal C, D. "Aumentó inversion en América Latina". La Nación, March 16, 2005, http://www.nacion.com/
Leitón, P. "El Salvador desbanca al país en potencial de crecimiento". La Nacion, October 28, 2003, http://www.nacion.com/.
Leitón, P. "Gobierno insta a sector privado a negociar aranceles con istmo". La Nación, Marzo 4, 2005, http://www.nacion.com/.
Lipsey, R.G. 1960. The Theory of Customs Unions: A General Survey. *Economic Journal* 70: 496–513.
Lipson, C. 1982. The Transformation of Trade: The Sources and Effects of Regime Change. In *International Regimes,* edited by SD. Krasner, 233–271. Ithaca and London: Cornell University Press.
Little, R. 1985. Structuralism and Neo-Realism. In *International Relations: A Handbook of Current Theory,* edited by M. Light and A.J.R. Groom, 74–89. London: Pinter Publishers.
Little, W. 1987. International Conflict in Latin America. *International Affairs* 63 (4) Autumn: 589–601.
Lizano, E. 1976. El Proceso de Integración Económica. In *Centroamérica Hoy,* edited by E. Torres Rivas, 160–229. México: Siglo XXI.
Lizano, E. 1979. Teoría y Práctica de la Integración Económica con Especial Referencia al caso de Centroamérica: Primera Parte. In *Temas sobre Integración Centroamericana,* edited by ICAP-BID, 17–53. San José: ICAP-BID.
Lizano, E. 1994. Centroamérica y el Tratado de Libre Comercio de América del Norte. *Integración Latinoamericana* 19 (204): 3–14.

Lizano, E. and Willmore, L.N. 1975. Second Thoughts on Central America: The Rosenthal Report. *Journal of Common Market Studies* 13 (3): 280–307.

López Contreras, C. 1984. *Las Negociaciones de Paz: Mi Punto de Vista*. Tegucigalpa.

Lusztig, M. 1998. The Limits of Rent Seeking: Why Protectionists become free traders. *Review of International Political Economy* 5 (1), Spring: 38–63.

Malamud, A. 2001. *Presidentialism and Mercosur: A Hidden Cause for a Successful Experience*. Paper presented at the Conference on Comparative Regional Integration, University of Southern Denmark, Odense, May 2001.

Mansfield, E.D and Milner, H.V. 1999. The New Wave of Regionalism. *International Organization* 53 (3), Summer: 589–627.

Mariscal, N. 1989. *Integracion Economica y Poder Politico en Centroamérica*. San Salvador: UCA Editores.

Martin, L.L. 1999. An Institutionalist View: International Institutions and States Strategies. In *International Order and the Future of World Politics*,edited by T.V. Paul and J.A. Hall, 78–98. Cambridge: Cambridge University Press.

Mattli, W. 1999. *The Logic of Regional Integration: Europe and Beyond*. Cambridge: Cambridge University Press.

Mazzei, U. 1998. Hemispheric Negotiations: What's in it for Central America?. *Capitulos SELA* 53, http://www.lanic.utexas,edu.

Mcclelland, D.H. 1972. *The Central American Common Market: Economic Policies, Economic Growth, and Choices for the Future*. London: Praeger Publishers.

Mcdowell, S.D. 1994. India, the LDCs, and the GATT negotiations on Trade and Investment in Services. In *Political Economy and the Changing Global Order*, edited by R. Stubbs and G.R.D. Underhill, 497–510. London: Macmillan.

Ministerio de Relaciones Exteriores de El Salvador. 1960. Memoria. San Salvador.

Ministerio de Relaciones Exteriores de El Salvador. 1992. Memoria. San Salvador.

Ministerio de Relaciones Exteriores de El Salvador. 1993. Memoria. San Salvador.

Ministerio de Relaciones Exteriores y Culto de Costa Rica. 1987. Memoria. San José, Costa Rica.

Menjivar, R. 1982. *Formación y Lucha del Proletariado Industrial Salvadoreño*. San José: Educa.

Milner, H.V. 1988. *Resisting Protectionism: Global Industries and the Politics of International Trade*. Princeton : Princeton University Press.

Milner, H.V. 1993. The Assumption of Anarchy in International Relations Theory: A Critique. In *Neo-Realism and Neo-Liberalism: The Contenporary Debate*, edited by D.A. Baldwin, 143–169. New York: Columbia University Press.

Milner, H.V. 1997. *Interests, Institutions and Information: Domestic Politics and International Relations*. Princeton: Princeton University Press.

Ministerio de Economia, Industria y Comercio de Costa Rica. 1996. *Costa Rica en la integración regional (1995)*. San José: Mieco.

Mittelman, J.H. 1996. Rethinking the "New Regionalism" in the Context of Globalisation. *Global Governance* 2 (2): 189–213.

Mittelman, J.H and Falk, R. 2000. Sustaining American Hegemony: The Relevance of Regionalism? In *National Perspectives on the New Regionalism in the North*, edited by B. Hettne et al, 173–193. London: Macmillan Press.

Monteforte Toledo, M. 1972. *Centroamérica 1: Subdesarrollo y Dependencia*. México: UNAM.

Morales, G.A. 1994. Integracion y Apertura: Nuevos Escenarios de Cooperacion y Conflicto en Centroamérica. *Centroamerica Internacional* 11: 2–12.

Moravcsik, A. 1991. Negotiating the Single European Act. In *The New European Community: Decisionmaking and Institutional Change*, edited by R.O. Keohane and S. Hoffmann, 41–84. Boulder: Westview Press.

Moravcsik, A. 1993a. Preferences and Power in the European Community: A Liberal Intergovernmentalist Approach. *Journal of Common Market Studies* 31 (4): 473–524.

Moravcsi, A. 1993b. Integrating International and Domestic Theories of International Bargaining. In *International Bargaining and Domestic Politics: Double-Edged Diplomacy,* edited by P.B. Evans et al, 3–42. Berkeley: University of California Press.

Moravcsik, A. 1995. Liberal Intergovernmentalism and Integration: A Rejoinder. *Journal of the Common Market Studies* 33 (4): 611–628.

Moravcsik, A. 1997. Taking Preferences Seriously: A Liberal Theory of International Politics. *International Organization* 51 (4), Autunn: 513–553

Moravcsik, A. 1998. *The Choice for Europe: Social Purpose & State Power from Messina to Maastricht*. London: UCL Press Limited.

Moravcsik, A. 1999. A New Statecraft? Supranational Entrepreneurs and International Co-operation. *International Organization* 53 (2), Spring: 267–306.

Moreno, D. 1990. *U.S. Policy in Central America: the Endless Debate.* Florida: Florida International University Press.

Moreno, D. 1994. *The Struggle for Peace in Central America.* Florida: University Press of Florida.

Morgenthau, H. 1971. *Politics in the Twentieth Century.* Chicago and London: The University of Chicago Press.

Morgenthau, H. 1992. State Interest Defined in Terms of Power. In *Basic Texts in International Relations*, edited by E. Luard, 287–293. London: Macmillan Press.

Muñoz G, M. 1994. La Seguridad de Costa Rica Hoy. In *De la Guerra a la Integración: La Transición y la Seguridad en Centroamérica,* edited by L.G. Solis Rivera and F. Rojas Aravena, 38–72. San José: Flacso-Chile/Fundación Arias para la Paz y el Progreso Humano.

Naisbitt, J. 1994. *Global Paradox: The bigger the world economy, the more powerful its smallest players.* London: BCA.

Nef, J. 1994. The Political Economy of Inter-American Relations: A Structural and Historical Overview. In *Political Economy and the Changing Global Order,* edited by R. Stubbs and G.R.D. Underhill, 404–418. London: Macmillan.

Nixon, R. 1978. *The Memoirs of Richard Nixon.* London: Arrow Book.

Northedge, F.S. 1976. *The International Political System.* London. Boston: Faber and Faber.

Nugent, J.B. 1974. *Economic Integration in Central America: Empirical Investigation.* Baltimore: Johns Hopkins University Press.

Nugent, N. 1993. The European Dimension. In *Developments in British Politics 4,edited by* P. Dunleavy et al , 40–68. London: Macmillan Press.

Nuhn, H. 1991. Conflictos en el Proceso de Industrialización en el Mercado Común Centroamericano. *Revista de la Integración y el Desarrollo de Centroamérica* 48: 53–84.

Nye, J.S. 1965. Patterns and Catalysts in Regional Integration. *International Organization* 19: 870–884.

Nye, J.S. 1967. Central American Regional Integration. *International Conciliation* 572: 5–66.

Nye, J.S. 1970. Comparing Common Markets: A Revised Neo-Functionalist Model. *International Organization* 24: 796–835.

Nye, J.S. 1987. *Peace in Parts: Integration and Conflict in Regional Organization.* New York: University Press of America.

Nye, J.S. 1993. *Understanding International Conflicts: An Introduction to Theory and History.* New York: Harper Collins College Publishers.

Obregón Loría, R. 1977. *Costa Rica en la Independencia y la Federación*. San José: Editorial Costa Rica.
ODECA. 1962. *Charter of the Organisation of Central American Status*. San Salvador: ODECA.
OECEI. 1968. *Mercado Común Centroamericano: Síntesis Económica y Financiera, No.2*. Buenos Aires.
Ohmae, K. 1995. *The End of the Nation State, the Rise of Regional Economies: How New Engines of Prosperity are reshaoing the Global Markets*. London: Harper Collins Publishers.
O'Nill, M. 1996. *The Politics of European Integration: A Reader*. London: Routledge.
Ortez Colindres, E. 1975. *Integración Política de Centroamérica*. San José: Educa.
O'toole, G. 2002. *Integration and Nationalism in Mexico during the Salinas Sexenio*. Paper presented at the Forum on Regional Integration in Latin America, Society of Latin American Studies Conference, University of East Anglia, 22–24 March.
Padelford, N. 1957. Co-operation in the Central American Region: The Organisation of Central American States. *International Organization* 11 (1), Winter: 41–54.
Paige, J.M. 1997. *Coffee and Power: Revolution and the Rise of Democracy in Central America*. Cambridge Massachusetts: Harvard University press.
Palacios L, J.J. 1995. El Nuevo Regionalismo Latinoamericano: El futuro de los Acuerdos de Libre Comercio. *Comercio Exterior* 45 (4): 295–302.
Panorama Centroamericano. 1998. Reporte Político, No.142, October .
Parker, F.D. 1964. *The Central American Republics*. London: Oxford University Press.
Pelupessy, W. 1991. Economic Adjustment Policies in El Salvador During the 1980s. *Latin American Perspectives* 18 (4), Fall: 48–78.
Pentland, C. 1973. *International Theory and European Integration*. London: Faber and Faber Limited.
Phillips, N. 2000. Governance after Financial Crisis: South American Perspectives on the Reformulation of Regionalism. *New Political Economy* 5 (3): 383–398.
Phillips, N. and Buxton, J. 1999. Introduction. In Development in Latin American Political Economy: States, markets and actors, edited by J. Buxton and N. Phillips, 1–10. Machester: Manchester University Press.
Pinder, J. 1968. Positive Integration and Negative Integration: Some Problems of Economic Union in the EEC. *The World Today* 24: 88–110.
Pleitez, W. 1994. El Protocolo al Tratado General de Integración Económica Centroamericana: Dónde Estamos y Hacia dónde Vamos'? *Tendencias* 26: 25–29.
Poitevin, R. 1977. *El Proceso de Industrialización en Guatemala*. San José: Educa.
Prebisch, R. 1962. Aspectos Económicos de la Alianza para el Progreso. In *La Alianza Para el Progreso: Problemas y Perspectivas,* edited by J.C. Dreier, 59–98. México: Editorial Novaro-México, S.A.
Prebisch, R. 1985. Crisis Mundial y Nuevas Fórmulas para la Integración. *Integración Latinoamericana* 98 (10): 50–55.
Presidencia de la República de Guatemala. 1986. Declaración de Esquipulas, Guatemala, 25 de mayo de 1986. In *Esquipulas, diez años después ¿Hacias dónde va Centroamérica?*, edited by J. Ordóñez and N. Gamboa, 269–271. San José: Educa-Csuca.
Presidencia de la República de Guatemala. 1987. Declaración de Esquipulas, Guatemala, 7 de agosto de 1987. In *Esquipulas, diez años después ¿Hacia dónde*

*va Centroamérica?*J, edited by Ordóñez and N. Gamboa, 260–268. San José: Educa-Csuca.
Presidencia de la República de Guatemala. 1991. Declaración de Antigua, Guatemala, 15–17 de junio de 1990. In *El Desafío del Desarrollo Centroamericano,* edited by E. Rodríguez et al, 233–244. San José: Euned.
Presidencia de la República de Guatemala. 1993. Protocolo al Tratado General de Integración Económica Centroamericana. *Integración Latinoamericana* 196 (18): 104–110.
Presidencia de la República de Costa Rica. 1991. Declaración de Puntarenas, Costa Rica, 17 de diciembre de 1990. *Pensamiento Centroamericano* 46: 72–78.
Presidencia de la República de Costa Rica. 1998. Declaración de San Isidro de Coronado, Costa Rica, 10–12 de diciembre de 1989. *Revista Centroamericana de Administración Pública* 22–23: 136–140.
Presidencia de la República de Nicaragua. 1993. Acuerdo de Managua. *Relaciones Internacionales* 46: 22: 99–100.
Presidencia de la República de Nicaragua. 1998. Declaración de Montelimar, Nicaragua, 2–3 de abril 1990. *Revista Centroamericana de Administración Pública* 22–23: 140–144.
Presidencia de la República de Panamá. 1997. Declaración de Panamá, 12 de julio de 1997. In *Centroamérica: La Integración que no Cesa,* edited by C. Sojo, 11–14. San José: FLACSO.
Procomer Costarricense de Comercio Exterior. 1997. *Costa Rican Export & Import Directory 1997.* San José: Comex.
Putnam, R.D. 1988. Diplomacy and Domestic Politics: The Logic of Two-Level Games. *International Organization* 42 (3), Summer: 427–460.
Quiñónez Amezquita, M. 1986. Guatemala: La Política Exterior del Gobierno Demócratacristiano (Conference). *Panorama Centroamericano/Pensamiento y Acción* 2: 47–53.
Ramírez Brenes, J.C and R.A. Sánchez Sánchez. 1995. *La Co-operación Internacional en la Coyuntura de la Política Exterior de la Administración Arias Sánchez 1986–1990.* Licentiate. Diss. Heredia, Costa Rica: Universidad Nacional.
Ramsett, D.E. 1969. *Regional Industrial Development in Central America: A Case Study of Integration Industries Scheme.* London: Frederick A. Praeger Publishers.
Raphael, D.D. 1970. *Problems of Political Philosophy.* London: Macmillan.
Reynolds, C. W. 1978. Fissures in the Volcano?: Central American Economics Prospects. In *Latin America and World Economy: A Changing International Order,* Vol.2, edited by J. Grunwald, 195–221. Beverly Hills- London: Sage Publications.
Rivera, R. 1995. Concertación Social e Integración Regional: Una Nueva Forma de Participación Social? In *Ilusiones y Dilemas de la Democracia en Centroamérica,* edited by K.D. Tangermann, 207–261. San José: FLACSO.
Robinson, H. 1977. *Latin America.* Plymouth: Macdonald & Evans.
Robinson, W.I. 2003. *Transnational Conflicts: Central America, Social Change, and Globalisation.* London: Verso.
Robson, P. 1998. *The Economics of International Integration.* London and New York: Routledge.
Rodas Martini, P. 2000. *Central America: Towards Open Regionalism or Towards an Opening without Regionalism?* Paper presented at the Workshop on Regional Integration in Latin America and the Caribbean, ILAS, London, July 08, 2000.
Rodríguez, E. ed. 1991. *El Desafío del Desarrollo Centroamericano.* San José, Costa Rica: EUNED.

Rojas Aravena, F. 1990a. *Política Exterior de la Administración Arias Sánchez 1986–1990*. San José: FLACSO.

Rojas Aravena, F. 1990b. *Costa Rica: Política Exterior y Crisis Centroamericana*. Heredia, Costa Rica: UNA.

Rosa, H. 1989. Estados Unidos y las Alternativas Económicas para El Salvador de Cara a la Década de los Noventa. In *El Salvador: Concertación y Nuevo Modelo Económico*. Cuaderno de Trabajo No.12, edited by CINAS, 45–67. México.

Rosamond, B. 2000. *Theories of European Integration*. London: Macmillan Press.

Rosenau, J. 1967. Foreign Policy as an Issue-Area. In *Domestic Sources of Foreign Policy*, edited by J. Rosenau, 11–50. New York: The Free Press.

Rosenau, J. N. 1992. Governance, Order, and Change in World Politics. In *Governance without government: Order and Change in World Politics*, edited by J, Rosenau and E. O. Czempiel, 1–29. Cambridge: Cambridge University Press.

Rosenthal, G. 1975. Algunos Apuntes sobre el Grado de Participación de la Inversión Extranjera Directa en el Proceso de la Integración Centroamericana. In *La Integración Económica Centroamericana*, edited by E. Lizano F, 272–296. México: Fondo de Cultura Económica.

Rosenthal, G. 1991. Un Informe Crítico a 30 Años de Integración en América Latina. *Nueva Sociedad* 113: 60–65.

Rouquié, A. 1994. *Guerras y Paz en América Central*. México: Fondo de Cultura Económica.

Rovira Mas, J. 1988. *Costa Rica en los años '80'*. San José: Porvenir-Flacso.

Rowles, J. 1980. *El Conflicto Honduras-El Salvador*. San José: Educa.

Sanahuja, J.A. 1992. *Los EE.UU. en Centroamérica, 1980–1990: ¿Ayuda Económica o Seguridad Nacional?* Bilbao: Hegoa.

Sanahuja, J.A. 1997. Integración Regional en América Central, 1990–1997: Los Limites del Gradualism. *América Latina Hoy* 17: 43–57.

Sanahuja, J.A. 1998. Nuevo Regionalismo e Integración en Centroamérica, 1990–1997. In *Integración y Desarrollo en Centroamérica*, edited by J.A. Sanahuja and J.A. Sotillo, 13–58. Madrid: IUDC/UCM.

Sánchez Sánchez, R.A. 2004. *Estado de Bienestar, Crisis Económica y Ajuste Estructural en Costa Rica*. San José: Euned.

Sancho, J. 1974. La Preparación Nacional de las Decisión Comunitaria. In *Temas sobre Integración Centroamericana*, edited by ICAP-BID, 190–266. San José: ICAP-BID.

Sancho, J. 1979. Anormalidad y Transición del Sistema Institucional Centroamericano. In *Temas sobe Integración Centroamericana*, edited by ICAP-BID, 99–117. San José: ICAP-BID.

Sartori, G. 1990. *Teoría de la Democracia: 1. El Debate Contemporáneo*. Buenos Aires: REI.

Schelling, T.C. 1960. *The Strategy of Conflict*. Massachusetts: Harvard University.

Schifter, J. 1986. *Las Alianzas Conflictivas: Las Relaciones de Estados Unidos y Costa Rica desde la Segunda Guerra Mundial a la Guerra Fría*. San José: Libro Libre.

Schmitter, P.C. 1969. Three Neo-functional Hypotheses about International Integration. *International Organization* 23: 161–166.

Schmitter, P.C. 1970a. A Rivised Theory of Regional Integration. *International Organization* 24: 836–868.

Schmitter, P.C. 1970b. Central American Integration: Spill-over, Spill-around or Encapsulation? *Journal of Common Market Studies* 9 (1): 1–48.

Schneider, G and Cederman, L.E. 1994. The Change of Tide in Political Co-operation: A Limited Information Model of European Integration. *International Organization* 48 (4), Autumn: 633–662.

Schulz, D.E. and Sundloff Schulz, D. 1994. *The United States, Honduras, and the Crisis in Central America*. Boulder: Westview Press.

Seligson, M. A. 1973. Transactions and Community Formation: Fifteen Years of Growth and Stagnation in Central America. *Journal of Common Market Studies* XI (3): 173–190.

Seligson, M.A. 1993. Actitudes de la Población Centroamericana frente a la Integración Política y Económica. *Anuario de Estudios Centroamericanos*, 19 (2): 7–24.

SICA. 1992. Protocolo de Tegucigalpa. San Salvador: SICA.

SICA. 1997. *Unión Centroamericana:Un Compromiso ante el Mundo*, Vol.1. San Salvador: SICA.

SICA . 2000. SGSICA Noticias, http://www.sgsica.org/noticias/27/10/ 2000.

Sideri, S. 1997. Globalisation and Regional Integration. In *Globalisation, Competitiveness and Human Security,* edited by K. Cristóbal, 38–82. London: Frank Cass.

SIECA. 1972. *El Desarrollo Integrado de Centroamérica en la Presente Década: Bases y Propuestas para el Perfeccionamiento y la Reestructuración del Mercado Común Centroamericano. Estudio No.5: Programa de Integración Física.* Guatemala: SIECA.

SIECA. 1973. *El Desarrollo Integrado de Centroamérica en la Presente Década: Tomo.1.* Buenos Aires: BID/INTAL.

SIECA. 1975. Algunas Consideraciones en torno a la Situación Jurídica del Mercado Común Centroamericano. In *La Integración Económica Centroamericana,* edited by E. Lizano, 374–412. Mexico: Fondo de Cultura Económica.

SIECA. 1982. El Proceso de Integración Económica Centroamericana: Evaluación Crítica de Algunas Experiencias. *Integración Latinoamericana* 7 (65): 4–13.

SIECA. 1989. *Carta Informativa* No.337. Guatemala: SIECA.

SIECA. 1990. *Hacia Una Estrategia de Integración Para el Desarrollo de Centroamérica* . Guatemala: SIECA.

SIECA. 1991. *Carta Informativa* No.349. Guatemala: SIECA.

SIECA. 1996. Avances de la Integración Económica Centroamericana. *Integración Latinoamericana* 18 (196): 117–119.

SIECA. 1998. *Situación de Centroamérica: El Proceso de Integración Económica Centroamericana y sus Perspectivas.* Guatemala: SIECA.

SIECA. 1999. *Avances de la Integración Económica Centroamericana 1995–1998.* Guatemala: SIECA.

SIECA. 2002. El Proceso de Unión Aduanera Centroamericana, http://www.sieca.org.gt,november.

Siri, G. 1984. *El Salvador and Economic Integration in Central America.* USA: Lexington Books.

Solano Orfila, R. 1982. Centroamérica: La Crisis de un Sistema Oligárquico. In *Centroamérica: Condiciones para su Integración*, edited by J.M. Alfaro et al, 85–98. San José: FLACSO.

Sol Castellanos, J. 1972. El Proceso de la Integración Económica Centroamericana. *Revista de la Integración Centroamericana* 4: 45–100.

Soto Acosta, W. 1990. Costa Rica: La Integración Centroamericana como Mecanismo de Reforzamiento del Estado-Nacional (Una Hipótesis). *Annales Des Pays D' Amerique Centrale Et Des Caraibes* 9: 45–69.

Soto Acosta, W. 1991. Negociación y Liderazgo: Esquipulas II 1986–1990. *Revista de Ciencias Sociales* 51–52: 9–22.

Soto Acosta, W. 1993. Export Promotion and Regional Co-operation in Costa Rica. In *Economic Maladjustment in Central America*, edited by W. Pelupessy and J. Weeks, 89–95. New York: St. Martin's Press.

Stevens, W.J. 1997. *Treinta y Cinco Años del Mercado Común Centroamericano (MCCA) Visto por un Europeo: Un Mercado Común que no se atreve a Indentificarse como tal*. Documento de Estudio No.1, Nueva Epoca. Heredia, Costa Rica: UNA.

Stopford, J and Strange, S. 1991. *Rival states, rival firms: Competition for world market shares*. Canada: Cambridge University Press.

Strange, S. 1994. Rethinking Structural Change in the International Political Economy: States, Firms, and Diplomacy. In *Political Economy and the Changing Global Order*, edited by R. Stubbs and G.R.D. Underhill, 103–115. London: Macmillan.

Strange, S. 1996. *The Retreat of the State: The Diffusion of Power in the World Economy*. Cambridge: Cambridge University Press.

Sullivan, M.P. 1988. Transnationalism, Power Politics, and the Realities of the Present System. In *International Relations in the Twentieth Century: A Reader*, edited by M. Williams, 255–274. London: Macmillan Education.

Taylor, P. 1983. *Limits of European Integration*. New York: Columbia University Press.

Teeple, G. 1995. *Globalization and the Decline of Social Reform*. New Jersey: Humanities Press.

Thielen, F. 1989. Estudio Comparativo del Sector Algodonero de Nicaragua y El Salvador. In *La Economía Agroexportadora en Centroamérica: Crecimiento y Adversidad*, edited by W. Pelupessy, 115–157. San José: FLACSO.

Torres Rivas, E. 1975. *Interpretación del Desarrollo social Centroamericano: Procesos y Estructuras de una Sociedad Dependiente*. San José: Educa.

Torres Rivas, E. 1999. Centroamérica en el Final del Siglo (Una Reflexión Egoísta, en Primera Persona). *Tendencias* 76: 24–27.

Trubowitz, P. 1998. *Defining the National Interest: Conflict and Change in American Foreign Policy*. Chicago: University of Chicago Press.

Truyol Y Sierra, A. 1990. *Escritos sobre Política Internacional*. Madrid: Editorial Técnos.

USCSI. 2002. *Written Testimony on the Central American Free Trade Agreement for the Trade Policy Staff Committee Office of the United States Trade Representative*, http://www.uscsi.org/02/12/2002.

Valle Martínez, M.A. 1999. Experiencias de la Unión Centroamericana y sus Limitaciones (1821–1993). *Cuadernos CRIES* 3: 31–52.

Varas, A. and Tulchin, J. 1994. Presentación. In *De la Guerra a la Integración: La Transición y la Seguridad en Centroamérica*, edited by L.G. Solis Rivera and F. Rojas Aravena, i-vi. San José: Flacso-Chile/ Fundación Arias Para La Paz.

Varas, A. 1995. Latin America: Towards a New Reliance on the Market. In *Global Change, Regional Response: The New International Context of Development*, edited by B. Stallings, 272–308. Cambridge: Cambridge University Press.

Véliz, C. 1980. *The Centralist Tradition of Latin America*. Princeton, New Jersey: Princeton University Press.

Villagrán Kramer, F. 1967. *Integración Económica en Centroamérica: Aspectos Sociales y Políticos*. Guatemala: Universidad de San Carlos.

Wagner, R.H. 1970. *United States Policy Towards Latin America: A Study in Domestic and International Politics*. Standford, California: Standford University Press.

Wallace, H. 1972. The Impact of the European Communities on National Policy-Making. In *European Integration: Selected Readings*, edited by M. Hodges, 285–303. London: Penguin.

Wallerstein, I. 1979. *The Capitalist World Economy*. Cambridge: Cambridge University Press.

Waltz, K.N. 1972. The Myth of National Interdependence. In *The International Corporation*, edited by C. Kindleberger, 205–222. Cambridge, Massachusetts: The Massachusetts Institute of Technology.

Waltz, K.N. 1986a. Political Structures. In *Neorealism and its Critics*, edited by R.O. Keohane, 70–97. New York: Columbia University Press.

Waltz, K.N. 1986b. Anarchic Orders and Balances of Power. In *Neorealism and its Critics*, edited by R.O. Keohane, New York: Columbia University Press.

Waltz, K.N. 2008. *Realism and International Politics*. New York and London: Routledge.

Webb, C. 1982. Decision Making in the EEC. In *Decision Making: Approaches and Analysis*, edited by A.G. Mcgrew and J. Wilson, 303–313. Manchester: Manchester University Press.

Webber, M. 1997. States and Statehood. In *Issues in World Politics*, edited by B. White et al, 24–44. London: Macmillan Press.

Whitman, M.V.N. 1979. *Reflections of Interdependence: Issues for Economic Theory and U.S. Policy*. Pittsburgh: University of Pittsburgh Press.

Willmore, L. 1975. El Patrón de Comercio y Especialización en el Mercado Común Centroamericano. In *La Integración Económica Centroamericana*, edited by E. Lizano, 214–231. México: Fondo de Cultura Económica.

Willmore, L. 1989. Export Promotion and Import Substitution in Central American Industry. *Cepal Review* 38: 49–67.

Willmore, L. and Matter, J. 1993. *Reconversión Industrial, Apertura Comercial y Papel del Estado en Centroamérica*. Cuaderno 15. Tegucigalpa: BCIE.

Wincott, D. 1995. Institutional Interaction and European Integration: Towards an Everyday Critique of Liberal Intergovernmentalism. *Journal of Common Market Studies* 33 (4): 597–609.

Wionczek, M.S. 1966. Integración Económica y Distribución Regional de las Actividades Industriales. *El Triméstre Económico* 33 (3), No.131: 469–502.

Wionczek, M.S. 1968. Requisites for Viable Economic Integration. In Regional Internationalism: Readings, edited by J. Nye Jr, 287–303. Boston: Harvard University, Little, Brown & Company.

Wynia, G. W. 1970. Central American Integration: The Paradox of Success. *International Organization* 24: 319–334.

Young, O.R. 1999. *Governance in World Affairs*. Ithaca and London: Cornell University Press.

Index

A

abolishing discrimination (economic), 1
anarchy: competition, conflict and self-help 1, 15; lack of central authority 1; relative
power, 2, 3, 13; relative gain, 13; neo-realism, 15; international politics, 1, 13, 15, 176
asymmetrical integration, 3, 101
asymmetrical bargaining, 2–3, 5,6, 17, 20, 21, 176, 182, 185
asymmetrical interdependence, 7, 89, 114
asymmetrical cooperation, xx, 8, 25
Aron, Raymond, 14
asymmetrical power, 16
asymmetrical negotiation, 20
Arias Peace Plan: as asymmetrical bargaining, 112, 125; convergence of preferences, 112; conflict resolution, 113, 115; protecting Costa Rican sovereignty, 115, 116; symmetry and simultaneity, 121; a success, 121–122; as negotiated policy-coordination,122; another Munich, 121
ARENA, 37, 147, 198n30, 167
ANEP, 39
authoritarian pattern of development, 53
Arbenz, Jacobo (President), 56, 61, 99
Arévalo, Juan José (President), 61
against foreign investment, 83
adjustment at the level of the CACM, 95
autonomous actor, 98
appendage of agro-exports, 98
agro-export model and sector, 98–99 see outward-led growth
agrarian reform, 99
automaticity, 100
absolute gains, 100
Act for Peace and Cooperation, 106, 107
Arias Sánchez, Oscar (President): as president, 108, 109, 110, 113, 161, 162; on strong
leadership for peace, 109, 110; close to Cerezo, 111; as mediator and spectator, 117; Nobel Peace Prize, 121
Azcona Hoyos, José (President): as president, 108, 120, 121; on signing the peace plan, 108, 120, 121; the Contras as state within the state, 120; on fear of exclusion, 120
Arias' foreign policy: active and independent, 111–112; disagreement with President Reagan,111; Contras the problem, 111; peace plan for, 111, 112; active neutrality, 111; avoiding hondurani-sation of, 111; on US training camps, 111
army (Salvadorian): unable to defeat guerrilla, 122; forced to negotiate, 122
American intervention, 124
Antigua (Guatemala), 134, 137, 166
Antigua, declaration of, 138
Arzú Irigoyen, Alvaro (President), 148
Ayala Agrimaldi, Eduardo, 149
alternative alliances, 184

B

bargain, 1
bargaining, 2, 11, 16, 168, 179
bargaining power, 91, 179

Buxton, Julia, 5
balance of power, 13
bandwagoning, 19, 74
billiard ball model, 20
Britain, 21, 107
Borbón, Jorge, 33, 42, 71
Baran, Paul, 53
balanced development: ambiguous and politicised, 53, 75, 89; dropped of, 159;
conception of, 183
Bodenheimer, Susan Jonas, 56
bilateral trade agreements: interdependence and early trade relations, 62, 66; fragmented
free trade area, 67; bilateral treaties, 98
Bulmer-Thomas, Victor, 84, 99, 189
balance of gains, 91
beef supplier to, 94
blaming the CACM for, 95
boomerang effect, 97
bilateralism, 97
bipolar power struggle, 98
backward linkages, 99
Belize, 107, 137
benign tolerance with, 111
Bush, George (President): support to the Arias peace plan, 11, 122
Barrios de Chamorro, Violeta (President), 118
Bolland Amendments, 119
Buzan, Barry, 128
border conflicts, 151, 174
borderless world, 156

C

Central America, 1, 2,3,10,21,24, 25, 28, 89
Central American regional integration: as regional integration, 1, 177; as of balanced
development, 55; modernisation, 60, 64; as political control, 51, 60–61, 147; as of
cooption, 60; reliance on agrarian sector, 62, as a rational response, 64; as cushion to crises, 67, 147, 178; as regional community, 68; as intergovernmental bargaining, 75-77,138, 140; impact of external/structural environment, 101, 136, 156, 178–179, 184; as of protectionism, 170–171; as open regionalism and globalisation, 134, 147, 152, 155,
156, 187; governments as actors, 134, 135, 186; social exclusion, 135–136; as bargaining chip, 136–137, 152, 178; no supranationality, 71, 72, 87, 138–139, 148, as trampoline for, 153
customs union theory, 1
competition, 1, 181
conflict and cooperation, 1
complex interdependence, 5, 15, 16, 43, 86
Central American Common Market (CACM): as Common Market, 3, 43, 51, 91–94, 95, 96, 98, 154, 155, 158, 162, 171, 174, 177; as of asymmetric cooperation, 51; as complex interdependence, 5, 15, 16, 43, 86; cooperation and power politics, 74; growth impact, 80; as of rebalancing development, 80–81; on gains for all, 81; on foreign
control, 44, 88; as of economic reform, 44, 45; trade deficits, 95; collapsing even without, 96
compromise 3, 4,16, 31, 49, 96, 115, 125, 127, 129, 162, 163, 164, 168, 173, 174, 182, 183, 185, 186, 187
convergence: as pre-condition for integration, 131; lack of, 172
coalitions: North Triangle, 6, 7; Esquipulas peace process, 5, 8
Costa Rica: as state, 7, 29, 31, 93, 94; as of outward- led model, 32, 34, 44, 45, 49, 105,
113, 143; support to producers, 32; sceptic partner, 32, 33, 34, 41, 42, 45, 49, 71, 162;
view of integration, 48, 114, 143–144–146, 161, 163; reluctant to compromising
sovereignty; 71, 72, 87, 115, 143, 161, 163; as of political union, 143, 143; the regional bloc, 161; national interest, 161; most social developed state, 33, 143; losing out ofintegration, 33, 34, 42, 43, 71; use of the territory by the US, 109–110; testing ground for neo-liberal policies, 110 ; policy change and

multinational firms, 143; reform of institutions, 148; right wing influence,162; bargaining and compromising, 162, 163, 164, 185; threat of exclusion from, 162–164; tariff reductions, 167; trade conflicts and integration, 46, 46, 47; countering the tripartite, 75
Central American bloc: as bloc; 9, 146; pooling sovereignty, 147, 158; fragmented and hollow, 147, 153, 189; as leverage, 158; Costa Rica's view of, 161
civil wars: impact on integration, 104; end of, 158
common external tariff, 9, 57
cognitive realism, 12,14
Carr, Edward, 13
correlation of, 15
credible commitment, 20, 157, 180, 183, 190
constraint on cooperation, 20
Cold War, 27, 28, 128, 129, 130, 132, 133, 136, 179, 187
Carreras, Rodrigo, 34, 150, 151
Castellanos, Jorge, 35, 69
Cristiani, Alfredo (President), 37, 122, 167
CA-4: El Salvador, Guatemala, Honduras and Nicaragua, 38, 43, 140, 142, 143, 161, 162, 174; migratory integration, 142; inward integration, 157; as of Nicaragua, 160
controlled interdependence, 43
Carazo, Rodrigo (President), 44
CADEXCO, 44
Caribbean Basin Initiative, 44
CCJ: Central American Court of Justice, 47, 139, 151, 174
centre and periphery, 54
customs union, 55, 174
common market, 55
Castañeda, Oscar (President), 61
Caribbean Pact: for integration, 61; against dictatorships, 61
Cueva, Agustín, 62
Committee for Economic Cooperation, 62
Central American clause, 66
Central American trade regime, 67
Castillo, Carlos Manuel, 71
Cerro Verde, 73
CABEI: Integration bank, 75, 78, 182; as incentive and threat, 78
CET: Common External Tariff, 84, 114, 154, 166, 167, 173, 187; bargaining for, 168
constitutional restrictions, 85
CAEC, 86, 90, 96
Comision Normalizadora, 86
consensus, 87, 163
Central American Social and Economic Community, 87
crisis of expectation, 88, 89
conflict resolution, 90–91
convention on fiscal incentives, 90
condition of backwardness, 90
creative effect, 90
Cohen Orantes, Isaac, 91
cultivation of coffee, 93
comprador class, 93
Cáceres, Luis René, 93
cultivation of cotton, 94
compromising sovereignty, 98
catalyst for integration,68, 69, 98, 128, 130, 183
community building, 100
countervailing measures, 101
currency devaluation, 104
Contras, 104, 105, 110, 111, 116, 117, 120, 121 see US foreign policy
Caribbean Basin Initiative (CBI), 105, 110
compensatory trade, 105
Contadora Group, 106, 107, 109, 111, 117
Contadora's failure, 112
Cerezo Arévalo, Vinicio (President): as president, 106, 107, 113, 115; search for leadership, 106, 107, 108; active foreign policy, 107; neutrality, 107
Caraballeda meeting, 107
Christian Democratic ideology, 108
Christian Democratic parties, 109
CIA, 110, 119, 133
Costa Rican neutrality, 109, 195n10, 111
concerted defection, 114, 181, 201n1 see opt-out
Central American Tariffs Council, 114, 168
Costa del Sol, 118
Christian Democratic Party (El Salvador), 119

Central American Monetary Council, 123
captive market, 125
Central American Economic Community, 134
Chávez, Hugo (President), 135
CAFTA, 135, 136, 147, 152, 169, 170, 171, 173, 184, 189
Cristiani, Alfredo (President): pragmatic view of integration, 146
Callejas, Rafael L (President): on market reform, 159; actions on integration, 159, 186
Calderón Fournier, Rafael A (President), 162, 163, 164
Calderón Sol, Armando (President), 167
Central American preference, 174
China, 179
cheating, 181
Castro Aragón, Mauricio, 189
competitiveness, 190

D

developing countries: dependent and structurally constrained, 2; dependency, 4,7,10, 25, 29; reducing and increasing of, 84, 178
distributional conflicts, 3, 4, 5, 7, 17, 21, 79, 89, 92, 100, 162, 177, 183, 184
disruption of integration, 91
democracy, 6
domestic constraints, 7
disintegration, 7, 101, 103, 125, 127
Dahrendorf, Ralf, 12
developed economies, 24
Delgado, Rosa, 36
Dillon, Douglas, 57
Development and Assistance Fund, 74
Delgado, Enrique, 75, 97
decentralised authority, 89
deficit states, 97, 100, 101
decree-97, 97
distorted industrialisation, 99
Duarte, Napoleón (President): as president, 108, 118, 119, 120; as of paying lip-service to the Arias plan, 119; on failing US foreign policy, 119; persuading President Azcona, 120
D'Escoto, Miguel, 113
de-emphasised intergovernmentalism, 114
diplomatic fiasco, 116
defecting from the agreement, 121
Dunkerley, James, 121
democratic governance, 124, 152
democracy promotion, 124
domino effect, 128
De la Ossa, Alvaro, 136
Dominican Republic, 137
deeper integration, 157
divergence, 172, 173
discrimination, 173
dominant actors, 179
defensive motivations, 180, 187

E

economic theory (integration): abolishing discrimination,1; customs union, 1 see trade
creation and trade diversion
economic regionalisation, 2
external actors: as catalysts for integration, 4, 68
El Salvador: as state, 7, 31, 93–94, 96–97, 184; as of free market, 32, 40, 41, 63; as
economically conservative, 32, 39; leading integrationist, 32, 35, 38, 48, 62, 64–65, 69, 146; of regional institutions' support, 35, 47, 48; consolidation of 48, 49;
entrepreneurial elite, 33, 63; businesses support for integration, 36; export dependence within the CACM, 38, 40, 167; of economic reform, 36, 37,39, 167; as of exports, 36, 37; growth potential, 37; banking and other services, 37, 38; of dollarisation, 39; pragmatic view of integration, 39,40; as of protectionist measures, 96; tariff reductions, 167, 168; bargaining power, 168, 169, 184
economic growth, 7, 99, 132, 165
Europe, 9, 14, 16, 25, 26, 177, 184
European Union (EU): 10, 15, 112, 136, 137, 177, 179, 189
European integration, 11, 24
endogenous variable, 12,13, 98
enlightened bureaucrats, 12
economic interdependence, 12,17, 161, 165, 177
exogenous variables, 13; constraints, 178

external environment: impact on integration, 15, 67, 98, 101; ignored by, 98, 101, 132;
integration as cushion to, 67;
export-led growth, 34
entrepreneurial class, 35
ECLAC: uneven terms of trade, 54; centre and periphery, 54; import-substituting industrialisation, 54; intellectual assistance for, 55; cooperation, 55; counter culture to US, 56–58; as catalyst for, 68–69; on open regionalism, 132
Eisenhower, Dwight D (President): 57; lack of interest in, 57; support for Honduras and
El Salvador, 72
Echandi, Mario (President), 43, 71, 72, 87, 182
executive board of big businesses, 53
export agriculture (EXA), 65, 84, 99, 101, 137
Esquipulas (Guatemala), 73, 107, 116, 117
El Poy, 73
EC, 86,89, 90
entrenched intergovernmentalism: as of Central America, 24–30, 59, 77, 82, 85, 86, 88, 89, 90 177, 179, 181
ECLAC's paradigm of integration, 89
economic policy preferences, 91
escalation of the conflict, 95
empty chair, 96, 101
economic sovereignty, 97, 163
environmental degradation, 99
external war, 99
economic depression, 101
economic convergence, 101, 131, 167
Esquipulas process of negotiation: as process of negotiation, 102, 106, 114, 127; as asymmetrical interdependence, 114; as intergovernmental bargaining, 115, 184; as of returning to integration, 122, 124, 125, 129; as policy coordination, 129
export promotion policies, 103, 110, 115
Esquipulas, Declaration of, 107, 108; as peace plan, 117
Esquipulas I: as summit, 107, 109; on peace and integration, 107
economic recovery of Costa Rica, 110
European Community, 112, 117
enforced vicinity, 115, 120
external debt, 125
East-West conflict, 128 see Cold War
Enterprise for the Americas, 133, 137, 164
Echeverría, Carlos M, 150
end of Cold War, 152
economic liberalisation, 158, 159
economic reform, 158, 165
economic gains, 160, 177

F

functionalism, 5
free trade area, 8, 55, 155
far-reaching integration, 13, 25
France, 21
Falleto, Elson, 29
federalist fear, 33
Flores, Francisco (President), 39, 152
Figueres, Olsen, José M (President): on reforming institutions, 148
fear of exclusion, 52
Fuentes Morh, Alberto, 54, 70
Figueres Ferrer, José (President), 61
foreign investment: losers and winners, 82–83, 172, 88; against of, 83
foreign corporations, 88
football war, 95
free trade, 97
free rider, 97
flexible arrangement, 101
fear and mistrust, 104
free market, 105
fall of Somoza, 107, 128
FMLN: major military operation in, 122
Fernández, Guido, 109, 112
FSLN, 118
fragmentation, 127
FTAA: Free Trade Agreement for the Americas, 147
federalist ideology: in the North Triangle, 158
FEDEPRICAP, 165, 200n21
FECAICA, 168
full integration, 174
functional theorists, 166
financial stability, 179

G

governmental commitment, 2, 3
governance (regional), 2
global economy, 1, 4, 5, 25, 187

global governance, 5, 6
globalisation: 5, 20, 127, 135, 138, 152
Guatemalan Protocol: as protocol, 3, 6, 9, 33, 157; CACM as free trade area, 155; new regionalism, 155; as of neo-liberalism and globalisation, 155
governments as strategic actors, 17, 18, 134–136, 138, 141
Globalised political economy, 6, 27, 180
Global integration, 7
Guatemala: as state, 8, 72, 93–4; bargaining on the tripartite, 73; dependent on the CACM, 114, 159; positive integration, 114; as of the North triangle, 159; economic interdependence, 159; as a broker on integration, 163, 186; on neutrality, 107; on leadership failure, 72, 109
General Treaty of, 9, 33, 156
Gill, Stephen, 10
grand theory, 11
governments' preferences, 13, 177, 183
Germany, 21, 184
global diplomacy, 25
geo-economic factors, 32, 33
GATT-WTO, 46, 114, 170, 173
gatekeepers, 62, 71, 86, 185
gap in levels of development, 91
gains from, 94
Guatemalan neutrality, 107
General Captaincy for, 107, 150
Guatemalan-Salvadorian axis, 109
Guatemala unable to lead, 109
guerrillas (Salvadorian), 119, 122, 128
Gamble, Andrew, 135
GS-SICA, 139, 183
global capitalism, 156
gradualist way of, 157
gradualism, 157,
geopolitics, 158
globalised world, 179
governments as political entrepreneurs, 186

H

handicaps, 4, 28
hegemony, 3, 19, 176
heuristic (power), 2, 10
high politics: high politics conflicts, 3, 4, 9,13, 128, 173, 174, 184, 190; states rivalries and competition, 1 ; power politics, 6; realism, 12
Huntington, Samuel, 11
Haas, Ernst, 11, 101
Hoffman, Stanley, 12, 52, 59, 60, 85, 90
harmonisation, 14, 172
Holsti, K.J, 22, 23, 29
Honduras government, 51
Honduras: as state, 65, 87, 91–93, 94, 96–97, 98, 120, 121, 184; isolated markets, 65, 93, 94; integration with El Salvador, 66, 70; 73; lagging on signing treaties, 71, 87, 90, 101; in the tripartite, 73–74; on balanced development, 87, 90, 101; failure to extract gains from, 92–93–94; lack entrepreneurial class and good leadership, 93; banana plantation state within the state, 93; a corrupted and rent-seeking elite, 93; blaming the CACM and the Salvadorians, 95; as of hostile relations with, 96; withdrawal from the CACM, 97, 98, as of costs of withdrawing, 98; as sanctuary for the Contras, 198n12, 120; cooperation with the peace plan, 120–121; as of rapprochement with El Salvador, 129; as of common security interest, 129; as of support to integration in the 1990s, 159; as of economic liberalisation, 159
high politics move, 97
honduranisation of Costa Rica, 111
high politics necessity, 128
Hettne, Bjorn, 135
Hurricane Mitch, 150, 151

I

Intergovernmentalism: as theory, 1,2 ,3,4,5,6,10,11,12,15,17,18,24 , 176, 177, 180, 181, 184; as bargaining power, 91, 179; as of asymmetrical bargain, 2, 3, 5, 17, 20–22, 176, 182, 185; as purposive choice of actors, 15; national preferences, 19; as of lowest-common denominator, 4, 21, 22, 31, 52, 112, 125, 174; as of preserving sovereignty, 7, 19, 20, 22, 23, 180; nation-state, 13,

85, 162; as of governments as strategic actors, 13, 17, 20; as of national interest, 5,6, 11, 13, 14, 15, 35, 177; joint governmental bargaining, 1, 3, 27, 157
International Relations, 1, 6, 176
interdependence (regional): state-led, 2, 85, 177
interstates bargaining, 3, 4,7,13; 102, 154, 157, 177, 180, 183, 184
internationalisation, 2
international economy, 2
international political economy, 2,6, 178
interests of the states, 5
intra-regional trade: growth in the 1950s and 960s, 68; unequal, 83; falling, 103, 105;
increased, 132
incremental logic, 12, 98, 176
international politics, 1, 13,15, 176 see anarchy
Ikenberry, John, 16
interdependence school, 16
institutionalists, 20
integration ideology, 35, 61, 182, 158, 160
imperialism: integration as 53, 58
import- substituting industrialisation: diminishing dependence, 54, 61
intellectual assistance for integration, 55 see ECLAC
integration industries: no replication of, 88; political conflicts, 88
industrialisation: convergent interests, 54, 61; supportive coalitions, 61
industrial growth and diversification, 80–81
international regime, 89
imperialism of the colón, 95
inflexible policies, 97
intensive social exclusion, 99
intra-regional openness, 100
isolating Nicaragua, 104 see US foreign policy
IMF-World Bank, 110, 155
involuntary propinquity, 115, 120
Iran-Contras scandal, 119
integration plateau, 127
integration as structure: Northern states' preference, 127
integration as process: Costa Rica's preference, 127
international relations of market, 132
inward integration, 157
integrationist rhetoric, 160
ideological convergence, 161 see integration ideology
inflexible rent seekers, 166

J
Jackson, Robert, 29
Judge and accused, 90
joint gains, 162

K
Kuhn, Thomas, 11
Keohane, Robert, 14, 16, 17, 89
Krasner, Stephen, 24
Kennedy, John, 57
Korean War, 67
Kirkpatrick, Jeane, 104

L
Latin America 3, 12, 25, 26, 28, 29, 90, 91
larger states: in Central America, 59, 157, 199n1
lowest-common denominator, 4, 21, 22, 31, 52, 112, 125, 174, 180, 182, 183, liberal intergovernmentalism, 4, 17, 20, 177, 180
Law, David, 10
loci of action, 11
low politics, 12, 14
logic of diversity, 13,14, 91, 180, 186
Lacayo, Miguel, 38
Liberal Morazanist states: El Salvador, Honduras and Nicaragua, 47, 148, 157, 199n.4; support for institutions, 47, 148; El Salvador as Brussels of, 148; full integration, 157
limited integration: Costa Rica's view of, 55, 161
Lemus, Tobias (President), 72, 73
La Palma (El Salvador), 73
location advantages, 87–88
lavish incentives to, 88
LDS, 91, 97
Lizano, Eduardo, 94
level of growth, 94
López Arellano, Oswaldo (President), 95
lagging far behind, 98
logic of the spill-over, 100, 184 see neofunctionalism

left-wing guerrillas, 102
legitimacy of governments, 102
López Contreras, Carlos, 128
level of convergence, 130, 131, 157, 161, 176, 190
level of regionness, 152
liberalisation in the CACM: as of industrial goods, 169, 171; in agriculture and services, 169, 170
level of openness, 172

M

Moravcsik, Andrew, 2,5,6, 11,12,15,16,17,19,20,22, 30, 56,59, 100, 114, 130, 157, 158, 165, 168, 177, 178, 180, 182, 183, 184, 186
Mercosur, 10
mid- range theory, 11
Morgenthau, Hans, 13
modified structural realism, 14,15
Milner, Helen, 17, 144
mutual gains, 18
Mattli, Walter, 25, 44
multinational businesses, 27, 179
Mora Porras, Juan R (President), 34
Menjivar, Rafael, 36
market liberalisation, 51, 124
Ministers of Economics: as technocrats 52, 54; as intergovernmental actors, 59–60
market-led integration, 55, 57, 58
Manichean, 62
multilateral treaties: leading role of, 70; overcoming opposition from, 70; opening
markets, 70–71
Managua's treaties, 76
McClelland, Donald H, 82
majority voting, 87
Modus Operandi, 87, 194n4, 97
mutual attrition, 91
misperception, 98
Molina government, 99
military intervention, 102
mutual recognition: 102
Mejía Víctores, Oscar A (President), 107
Monge, Luis Alberto (President), 109–110
Madrigal Nieto, Rodrigo, 112
Mexico: an obstacle to the Arias peace plan, 117
main Nicaraguan bargain, 118
macroeconomic cooperation, 129; 132
Mittelman, James, 135, 188
Montelimar (Nicaragua): from security to economic integration, 137, 165
marketisation, 138
Managua, Declaration of, 149, 160, 161
muddling through, 156
Morazanist states, 158
Morazán, Francisco, 160, 161

N

negative externalities, 2, 26, 50, 177, 190
non-governmental actors, 3, 14, 27, 154
Nye, Joseph, 1, 15, 59, 85, 98
national interest, 5, 6, 11, 13, 14, 15, 35, 177
neo-liberal principles, 6, 124, 129, 155 see neo-liberal economics
North Triangle states: 199n3; coalition, 6; quicker integration, 142; as of bargaining, 157, 162; federalist ideology, 158, 160; as of Nicaragua, 160; as of excluding Costa Rica, 164 new regionalism: as complex patchwork of, 132–133; as of Latin America, 133–134; avoiding exclusion from, 136–137, 178
normal science, 10, 11
major states, 11
neo-functionalism, 11, 12, 13,14,16,20, 139 see neo-functional theory
neo-functionalist logic: neo-functionalism, 11,12,13; supranational authority, 11; spillover,12; incremental logic, 12, 184; federal government, 12; political union, 12; supranational governance, 13; sectors' integration, 157; supranational planning, 157
neo-functional theory, 89, 90, 96
neo-functionalists, 100
negative integration, 13, 114, 146
neo-realists, 15 see anarchy
national preferences, 19
negotiated policy coordination, 19, 77, 122, 180
NAFTA: North American Free Trade Agreement, 20, 137, 164, 179

negative policy externalities, 21, 157, 199n2, 165, 177
non-traditional goods, 44, 45, 113, 114
National Liberation Party: supporting integration, 45, 71, 76
negative list of goods, 74
northern bloc: the tripartite, 75
Nicaragua: bargaining on the tripartite, 75–76; trade deficit, 95; on balanced development, 75, 101; empty chair tactic, 96, 101; as of CA-4, 160; as of integration ideology, 160; as of beef supplier to, 94
Nugent, Jeffrey, 84
nation-state, 85, 162
non-cooperation, 88, 95
non preferential treatment, 91
nation-building, 93
nationalism: unilateral action, 95, 101, 103
net importer of basic grains, 96
negative trade balances, 99
net gains, 100
neo-liberal economics, 1001
Nicaraguan revolution: regional divergence, 104; as of domino effect, 128
National Bipartisan Commission on Central America, 105
Northedge, F.S, 115, 162
Nobel Peace Prize to, 121
negative rates of growth, 125
new generation of governments, 125
new convergence of interests, 126
northern states: inward integration, 127, 157 see North Triangle states
new wave of integration, 132 see new regionalism
New Right, 146
national officials as entrepreneurs, 157
non-tariff barriers, 172

O

ODECA, 32, 35, 61, 85, 138, 139
OAS, 57, 152
Osorio, Oscar (President), 61
option of voice: traditional producers, 62
outward-led growth: reliance on the outside world, 67; as source of growth, 134
option of exit, 62
oligarchy, 99
Ortega, Daniel (President), 108, 112, 113
opt-out, 114, 163, 186 see concerted defection
open regionalism, 127, 132, 134, 156, 188 see new regionalism
official integration, 136
Ocotepeque agreement, 141
Orlich, Francisco (President), 182

P

parsimony (explanatory), 2, 18
policy interdependence, 2, 15
preference intensity, 2, 3, 16,20, 102, 176, 180, 182, 185
policy convergence, 3, 6, 18, 164, 182, 183, 184
poor states, 4 see smaller states
political project (integration), 5
peace process, 5, 8 see Esquipulas process of negotiation
Phillips, Nicola, 5
power politics, 6, 7, 13, 18, 20, 176 see realism
political response by, 8 see governments as strategic actors
patterns of interdependence, 10, 177
perspective, 10, 11
paradigm, 10, 11, 34
political union, 12
policy cooperation: as measure for integration, 14, 103
purposive choices of actors, 15 see intergovernmentalism
Panama: presidential summit, 148, 149; reforming SICA, 148
Power: as control, 16; as bargaining, 17; political power, 11; unequal distribution of, 179
Putnam, Robert, 17, 163
political commitment, 18, 183
positive gains, 19
politics of integration, 19
political gain, 19
pooling sovereignty, 19, 23, 180
preferences and power, 20
preference formation, 20, 180, 181
policy coordination: as measure for integration, 103; as declining, 103
protectionism, 25, 32, 34, 97, 170, 124
protectionist measures, 94, 95, 106
presidentialism, 25

Peace Accords (El Salvador), 36, 122, 158
Pacheco, Amparo, 46, 144, 172
Prebisch, Raul, 54
peripheral countries, 54
path of least resistance: ECLAC following governments' lines, 56, 183; 68
positive list of goods, 74
premature over politicisation, 85, 86
political conflict, 88
preferential treatment: granted to 91; asked by, 96
pressure groups, 98
politicisation of welfare, 100
price of oil: as of financial crisis, 102–103
President Carter: view of political conflicts, 104; as for human rights, 128; progressive regimes, 104
PARLACEN, 108, 114, 115, 117, 138, 139, 141, 148, 151, 160, 162, 183
positive integration, 114
presidential summits: as intergovernmentalism, 117 see political cooperation
Plan de Acción Inmediata: aid for reconstruction, 123
Palma Gámez, Roberto, 128
Pérez Caldaso, Eliseo, 128
peace treaty: El Salvador- Honduras, 129
political cooperation, 129, 197n4 see presidential summits
PAECA (Central American economic Action Plan): economic convergence, 131, 132, 165, 166
post-Cold War, 134
Payne, Anthony, 135
periphery customs, 142
plateau, 152, 160 see integration plateau
Pacheco, Abel (President), 162
preferential treatment, 173
political economy, 180
polarisation, 188

Q
Quiñones Amézquita, Mario, 107

R
regionalisation, 2, 156, 168
regional interdependence, 2, 24, 26, 178
regional governance, 2, 28
relative power,2, 3, 13,15,16, 27, 88, 102, 114, 125, 183
recalcitrant governments, 4,6, 180, 190
regional bureaucrats: against reforms of institutions, 151
regional technocrats, 4, 184 see neo-functionalism
regionalist project, 5 see new regionalism
regionalism, 6, 28, 127, 128, 132, 147, 156, 176
re-launch of regionalism/integration, 5,6,8, 157, 158, 164, 182, 185
regional integration: as policy coordination, 130 see political cooperation and policy
cooperation
regional building, 6
regional security complex, 8, 60, 123, 128
regional institutions, 12,
rational choice by, 30, 176 see intergovernmentalism
realism, 12,13,15,18,20,
realist view of: position of the states, 13; anarchy,1; balance of power, 13,
capabilities, 16; neo-realism, 15
regime formation, 15
regional paymaster, 25
regional trade conflicts, 46,47
regionness, 50, 67, 130, 131, 132, 143
reciprocity, 55, 90
regime of integration industries, 58, 87
rigid system of control, 60, 61 see intergovernmentalism
re-balanced economic development, 80–81
road networks, 82
Reynolds, Clark W, 84
rent-seeking state, 93
rivalry, 1, 95, 176
rolling back, 97
repression, 99
relative gains,100
recession: price of oil and crisis, 102, 103
Reagan administration: military response to crisis, 104; conflicts as East-West, 104; isolating Nicaragua, 105, 109–110, 121, 125; disinterest in the CACM, 105, 106; preference for global

integration, 105, 125; rejection of Contadora's diplomacy, 106, 118; rejection of the Esquipulas process, 121; on punishing governments, 121; exclusion of the left, 125
regionally driven alternative for peace, 106 see Esquipulas process of negotiation
Rios Montt, Efraín (President), 107
Reagan' counterinsurgency strategy, 110
Rojas Aravena, Francisco, 114
rebuilding payment system: European Community support, 123; strengthening Honduras
and Nicaraguan exports' capacity, 123
Robinson, William I, 124, 146, 187
rise of the left, 128
Rodríguez Echeverría, Miguel A (President): against the Brussels model, 149, 150
Rodríguez-Arzú bloc: against reforming and relocating institutions, 150
region states, 156
reluctant state, 157, 199n5, 177, 184
right wing interests, 162
remittances, 167, 200n26
Robson, Peter, 184
regional blocs, 188, 190
Rio Group, 189

S

self-help system: international system,1; competition, 1; anarchy, 1; international politics, 1, 13, 15, 176; states' preferences,1,6,15,16, 178, 179, 180; realism, 12, 13, 15, 18, 20 see neo-realists
side-payment, 3, 6, 21, 160, 177, 181, 184
System of Central American Integration (SICA), 4, 8, 127, 138, 139, 140, 141, 148, 149, 150, 155, 158, 183, 185, 186, 187, 190
strategic environment, 2,6,7,13,15, 25, 26, 29, 177, 178, 179, 180
strategic interdependence,3,6, 26, 27, 97, 110, 120, 122, 125, 177
structural constraints, 2,6 see structuralism
structural environment, 4,9, 10,17,18, 26, 28, 152, 156, 161, 164, 178, 179, 180
structural intergovernmentalism, 4
structural factors and Central America, 5
strategic actors: governments as, 6, 18
smaller states, 6, 24, 25, 177, 179
sovereignty, 7, 20, 22, 23
Special Action Plan (PAECA), 9
South America, 10
supranational authority, 11, 13, 43, 86, 176 see neo-functional theory and neo-functional logic
spillover, 12,14,18, 28, 34, 86, 96, 101, 123, 132
Sartori, Geovani, 12
structuralism, 15, 30, 176
Schelling, Thomas, 15, 17
strategic interactions,16,17, 25, 177, 178, 179
structural power, 16
self-interested governments, 19 see intergovernmentalism
Stopford, John, 27,
Strange, Susan, 27
strategic paradigm, 27
strategic bargaining, 27
San José protocol, 32
Salvadorian capitalism, 33
Sorto, Francisco, 35, 134
Superimposed development, 36, 52, 62
Social Christian Party (Costa Rica), 42
strategic liberalisation, 44
sociological analysis: social forces, 52, 53; integration and imperialism, 52; market
determinant, 53
Somoza, Anastacio (President), 72, 73,96
Southern bloc: countering the tripartite, 75
system overload, 80, 90
SIECA, 88, 89, 90, 141, 150, 151, 155, 171, 183
structural failure of the CACM, 92
San Pedro Sulas, 93
Schmitter, Philippe C, 96, 100, 139
spill-around, 96
self-encapsulation, 96
spill-over syndrome, 96
surplus states, 97, 105
state with restricted markets, 98
social mobilisation, 99
self-sustainability, 100
state subsidisation, 104

security dilemma: fear and mistrust, 104; increased military budgets, 104
structural adjustment programme, 105, 113, 131
Sandinistas: defeat of, 117, 118, 123
symmetry and simultaneity, 121 see Arias peace plan
sub-regional bloc: El Salvador, Guatemala and Honduras, 129
Solis Rivera, Luis Guillermo, 130, 135, 144, 146, 147
SICA's Consultative Committee (SICA-CC), 135, 140, 141
Solano, Patricia, 143, 151, 158
single treaty, 149, 150
stop- and- go logic, 153
state monopoly, 170
sensitive products, 172, 173
security community, 175, 176
state-centric, 23, 179

T
threat of exclusion, 3, 6, 20, 21, 163, 164, 177, 182, 183, 190
trade disputes, 9
theoretical perspective, 10
theory, 10
traditional realism, 12, 13 see realism
transnational forces, 14, 20
theory of integration, 15, 16
two-level game, 21
trade dependent, 22, 190
triangular diplomacy, 27
technocratic view of integration: ECLAC's functionalism, 53, 54; technical view of integration, 101, 132
terms of trade, 54
Tegucigalpa treaties, 57, 192n2, 71, 72, 87
trade diverting effect, 57, 58
trade creation, 58, 103
trade relations: as protected, 59, 60
Torres Rivas, Edelberto, 63
tripartite treaty: El Salvador, Guatemala and Honduras, 72–73, 182; as strategic bargaining, 75; compromise with, 75
tortuous ratification procedures: entrenched intergovernmentalism, 85–88, 90
traditional exports, 94 see EXA
trade deficit, 95
tariff reduction, 98, 173
technocratic theses, 100 see ECLACs paradigm and neo-functional theory
trade diversion, 57, 58, 103
trade war, 103
trade debts, 105
Tegucigalpa Group, 111, 196n15
Thatcher, Margaret (Prime Minister), 112
Trifinio: El Salvador, Guatemala and Honduras, 129, 142
transition to democracy: democratic legitimacy, 130–131
Tulchin, Joseph, 132
transnational state, 135, 187
transformative regionalism: against US hegemony and inequalities, 135
Tegucigalpa Protocol, 138, 161
transnational capitalist class, 156
Transitional Multilateral Trade Accord, 159
tariffs policy, 167, 168
tariff reform: bargaining for, 164, 165, 166, 168, 169, 173, 182
Temporal Protection Tariff (TPT), 166
trade disputes, 173 see trade wars
territorial state, 176
trading blocs, 179, 187

U
underdevelopment, 4, 10, 25, 29, 90, 98, 165, 178
utilitarian actors, 19,
uneven development, 53
US (United States of America): against ECLAC' integration, 56; free trade and capital movement, 56–58; trade creation over trade diversion, 57–58; unwilling to support price stability regime, 67
unanimity, 85, 87, 163, 189
unfair trade practices, 90, 172
upgrading the common interest, 90
uncompromising policy of reforming the CACM, 97
US foreign policy: on hegemony, 56–58, 133; isolating Nicaragua, 104; Contras' war, 104; assistance to Costa Rica, 110; use of Costa Rican territory, 109–110; on regionalism, 133; rapprochement with Latin America, 133, as of Central America as a bloc, 164

Una Hora para la Paz, 112
UN (United Nations), 123

V

Veto: veto power, 3, 19, 87, 91, 121, 185
vetoing decisions/proposals, 3, 4, 180, 181, 184
variable geometry, 6, 127, 153, 163, 186
variable-sum game, 14
Villeda Morales, Ramón (President), 72, 73
vulnerability, 106
Vaky, Viron, 128
Varas, Augusto, 132

W

Waltz, Kenneth, 2
Wincott, Daniel, 11
Wallace, Helen, 12
Webb, C, 12
world politics, 13
World War I, 14
win-set, 18,19,22, 56, 114, 163, 164
Westphalia, treaties of, 22, 29
WTO, 46, 143, 172, 173, 174, 179
Wynia, G.W, 60
Willmore, Larry, 94
withdrawal from the CACM, 97, 98
Wright, Jim, 120
Washington Consensus, 155, 187
workable compromise, 190

Y

Ydígoras Fuentes, Miguel (President): attempt at leadership, 72; embracing Salvadorian
proposals, 73
Young, Oran R, 89

Z

Zero-sum game: Honduran and Salvadorian relations, 96; inflexible policies, 97

For Product Safety Concerns and Information please contact our EU representative GPSR@taylorandfrancis.com
Taylor & Francis Verlag GmbH, Kaufingerstraße 24, 80331 München, Germany

www.ingramcontent.com/pod-product-compliance
Ingram Content Group UK Ltd.
Pitfield, Milton Keynes, MK11 3LW, UK
UKHW022000180926
475701UK00003B/126

* 9 7 8 0 4 1 5 6 2 1 5 9 5 *